202 SERVICES YOU CAN SELL FOR BIG PROFITS

Other titles by James Stephenson

- *202 Things You Can Buy and Sell for Big Profits*
- *Ultimate Homebased Business Handbook: How to Start, Run and Grow Your Own Profitable Business*
- *Ultimate Small Business Marketing Guide: 1500 Great Marketing Tricks That Will Drive Your Business Through the Roof*
- *Ultimate Start-Up Directory*

Coming Fall 2005

- *202 Things You Can Make and Sell for Big Profits*
- *202 Ways to Supplement Your Retirement Income*

202 SERVICES YOU CAN SELL FOR BIG PROFITS

JAMES STEPHENSON

EP
Entrepreneur. Press

Managing editor: Jere L. Calmes
Cover design: Beth Hansen-Winter
Composition and production: Eliot House Productions

Library of Congress Cataloging-in-Publication Data

Stephenson, James, 1966–.

202 services you can sell for big profits/by James Stephenson.

p. cm.

Includes index.

ISBN 1-932531-52-1 (alk. paper)

1. Business planning. 2. New business enterprises—Planning. 3. Service industries—Planning. I. Title. II. Title: Two hundred two services you can sell for big profits.

HD30.28.S72823 2005

658.1'1—dc22 2005007330

Printed in Canada

11 10 09 08 07 06 05 10 9 8 7 6 5 4 3 2

58729580

CONTENTS

PREFACE

Why are businesses that sell services in the United States and Canada booming, leaving many struggling just to keep up with demand?

There are mainly two reasons—aging demographics, and the shift from a manufacturing- and production-based economy to a services-based economy. In the United States and Canada the aging of the population has created the fastest-growing demographic group in both countries. Millions of people are retiring or nearing retirement, and as a general rule they are more in need of services, and are often better off financially to hire providers of every service imaginable—cleaners, house painters, nonmedical home care, and taxi services. But that's only half the story, because people are also living longer and are much healthier than in decades past, resulting in retired folks also kicking up their heels and having lots fun. They are booking trips, taking dance lessons, hiring personal trainers, learning new languages, and taking computer classes—again driving the need for more service providers.

Over the past two decades there has also been a shift in the United States and Canada away from our traditional manufacturing- and production-based economies, to services- and technology-based economies. In short, this means manufacturing jobs are being swallowed up by overseas economies with cheaper labor, raw materials, and production costs. Depending on your outlook, the fallout of this shift in the economy has been both negative and positive. On the negative side, many manufacturing jobs have disappeared, never to return, displacing many people from their jobs. On the positive side, America leads the world in technology, which is exported to foreign countries to drive their new manufacturing and production economies at considerable profits to the technology providers. The profits gained from exporting technology stays in the country and is spent on services of every kind—gardeners, dog walkers, IT consultants, and caterers, for example.

People from every walk of life, level of education, age group, and those displaced by the shifting economy are choosing to sell services rather than fight it out to get a traditional job and then fight even harder to keep it. Many people who sell services are quickly discovering they can work less, earn more, be the boss, gain security, and be a lot happier in the process. With the help of this book you can also learn how to cash in on the boom in selling services. The choice is yours to make. You can sell services full-time and replace, or in all probability, increase your current income. You can sell services part-time to help pay your way through college, pay down the mortgage, or save for your kids' educations. You can sell services to supplement your retirement income so you can enjoy your golden years to the fullest, pursuing the things you never had time for in the past. Or you can sell services seasonally, leaving you more time to pursue other interests like travel, education, and recreation. All of this is easily within your reach and can be achieved by starting and operating your own business selling services.

My objective in creating this book was clear: Identify the best services to sell and include the information and tools that you need to successfully market and sell your services for maximum profit. There are numerous books available on the topic of starting a business; in fact, I have written a couple, but *202 Services You Can Sell for Big Profits* is one of the few books that is solely focused on selling services, not to mention the most up-to-date and resource-packed opportunities. The information included has been specifically developed to walk you through every step needed to start and run a business for success and profit. The book explains the best services to sell, the best way to sell them for maximum profits, and how you can get and keep customers for life.

Overall, after completing this book, you will have acquired valuable information and knowledge about all the critical topics, including legal and financial issues, business and marketing planning, setting up shop, sales and marketing, and the best 202 services to sell for big profits.

Legal and Financial Issues

You will discover information that demystifies all those tough legal and financial issues. You will learn what licenses and permits are needed to start your business and sell services, and how and where they may be obtained. You will also determine what legal business structure is right for your needs: sole proprietorship, partnership, limited liability corporation, or corporation, and the pros and cons associated with each of them.

Do you need insurance to sell services? Yes, and you will learn what insurance coverage is needed to best protect your assets, and where you can get it. Of course, you also need to know how much money will be required to start your new enterprise, and what funding sources are available to you. We will show you how to start your new venture for peanuts and where you can find the money you need to get rolling, and even how to grow your venture in the future.

Likewise, money management issues are discussed, and you will learn how to set up your books, work with accountants and bookkeepers, and open commercial bank accounts. You will discover how to establish merchant accounts so you can provide your customers with convenient purchase payment options, including credit cards, debit cards, electronic money transfers, and retail financing and leasing options. You also need to know how much you can charge for your services and how to determine your pricing strategy; information on both is included so you can learn how to sell your services for maximum profit.

Business and Marketing Planning

A business can only be as strong as the research and planning that go into it right from the start. To establish a rock-solid business foundation to build upon, you will find out how to develop a business plan in step-by-step detail, one that can be used to secure start-up funding and also act as a roadmap to guide your new business to success and profitability. Who is your target audience and where do you find them? Don't worry—inside you will learn to identify your target customers—who they are, where they live, how many there are, how they make buying decisions, and how to build lifelong selling relationships with all of them.

As well, you'll learn to identify competitors in the marketplace who also want to sell their services to the same target audience as you. You'll discover the tools and tricks the pros use to build competitive advantages that leave the competition in the dust. Finally, when it comes to business and market planning, it is critical that you also know how to implement your new business and marketing strategies. Therefore, inside you will learn how to create an action plan and measure results so you can stay on track and meet and exceed your sales and marketing goals and objectives.

Setting Up Shop

Every business also needs a base of operations to work from, and in Chapter 4 you will learn how to select the right location for your business: homebased, office, and storefront locations are discussed, along with the pros and cons of each option. Once you have chosen your location, you also need to know what type of equipment is needed and how to organize your workspace so that you can maximize efficiency and productivity—topics that are discussed in detail.

An operating location can also be on the web, so we'll show you how to get on the internet and start doing business there. Topics such as building your web site, selecting the right domain name, and registering with search engines are all covered. You will also discover the technologies to help increase sales and profits, put you light-years ahead of competitors, and save you time and money.

Every business uses products and services in the day-to-day operation of the business. Most businesses also need to purchase products for resale, and inside you will learn how to pick the right suppliers, purchase quality products and services, and buy on terms with no money upfront, all while being able to negotiate and receive the lowest price possible—helping to add hundreds and even thousands to your bottom line profits.

Sales and Marketing

The lifeblood of every business, regardless of size or what products or services it sells, is sales and marketing. Think of it as oxygen; businesses simply cannot survive without it. Consequently, a great deal of sales and marketing information has been specifically developed for the service provider in Chapter 5, as well as in other sections throughout the book. You will soon discover what is required to market and sell your services like a seasoned pro! Included is information such as customer service tips that are guaranteed to keep every customer for life, and amazing advertising secrets that will show you how to write great copy, create attention-grabbing newspaper ads, get on the radio, and create red-hot fliers to promote your services.

You will learn to use public relations tools such as news releases, talk radio, and community sponsorships to secure free and valuable publicity in print, on air, and on the web. You will also be privy to secrets that top sales professionals use daily to prospect for new and qualified business, put together perfect presentations, overcome all objections, master negotiations, and close every sale, every time. Events such as trade and consumer shows, seminars, and contests are extremely effective ways for small business owners to promote and sell their services, and in these pages you will discover how to use event marketing to boost revenues and profits for your business.

The Best 202 Services to Sell

This is where the fun begins, because Chapter 6 is completely devoted to informing you about the best 202 services to sell, including a complete description of each service featured, a skill level recommendation needed to provide the service, how to effectively market and sell the service, and the current rates that other service providers are charging. You will also find hundreds of valuable resources throughout the book, including American, Canadian, and international private corporations, business associations, government agencies, individuals, web sites, publications, products, services, and lots more.

All the resources featured throughout were active web links, telephone numbers, and mailing addresses at the time of publication. Over time, however, some information changes or is no longer available. In an effort to ensure that resource information remains beneficial and active for the long term, I have endeavored to find reputable businesses, organizations, publications, and individuals to feature as resources. However, featuring a resource in this book is by no means an endorsement of the company, organization, product, or service. It is the responsibility of every entrepreneur to make sure he or she is doing business with reputable firms and individuals, as well as purchasing quality products and services.

Resource icons used represent the following:

- A mouse icon represents an online resource web site address.
- ☎ A telephone icon represents a resource's contact telephone number.
- A book icon represents a book or other publication that offers further information.
- ★ A star icon represents a franchise or business opportunity.

■ ■ ■

202 Services You Can Sell for Big Profits is the most authoritative and comprehensive service providers' book available. It gives you the ability to identify the best services to sell, how to get started, and the information and tools you need to sell your services for maximum profits. Harness the power of this book by putting it to work for you today!

CHAPTER

GETTING STARTED WITH SELLING SERVICES

Who can sell a service? The answer is simple—anyone and everyone. Everyone is qualified because each of us has skills, knowledge, or experience that other people are willing to pay for in the form of a service; or they are willing to pay you to teach them your specific skill or knowledge. Selling services knows no boundaries—anyone with a need or desire to earn extra money, work from home, or start and operate a full-time business can sell a service(s), regardless of age, business experience, education, or current financial resources.

That is the purpose of this chapter and the entire book—to show how you can identify your strengths, learn the basic business information and practices you need to know to start and operate a business, and combine these to determine the best service(s) for you to sell for big profits. The information that follows is designed to inform you about the advantages associated with selling services, and how you can capitalize on your existing skills. It helps you identify what the best time commitment might be for you—part-time, full-time, seasonal, or in retirement. The need for financial compatibility, and the importance of finding a good business match are highlighted. And, finally, the pros and cons of starting a business from scratch are discussed, as opposed to buying a business or purchasing a franchise or business opportunity.

What Are the Advantages of Selling Services?

There are many advantages associated with starting your own business selling services. Perhaps the biggest advantage is that you become your own boss, take control of your future, and in effect become the master of your destiny. I have been self-employed for a number of years, and for me the lure of self-employment is the freedom and independence that calling the shots affords, which can be difficult to achieve when you work for others.

Operating your own business also gives you the potential to earn more money, in some instances two, five, or even ten times more than you are currently earning. Why? Simple duplication. When you work for someone else, there is only you and only so many hours in the day to work for an hourly wage or a commission. When you operate a business, you can duplicate yourself by hiring employees and salespeople to increase revenues; you can duplicate your customers and find more just like them to purchase your services; and you can duplicate your business model and open in new geographical areas to service more customers and earn more profits. These are all things that you cannot do when you work for others, and if you do, chances are it will financially benefit the boss a lot more than you.

Starting a business also qualifies you for any number of the tax benefits associated with operating a business, even if you work a regular job and only operate your business part-time and from home. For instance, if you operate a business from home, a portion of your utility bill is tax-deductible against business revenues. A portion of home maintenance and your yearly property tax bill is also tax-deductible, and a portion of your transportation costs equal to the percentage that your car is used for business is tax-deductible. These are all very strong incentives for starting your own business selling services. Again, even if it is only part-time to get going, if you find that it suits you and you are happy, you have the opportunity to build the business into a major concern and fulfill many business and life goals. But none of this will happen unless you take that first step toward self-employment.

Capitalize on Your Skills

Do not worry if you lack business skills and experience in areas such as time management, personal-contact selling, negotiating, bookkeeping, and the ability to create effective advertisements. There's no question that these are all important skills to have, but at the same time they are also skills that with practice can be learned and mastered. More important is the question, "What skill(s) do you have that can be sold in the form of providing it as a service?" Any skill(s) that you possess can be your best, and by far your most marketable, asset. If you know how to safely walk a dog, that is a skill that people are willing to pay you for. If you know how to plan and throw one heck of a party, that is also a skill that people are willing to pay you for as their event and party planner. If you know how to play the piano, this is a skill that other people will pay you to teach them. If you know how to sell products and services online, once again that is a skill that people are willing to pay you for as an online marketing consultant. All are examples of skills that people pay other people to perform, or teach them how to learn.

Every person has one or more skills that other people are prepared to pay for in the form of a service provided to them, or to learn. However, with that said, most people have a tendency to underestimate the true value of their skill sets and experiences. You have to remember, what may come naturally to you may not come so naturally to others. Likewise, you might think that your particular knowledge or expertise may be of little value, but if someone else needs or wants to learn about that knowledge, it is very valuable to them.

Selling Services Part-Time

The first option is to start off selling your services on a part-time basis, which is a good idea because it enables you to eliminate risk by limiting your financial investment. It allows you to test the waters to make sure that being self-employed is something you enjoy and want to pursue. If all goes well, you may decide to transition from your current job, devoting more time to your new enterprise each week, all the while decreasing the time at your current job until you are working at your new business on a full-time basis. There are many advantages to starting off part-time, including keeping income rolling in, taking advantage of any current health and employee benefits, and building your business over a longer period of time, which generally gives it a more stable foundation. If it turns out you are not the type of person who is comfortable being the boss, you have risked little and still have the security of your job.

Of course, if your ambitions are only to generate extra money to pay down the mortgage, save for retirement, put yourself through school, or pay off those pesky credit cards after Christmas, selling services part-time is the perfect choice. It is important to do what you want to do and what best suits your individual needs. If selling services part-time works for you, then go for it.

Selling Services Full-Time

You can also jump in with both feet and start your new business selling services full-time. This option would appeal to people without a current job or people who are confident about being the boss and operating a business. There is nothing wrong with starting off full-time, especially if you take the time required to research the business, industry, and marketplace. You must also develop a business and marketing plan, and have the necessary financial resources to start the business and pay yourself until it becomes profitable.

The main downside to starting off full-time is risk. If you jump ship and leave your job, you risk loss of current employee benefits and have no guarantee of steady income, contributing spouses or partners excluded. The upside to starting off full-time is potential rewards, including the opportunity to make more money than you can at your current job, and to gain control of your future. Your decision to operate your new business on a full-time basis will largely be determined by your current financial situation, your own risk-reward assessment, and your goals and objectives for the future. Jumping in full-time will appeal to the true entrepreneurial mindset—people who prefer to blaze the trail rather than follow behind in the wagon train.

Selling Services Seasonally

Another option is to start a seasonal business selling services, which can be operated with a full- or part-time effort. But most are run full-time to maximize revenues and profits over a normally short time span. Examples of seasonal businesses selling services would include snow removal in winter, yard maintenance in summer in northern climates, income tax preparation service in spring, and serving as a vacation property rental agent. Just about any business can be run seasonally or occasionally, but some are obviously better suited to it than others.

A seasonal venture will appeal to people who want the ability to earn enough money during part of the year in order to do as they please with the remainder of the year—travel, pursue education, or work a job in another season. The potential to earn a very good living operating a business only part of the year is a genuine opportunity, as proven by the thousands of people who are currently doing it. The main downside to a seasonal business, especially one that can be operated year-round, is that you do not want to spend thousands of dollars and hundreds of hours promoting your business only to shut it down for half the year, sending current and potential customers running to your competitors while your business is closed. It may prove very difficult to lure them back when you reopen for business.

Selling Services to Supplement Your Retirement

The fourth option is to sell services to supplement your retirement income or just to have fun and stay active in your golden years. Retirement businesses have become extremely popular in the past decade, mainly because the cost of living has dramatically increased, often outpacing wages and retirement savings. The result is that many people head into retirement needing a little extra income to cover expenses and provide an adequate lifestyle or to maintain their preretirement lifestyle.

People are living longer and much healthier now than in decades past, and because of this many are seeking new challenges; starting and operating a business is a way to stay active physically and mentally. Older people also have a proverbial ace up their sleeves when it comes to starting a business and selling services. This ace up the sleeve is simply a lifetime of knowledge and experience that can only be acquired by spending lots of time on this planet. Because of the value of these skills, many people are willing to pay big bucks for them. This is why many people who are reaching or have reached retirement age have chosen to start a consulting business selling their experiences, knowledge, and skills for the benefit of their clients.

Financial Compatibility

Before you decide to get into business for yourself selling services, there are two issues to consider regarding financial compatibility—income and investment money. First, when deciding what type of services to sell, you have to consider how much money you *want* to earn, and how much money you *need* to earn. If you need to earn $75,000 per year to pay your personal expenses, there is little sense in starting a dog-walking service. Perhaps there are a few dog walkers earning this much, but at the same time, it is not a realistic expectation. How much money do you want to earn—that is, how ambitious are you? Again, you must be realistic and relatively sure that the service you choose to sell has the potential to generate enough income to live on in the short-term, and the potential to match your income goals in the longer term. Income does not have to factor into the business start-up equation for everyone. If you want and need to earn only a little money from a part-time or retirement business, the income equation will not factor as heavily as other issues.

The second big financial compatibility issue affecting your decision about which business to start or purchase is the amount of money needed to start or purchase the business. Not only will you need to have or have access to the investment needed to get rolling, but you will also need extra money for working capital to cover day-to-day operating expenses until the business achieves positive cash flow. This can take a week, a month, or even a year. In Chapter 2, you will learn how to obtain money from various sources to start and operate your business. Ultimately, financial compatibility is important when starting a business and deciding what services to sell. If you cannot afford to start the business and do not have the financial resources to pay operating expenses and your wages until the business can break even, you will probably have to look at alternative options, such as starting part-time, choosing a different business to start, or waiting until you have acquired the money needed to get started. The one thing that I have learned over the years is there is no sense in shooting yourself in the foot if you do not have to. Depending on the venture, it may be only $500, or $500,000, but money, or access to money, is needed to start or buy, and operate a business, period.

Finding a Good Match

You also must be well suited to start and operate the business and services you are considering providing. You and your business must be a good match. You may have an interest and even experience in a specific business or in providing a specific service, but that does not necessarily make it a good match. Here are a few points to consider when determining a good business match. Many of these issues are covered in greater detail in other chapters.

- Do you have the financial resources to start or purchase the business, and enough money to pay the day-to-day operating expenses until the business breaks even and is profitable? If not, it is probably not a good match, and you should consider alternatives.
- Does the business have the potential to generate the income you need to pay your personal expenses, and does it also have the potential to generate the income you want to earn? This is very important, because if you cannot pay

your own personal bills, you will soon be in trouble; and if, over time, you cannot earn the income that you want to earn, you will lose interest in the business—a recipe for disaster.

- Are you physically healthy enough to handle the physical strains of starting and running the business? If not, you may end up having to hire people for the job, which can be problematic if the business revenues are not there to support both management and employee wages.
- Do you have experience in this type of business or service, and do you have any special skills that can be utilized in the business? You can gain experience and knowledge on the job, but skills that can be utilized and capitalized upon right away are extremely valuable.
- Are there any special certificates or educational requirements to start and operate the business, and are these readily available? Find out the upfront costs associated with these, how they can be obtained, and the time frame needed to obtain specific certificates. Training and certification should not be viewed negatively, because often the return on time and investment is substantially rewarded financially. Anything worth doing is worth doing well.
- Would you enjoy operating the business, and does it match your personality type and level of maturity? This is very important. If you do not think that you would enjoy it, then don't start. Again, the loss of interest in a business is almost certainly the kiss of death. You can't stay motivated and rise to new challenges if you don't like what you're doing.

Starting a Service Business from Scratch

Your first option is to start a business selling services from scratch, which is by far the most common route for first-time entrepreneurs. People who feel the need to find new frontiers rather than follow behind in the wagon train will be pleased to know that there are numerous advantages to starting a business from scratch, as opposed to purchasing an existing business, franchise, or business opportunity. Depending on the venture, operating location, and equipment needs, less money is generally needed to get rolling when starting from scratch. You can usually get something started that has good growth and profit potential for less than a $10,000 initial investment. Additionally, starting a business from scratch allows you to have full control and independence, unlike most franchises and some business opportunities that impose strict management and reporting guidelines.

I would like to tell you that there are no disadvantages to starting a business from scratch, but I cannot. Unfortunately, things like low initial investment, little regulation, and quick start-up that attract first-time entrepreneurs to starting a business from scratch are also the same things that can kill the business. Why? Mainly because you can literally have a business start-up idea today and be open for business tomorrow, which leaves little if any time for two business essentials: research and planning. Additional disadvantages include the fact that you will be heading into uncharted waters: with no previous operating history, there is no system of checks and balances in place to measure progress beyond your research and business and marketing plans. And unlike buying an operating business, there are no existing revenues to help pay for or offset fixed operating costs. You have to build the business to the break-even point and profitability from scratch. Finally, unlike purchasing a franchise or existing business, there is no road map that clearly identifies the steps that need to be taken to get the business started, operational, manageable, and profitable.

If the idea of starting a business selling services from scratch appeals to you, check out Chapter 6, where you will find the best 202 services to sell for big profits, along with numerous helpful resources to get you started. If you think none are suitable, although more than a few are bound to be, I suggest that you purchase a copy of *Entrepreneur's Ultimate Start-Up Directory* (Entrepreneur Press, 2001), which contains information about 1,350 business start-up ideas.

Buying a Service Business

A second option is to purchase an existing business, one that has customers and is generating revenues. For people who want instant results and do not want to invest the time required to start a business from scratch and have to go through the process of research, planning, setting up shop, and finding customers, the purchase of a currently operating business is probably a better choice. But if you choose this route, no less planning and research has to go into finding the right business to buy than if you were starting a business from scratch. Perhaps even more planning and research are necessary because buying an operating business usually means investing a larger amount of money, which warrants careful research and planning to minimize financial risk. So you still need to research the marketplace, create a target customer profile, identify competitors, and develop business and marketing plans as you would for any business venture. A big advantage of purchasing an operating business is that you can often negotiate terms, meaning you pay a portion of the purchase price upfront and the balance in installments or balloon payments. This gives you the ability to pay the installments out of business revenues. In effect, you will actually be purchasing the business for no more than your down payment.

Before signing on the dotted line to buy any business, make sure to hire a lawyer to go over the purchase agreement, and an accountant to review all financial statements and conduct a business valuation. Also make sure to do your own investigative work by talking to customers, employees, suppliers, and the Better Business Bureau. Additionally, make sure all current agreements and contracts with clients, suppliers, and manufacturers are transferable, and stay with the business and do not leave with the exiting owner. It is also a good idea to have the current owner stay on after the sale for a reasonable amount of time to train you in the operations of the business and to help in the transition. Finally, make sure that you have a noncompetition clause built into the sale agreement. Noncompetition clauses prevent the past owner from starting a similar type of business or selling similar goods and services within a set geographic area, generally within the same state, and for a fixed period of time, generally three to five years.

If you decide to buy an operating business, you can search for suitable candidates in a number of ways, including real estate agents, newspapers, and business-for-sale specialty publications. You can also contact The International Business Brokers Association, www.ibba.org, which has links to more than 1,100 independent business brokers around the world. You might also want to visit Biz Buy Sell, www.bizbuysell.com, which is billed as the internet's largest business-for-sale portal, with over 20,000 listings.

Buying a Service Franchise

Another option is to purchase a franchise or business opportunity, which can cost anywhere from a low of a few hundred dollars for a basic business opportunity, to well into the seven-figure range for an internationally known franchise. Purchasing and operating a franchise is a great option for people who want a proven management system, initial and ongoing training and support, and the benefits associated with branding on a large-scale basis. With a franchise operation you usually have the combined strength of many franchisees as opposed to the possible weaknesses of one independent small business. The combined strengths can help lower costs, as goods and services are purchased in bulk, enabling you to reach a broader audience through collective advertising.

Unfortunately, there are also disadvantages associated with purchasing a franchise. When you own and operate a franchise, you have much less control and independence in all areas of your business than you do in an independent business. This is because one of the doctrines of the franchise model is conformity through consistent brand management. Consequently, if you are the stubborn and independent type, you might find operating a franchise to be little more than managing someone else's business.

Even if you decide to purchase a franchise, you still have to take the same precautions that you would when starting or purchasing any other type of business.

Before buying any franchise, you should be sure it's something you want to do and believe you would enjoy. A good match is still a key requirement for success, whether the business is a franchise or not. Also visit and talk to other franchisees to get firsthand feedback about the business, franchisor, and management systems, and become a customer to make sure that you like and believe in the services being sold. Additionally, conduct your own market research to make sure that the local market will support the franchise and that the franchisor's research, statements, and forecasts are correct. Finally, always enlist the services of a lawyer to go over the franchisor's Uniform Franchise Offering Circular and decipher the legalese for you. Remember, the devil is in the details.

Along with the best 202 services to sell featured in Chapter 6, I have included many franchise and business opportunity resources. You can also contact the International Franchise Association, www.franchise.org, or the Canadian Franchise Association, www.cfa.ca. Both organizations can provide information to help you find a franchise that is right for you.

CHAPTER

2

COVERING LEGAL AND FINANCIAL ISSUES

Selling a service is like starting and operating any other type of business—there are legal and financial issues that must be considered and complied with in order to stay out of hot water with Uncle Sam and the other Powers That Be. In short, you have to do everything to the letter of the law, whether you are selling services full-time or just occasionally—no excuses! A few of the legal and financial issues that you will need to deal with are: registering a business name and selecting a legal business structure, obtaining a business license, obtaining a sales tax ID number if you will also be selling products, obtaining insurance coverage, opening a commercial bank account, and preparing and filing business and income tax returns. Money spent on professional legal and financial advice when dealing with these issues is money well spent. Lawyers with small-business experience will be able to advise you on which legal business structure best meets your specific needs, insurance and liability issues, drafting of legal documents, supplier agreements, and many other legal issues. In a nutshell, they will decipher legalese for you and help make sense of complicated matters pertaining to business. Likewise, accountants will decipher the tough financial information you need to know in order to comply with state and federal tax regulations, as well as help establish and maintain financial record-keeping. In this chapter you will learn about legal business-structure options, business license and permits, insurance, business financing, banking, and money management.

Legal Business Structure Options

The starting point for getting your business off the ground from a legal standpoint is to choose and register a business name, as well as select a business structure—sole proprietorship, partnership, limited liability corporation, or corporation. Issues such as budget, business goals, and personal liability will be determining factors for most entrepreneurs when selecting a business structure. Many people choose a sole proprietorship if they are on a tight budget and comfortable with liability issues. A partnership is the right choice if you will be running your new business with a spouse, family member, or friend. A limited liability corporation (LLC) or a corporation will be the right choice if your plans include expansion and you want to minimize personal liability concerns.

Registering a Business Name

Regardless of the legal structure you choose, you will also need to select and register a business name. You can name the business after your legal name, such as Jim's Window Cleaning, or you can choose a fictitious business name, such as West Coast Window Cleaning. Do make sure to have two or three name options ready to go, in case another business is already using your first choice. Business registration costs vary by state and province, though generally they are less than $200 to register a sole proprietorship, including name search fees. Normally, you have to show proof of business registration in order to establish commercial bank accounts, buy products wholesale, and open a credit card merchant account. So there are no shortcuts; you have to register your business. In the United States you can register your business name through the Small Business Administration (SBA). Log on to www.sba.org to find an office near you. In Canada you can register your business through a provincial Canadian Business Service Center. Log on to www.cbsc.org to find an office near you. More than anything else, your business name will promote your business and get used the most in print and conversation. So the importance of having the right business name cannot be overstated. The name you choose is the name that you will have to work with for a long while. Therefore, your business name should be descriptive so that it becomes an effective marketing tool. It should also be short, easy to spell, easy to pronounce, and very memorable. When naming your business, you have to think visual impact and word-of-mouth referral, as both rely on short, easy-to-spell-and-remember, descriptive names. Keep your business name geographically universal so that you do not limit growth potential; your business name should also convey the appropriate image you want to project.

Sole Proprietorship

Sole proprietorship is the most common type of legal business structure, mainly because it is the simplest and least expensive to start and maintain. A sole proprietorship means your business entity and your personal affairs are merged as one—a single tax return, personal liability for all accrued business debts and actions, and control of all revenues and profits. But it is still important to separate your business finances from your personal finances for record-keeping and income tax reasons. The biggest advantage of a sole proprietorship is that it is very simple and inexpensive to form and can be quickly and inexpensively started, altered, bought, sold, or closed at any time. Also, outside of routine business registrations, permits, and licenses, there are few government regulations. The biggest disadvantage of a sole proprietorship is that you are 100 percent liable for any number of business activities that go wrong. This can mean losing any and all personal assets, including investments and real estate, as a result of successful litigation or debts accrued by the business.

Partnership

A partnership is another popular type of low-cost legal business structure because it allows two or more people to start, operate, and own a business. If you do choose to start a business with a family member or friend, make sure the partnership is based on a written partnership agreement, not just a verbal agreement. The agreement should address issues such as financial investment, profit distribution, duties of each partner, and an exit strategy should one partner want out of the agreement. Like a sole proprietorship, business profits are split among partners proportionate to their ownership and are treated as taxable personal income. Perhaps the biggest advantage of a partnership is financial risks and work are shared by more than one person, which allows each partner to specialize within the business for the benefit of the collective team. Record-keeping requirements are basic and on par with a sole proprietorship. Unfortunately, partnerships also have disadvantages. The most significant is that each partner is legally responsible and personally liable for the other partners' actions in the business; a nonincorporated partnership offers no legal protection from liability issues. All partners are equally responsible for the business's debts, liabilities, and actions.

Limited Liability Corporation

A limited liability corporation combines many of the characteristics of a corporation with those of a partnership in that like a corporation, it provides protection from personal liabilities and the tax advantages of a partnership. Limited liability corporations can be formed by one or more people, called LLC members, who alone or together organize a legal entity separate and distinct from the owners' personal affairs in most respects. The advantages of a limited liability corporation over a corporation or partnership are that it is less expensive to form and maintain than a corporation, offers protection from personal liability that partnerships do not provide, and has simplified taxation and reporting rules in comparison to a corporation. Because of these advantages, limited liability corporations have become the fastest-growing form of business structure in the United States. In the United States you can file online using a service such as Corp America, www.corpamerica.com, or contact the American Bar Association, ☎ (202) 662-1000, www.abanet.org, to find a lawyer who specializes in filing in your area. In Canada you can file online using a service such as Canadian Corp, www.canadiancorp.com, or contact the Canadian Bar Association, ☎ (800) 267-8860, www.cba.org, to find a lawyer who specializes in filing in your area.

Corporation

The most complicated business structure is the corporation. When you form a corporation, you create a separate and distinct legal entity from the shareholders of the corporation. Because the corporation becomes its own entity, it pays taxes, assumes debt, can legally sue, can be legally sued, and, as a tax-paying entity, must pay taxes on its taxable income (profit) prior to paying any dividends to the shareholders. But the company's finances and financial records are completely separate from those of the shareholders. The biggest advantage to incorporating your business is that you can greatly reduce your own personal liability. Because a corporation is its own entity, it can borrow money and be held legally accountable in a number of matters. In effect, this releases you from personal liability. The major disadvantage is double taxation. Corporation profits are taxed, and then the same profits are taxed again in the form of personal income tax when distributed to the shareholders as a dividend. Unfortunately, the same does not hold true if the corporation loses money. Financial losses cannot be used as a personal income tax deduction for shareholders. In the United States you can file online using a service such as Corp America, www.corpamerica.com, or contact the American Bar Association, ☎ (202) 662-1000, www.abanet.org, to find a lawyer who specializes in filing in your area. In Canada you can file online using a service such as Canadian Corp, www.canadiancorp.com, or contact the Canadian Bar Association, ☎ (800) 267-8860, www.cba.org, to find a lawyer who specializes in filing in your area.

Licenses Needed to Sell Services

Whether you are selling specialized consulting services or operating a part-time window cleaning service, you are classified as a business, and all businesses must be licensed. In all probability you will need to obtain several licenses and permits, depending on the type of service(s) you sell and how the service(s) is sold. At minimum, you will need a business license, and if you sell products in addition to services, you will also need a vendor's permit and a resale certificate or sales tax permit ID number. Additional permits and licenses that may be needed can include professional and trade certificates if your profession or trade is regulated; a health permit if you sell or prepare food; a police clearance certificate if you sell home security services and products; a home occupation permit is required to work from home in some states as is a building permit if you significantly alter your home to suit your new venture. And if you are thinking about skipping any of the required licenses and permits, don't. You need these to buy products, open commercial bank accounts, open merchant credit card accounts and a lot more.

Business Licenses

As mentioned above, to legally operate a business in any municipality of the United States or Canada, you will need to obtain a business license. Business license costs vary from $50 to $1,000 per year, depending on your geographic location, expected sales, the type of business you are engaged in, and the types of services and products you sell. Because they are issued at the municipal level, contact your city/county clerk's or permits office for the full requirements for a business license. The Small Business Administration (SBA) also provides an online directory indexed by state, outlining where business licenses may be obtained, at www.sba.gov/hotlist/license.html. Additionally, in the United States and Canada you can contact the chamber of commerce to inquire about business license requirements and fees. Contact the United States chamber at ☞ www.chamber. com, or in Canada at ☞ www.chamber.ca

Permits

The name may vary depending on geographic location—resale certificate, sales tax permit, ID number—but whatever you want to call it, you need a permit to collect and remit sales tax if you will be selling any products and even some services. Almost all states and provinces now impose a sales tax on products sold directly to consumers, or end users. It is the business owner's responsibility to collect and remit sales taxes. The same sales tax permits are needed when purchasing goods for resale from manufacturers and wholesalers so the goods can be bought tax-free. (Taxes will be paid by the retail customer when resold.) The SBA provides a directory indexed by state outlining where and how sales tax permits and ID numbers may be obtained, including information on completing and remitting sales tax forms. This directory is located at ☞ www.sba.gov/hotlist/license.html. In Canada there are two levels of sales tax. One, the harmonized sales tax (HST) is charged by most provinces on the sale of retail products to consumers, and the second is charged by the federal government. The latter is known as the goods and services tax (GST) and is charged on the retail sale of all goods and most services. You can obtain a federal HST/GST numbers by contacting the Canada Customs and Revenue Agency at ☞ www.ccra-adrc.gc.ca.

Insurance Coverage

Spending money every month for intangibles like insurance can be painful, especially for a new business start-up with limited cash flow, but you must consider this expense as an absolute must. Purchasing appropriate insurance is the only way that you can be 100 percent sure that in the event of a catastrophe, your business, assets, and clients will be protected. Tracking down the right insurance for your specific needs can be a time-intensive endeavor because of the sheer number of insurance companies and coverage types available. Consequently, it makes sense to enlist the services of a licensed insurance agent to do the research and legwork for you. Not only will the agent be able to decipher insurance legalese for you, but she will also be able to find the best coverage for your individual needs at the lowest cost. To find a suitable insurance agent in the United States, you can contact the Independent Insurance Agents and Brokers of America at ☞ www.iiaa.org. In Canada, you can contact the Insurance Brokers Association of Canada at ☞ www.ibac.ca. Discussed below are a few of the more important types of insurance coverage—property, liability, workers' compensation, and disability insurance.

Property Insurance

Property insurance generally covers buildings and structures on the property as well as the contents, regardless of whether you rent or own your business location. Most property insurance policies provide protection in the form of a cash settlement or paid repairs in the event of fire, theft, vandalism, malicious damage, flood, earthquake, wind damage, and other acts of God. Floods and earthquakes generally require a separate insurance rider. Property insurance is the starting point for business owners, branching out to include specialized tools and equipment, office improvements, inventory, and various liability riders depending on what you sell. As a rule of thumb, property insurance should protect buildings, property, improvements, tools, equipment, furniture, cash on hand, and accounts receivable and payable, as well as restricted liability, which is discussed in greater detail below. Additionally, special riders will be needed to cover working at your clients' locations, as well as tools and equipment in transit to work sites. All insurance companies provide free quotes, but it is wise to obtain at least three so you can compare costs, coverage, deductibles, and reliability. If you are going to run your business from home, make sure to contact your current insurance agent and ask questions specific to the business you will be operating. In most cases, you will want to increase the value of the contents portion of the policy if you use expensive computer and office equipment in your business, as well as the amount of liability insurance if clients will be visiting your home.

Liability Insurance

No matter how diligent you are in taking all necessary precautions to protect your customers and yourself by removing potential perils from your business and the products and services you sell, you could still be held legally responsible for events beyond your control. Product misuse, third-party damages, and service misunderstandings have all been grounds for successful litigation in the United States and Canada. As the old saying goes, "It's better to be safe than sorry." The best way to protect yourself is to get liability insurance that specifically provides protection for the type of business you operate and the services you provide. Extended liability insurance is often referred to as general business liability or umbrella business liability, which insures a business against accidents and injury that might occur at the business location, at clients' locations, or other perils related to the products and services sold. General liability insurance provides protection for the costs associated with successful litigation or claims against your business or you, and covers such things as medical expenses, recovery expenses, property damage, and other costs typically associated with liability situations.

There are also more specific types of liability insurance protection that some business owners will need in the event of misadventure, especially professional liability insurance. Professional liability insurance, also commonly known as errors and omissions insurance, is designed to protect you and your company from the financial losses that might arise if you are sued by a client(s) due to alleged negligence on your part while rendering professional services or advice. In many states and provinces, professional liability insurance, or errors and omissions insurance, is mandatory. Without it you cannot legally practice. At one time, only practicing professionals such as lawyers, notary publics, certified accountants, and engineers carried professional liability insurance, but it is now commonplace for just about every type of business professional and consultant to carry such insurance. Basically, anyone who charges a fee for advice or professional services should carefully consider obtaining professional liability insurance. American Professional Online, www.americanprofessional.com, provides visitors with free professional liability quotes.

Workers' Compensation Insurance

In the United States and Canada, workers' compensation insurance is mandatory for all the people your business employs, regardless of whether they work full-time, part-time, or seasonally. Workers' compensation insurance protects employees injured on the job by providing short- or long-term financial benefits as well as covering medical and rehabilitation costs directly resulting from an on-the-job injury. If you have no employees and operate your business as a sole proprietorship or partnership, workers' compensation insurance is not mandatory; unless your business is incorporated, officers and any employees must be covered. Rates are based on industry classification, which generally means the more dangerous the work, the higher your premiums will be. Likewise, the more claims for workers' compensation that your business files, the higher your rates will go. Workers' compensation classifications, forms, and guidelines can be especially confusing for first-time entrepreneurs. Fortunately, information about workers' compensation coverage can be found at U.S. Department of Labor, Office of Workers' Compensation Programs online, www.dol.gov/esa/owcp-org.htm. This web page has links to all states and the District of Columbia, explaining workers' compensation rules and regulations. In Canada, log on to www.awcbc.org. The Association of Workers' Compensation Boards of Canada provides links to all provincial and territorial workers' compensation offices.

Disability Insurance

If you were sick or injured and could not work, would you have the ability to pay your business expenses and wages? If not, chances are you need to obtain disability insurance coverage. Disability insurance is especially important to service providers because often jobs involve physical work. Disability insurance makes payments to you in the event that a physical or mental illness, or bodily injury prevents you from working. Policy benefits and costs vary, depending on coverage, but regardless of the policy you choose be sure to have a cost-of-living clause built into the policy, which increases benefits proportionate to the consumer price index. Also tell your insurance agent that you want your disability coverage to include partial disabilities, which enables you to collect partial benefits while working part-time in your business if you cannot return to full-time active duty. And build in a clause that gives you the right to increase your disability insurance benefits as your business and income grows. This is known as an additional purchase option and can be extended to include key employee disability insurance as well.

Financing Your New Business

How much money do you need to start your business? It depends on the type of service you will provide, equipment requirements, business location, transportation needs, and marketing. I have included a handy start-up costs worksheet in Chapter 3, Business and Marketing Planning, to help you calculate how much money will be needed to start your business. If this is your first foray into business ownership, you should also know that there are generally three funding requirements—start-up, working capital, and growth capital. All are important and serve their own function.

Start-Up Capital

Start-up capital is the money used to start a business, buy a business, or buy a franchise. Start-up capital is needed to purchase equipment, rent business premises, buy office furniture, meet legal requirements, and pay for training. There are ways of limiting the amount of start-up capital, as you will see later in this section, but you will require some money to start or purchase a business.

Working Capital

Working capital is most important because it's the money you need to pay all the bills and your wages until the business reaches a break-even point. More than a few entrepreneurs have failed in business because a lack of operating capital prevented the business from reaching positive cash flow.

Growth Capital

Growth capital is the money needed should you decide to expand your business. Even if your plans are not to expand, lack of growth capital can become problematic when forces beyond your control, such as new competition or new government regulations, take effect. You may not want to grow, but forces beyond your control may necessitate growth in your business, if for no other reason than just to survive and remain viable. It is not necessary to have growth capital sitting in the bank, but it's a good idea to have a plan in place that could give you access to growth capital should the need arise.

Personal Savings

The first and perhaps best way to finance your business venture is by using your own personal savings or tapping investments. Self-funding enables you to stay in control of how, when, and why funds are distributed; you do not have to satisfy a banker's or investor's requirements; you will not feel anxious about whether you can get the proper funding; you do not have to worry about debt accumulation; and there is no bank or investor loan and interest repayment to make each month. To fund your business start-up personally, the money can come from your savings account, investment certificates, retirement funds, mutual funds and stocks, or insurance policies. Keep in mind, though, that in some instances money that you remove from fixed certificates or retirement investments may be subject to additional personal income tax or penalties for early withdrawal or cancellation. It is always wise to consult with an accountant prior to cashing, selling, or redeeming any personal investment. Depending on the investment you want to liquidate, you might actually be earning a higher rate of return than the interest rate you can secure for a start-up business loan. You can also sell or borrow against other personal assets such as real estate, antiques, or boats to fund a business start-up or purchase. At the end of the day, you will have to decide to what lengths you are prepared to go in personally financing your business ambitions.

Love Loans

Another way to fund your business is to ask family members or friends for a loan, which is often referred to as a love loan. However, there is a potential downside to this method of financing: if your business venture were to fail, would you still be able to pay back the loan? If not, the relationship could be damaged beyond repair. But with that said, many successful business ventures have been built upon love loans. If you decide to borrow from friends or family to fund your business, treat the transaction as you would if you were borrowing from a bank. Have a promissory note drawn up and signed (see Figure 2.1), noting the details of the agreement.

Bank Loans

If your credit is sound, you can apply for a bank loan to fund your business. Business loans can be secured or unsecured. Secured loans are guaranteed with some

FIGURE 2.1: Sample Promissory Note

This loan agreement is by and between:

Borrower Information

Name ______________________________

Address ______________________________

City ____________ State ____________ Zip Code __________ Tel ____________

Lender Information

Name ______________________________

Address ______________________________

City ____________ State ____________ Zip Code __________ Tel ____________

I, (borrower's name here), promise to pay (lender's name here) the sum of $ __________, bearing interest at the rate of __________% per annum, and payable in __________ equal and consecutive monthly installments, commencing on the __________ day of each month until paid, with a final installment of $ __________ on the _____ day of _____, 20_____, upon which the loan shall be repaid in full with no further principal or interest amounts owing.

____________________	__________	____________________	__________
Borrower's Signature	Date	Lender's Signature	Date

____________________	__________
Witnessed by	Date

other type of investment, such as a guaranteed investment certificate. Unsecured loans are not secured with any investments or assets, and funds are advanced because of your creditworthiness. The advantage of a secured loan is that the interest rate is generally lower, by as much as 5 percent. The disadvantage of a secured loan is that many first-time entrepreneurs do not have investments to secure the loan; otherwise, they would be able to self-finance the start-up. You can also talk to your bank or trust company about setting up a secured or unsecured line of credit. One advantage of a line of credit over a standard business loan is that you only have to repay interest based on the account line balance and not the principal. This is exactly the type of funding flexibility new business start-ups need to get established and grow without the pressure of high-debt repayment. If you decide to seek a business loan or line of credit, go armed with a bulletproof business and marketing plan. Bankers want to know that they are investing in sound and well-researched ideas that have the potential to succeed. Many banks offer entrepreneurs small business loan programs, including Bank of America, www. bankofamerica.com, and Royal Bank, www.royalbank.com/sme/.

Government Business Loans

In the United States and Canada there are government programs in place to assist people in starting a new business or to provide growth funding for existing small businesses. In the United States these programs are administered through the SBA. There are three financial assistance programs offered by the SBA aimed specifically at small businesses—Business Loans, Investment, and Bonding Programs. In Canada, most small business financial aid and incentive programs are administered through the Business Development Bank of Canada.

SBAs Business Loans Program

This program is available to new business enterprises with start-up funding loaned from microlending institutions (participating banks and credit unions), and guaranteed in full or in part by the government. There are various levels of qualification for the Business Loans Program, so check with your local SBA office for more details to see if you qualify.

SBAs Investment Program

This program supplies new business ventures with funding, and existing small- to medium-sized businesses with venture capital that can be used to fuel growth and expansion. There are various programs available and qualifications to meet, so contact your local SBA office for details.

SBAs Bonding Program

The SBA also offers a Security Bond Guarantee (SBG) program, which provides small and minority contractors with the opportunity to bid on supply and service contracts. Contact your local SBA office for details.

Even though these government programs are in place in the United States and Canada to meet the funding needs for new and existing small business ventures, they offer no guarantees of securing financial assistance. Each application is based on the potential of the venture and the principals. All the usual steps, such as a complete business and marketing plan, are required if you intend to pursue government small business funding.

United States
U.S. Small Business Administration (SBA)
Financial Programs
409 Third Street SW
Washington, DC 20416
☎ (800) 827-5722
www.sba.gov/financing/

Canada
Business Development Canada
BDC Building
5 Place Ville Marie, Suite 400
Montreal, Quebec H3B 5E7
☎ (877) 232-2269
www.bdc.ca

Private Investors

Start-up funds can also come from private investors, but almost always with strings attached. Private investors may want an incredibly high rate of interest, an equity or even controlling interest in the business; they may want to work in the business, or a combination of any or all of these conditions for funding. So if you go looking for private investors to help you float your business dream, be prepared to make sacrifices. If you decide to take in a private investor who wants to remain silent in the business, then a good match between you is of less concern. However, if the investor will be taking a hands-on role in the business, effectively making him a partner, there are more issues to consider. You will need a formal partnership agreement and all parties should share a similar excitement for the business and have similar future goals and ambitions. Finally, the investor should have specific experiences and resources that can be utilized in the business. The most common way that people find investors to help finance a business start-up or expansion is by placing a classified advertisement in their local newspapers or an industry magazine, especially for deals involving amounts less than $100,000. There is also a great number of venture capital web sites, such as Venture Directory Online, www.venturedirectory.com, or V Finance, www.vfinance.com, listing entrepreneurs or venture capitalists (also known as business angels), who are seeking to invest in new and existing businesses.

Bootstrapping Techniques

Bootstrapping is also a way for financially challenged entrepreneurs to fund their business ventures. The four main bootstrapping techniques include using credit cards, barter, leasing or renting, and supplier terms to help reduce the amount of money initially needed.

Credit Cards

The obvious drawback to using credit cards to fund your business enterprise is that most have high annual interest rates, some as much as 20 percent. But if money is in short supply and you feel confident that your business will fly, using your credit card may be your only option. If you are going to use credit cards to finance some or all of your business start-up, then plan early. Try to pay off your credit cards to a zero balance while you are still working. Doing so leaves you carrying less debt, with lower monthly obligations, and the opportunity to borrow more money against the cards to start your business. Also, shop for credit cards with the lowest interest charges and no annual fees, and cards that reward purchases with air miles or redeemable shopping points. I would also suggest that you apply for credit cards that are specifically for small business use, such as the Visa Small Business Card, www.usa.visa.com/business, or American Express Small Business, www.americanexpress.com. Business credit cards generally charge a lower annual interest rate and include useful small business features such as online bookkeeping and access, business travel features, business insurance options, and no extra charges for cash advances.

Barter

Bartering your way into business is yet another option for the more creative entrepreneurial set. Barter clubs for small business owners such as National Trade Association, www.ntatrade.com, and First Canadian Barter Exchange, www.barterfirst.com, have become extremely popular, because all it takes is a simple click of the mouse. The premise behind barter is basic: you offer the goods or services that you sell in exchange for goods and services that you need to start, operate, or promote your business. Bartering with other businesses will not supply all the money you need to start and operate your new business, but it can greatly help.

Leasing and Renting

Leasing or renting equipment is another strategy that will not completely fund your entire start-up, but like barter, it can greatly reduce the amount of cash that you need. Renting or leasing equipment, tools, or fixtures enables you to save your precious money for other business-building activities such as marketing. An additional benefit of renting or leasing equipment is the fact that in most cases the total rental or lease payment is a 100 percent business expense, as opposed to the sliding scale of depreciation on owned equipment for tax purposes. When the lease or rental term is over, you can upgrade to a new model without having to worry about selling or trading in the old one, or simply turn it in and be done with it.

Supplier Terms

Another way to bootstrap your way into business is to ask your suppliers for a revolving credit account that gives you up to 90 days to pay for goods and services you need to start or operate your business, or that can be resold to customers for a profit. More times than not, however, asking nicely will not work until you have demonstrated to suppliers that you are a worthy credit risk. This is usually accomplished by the supplier conducting a credit check on you, or through some sort of security guarantee that you provide. If your credit history is good, in some cases you can establish revolving credit accounts with suppliers that will give you up to 90 days to pay.

Getting Paid and Money Management

Getting paid and money management can be tricky business because, in addition to customers, cash flow and managing your accounts properly is what keeps your business humming along. Consequently, getting paid in full and on time, as well as understanding money management, has to become a priority, even if you elect to hire an accountant or bookkeeper to manage the books. You will still need to familiarize yourself with basic bookkeeping and money management principles and activities such as understanding credit, reading bank statements and tax forms, and making sense of accounts receivable and payable. You also have to give careful consideration to the purchase payment options you offer customers, including cash, checks, debit cards, credit cards, and online payment options, as well as establishing payment terms and debt collection in the event of nonpayment. All are discussed in further detail below. Information about pricing your service can be found in Chapter 5.

Opening a Bank Account

Once you have chosen a name and registered your business, you will need to open a commercial bank account. Setting up a business bank account is easy. Start by selecting the bank you want to work with, think small-business-friendly, and call to arrange an appointment to open an account. There is not much more required than that. However, when you go, make sure you take personal identification as well as your business name registration papers and business license, because these are usually required to open a commercial bank account. The next step will be to deposit funds into your new account (even $100 is okay). If your credit is sound, also ask the bank to attach a line of credit to your account, which can prove very useful when making purchases for the business or during slow sales periods to cover overhead until business increases. While you are there, also be sure to ask about a credit card merchant account, debit account, and other small business services.

Bookkeeping

When it comes time to set up your financial books, you have two options—do it yourself or hire an accountant or bookkeeper. You might want to do both by keeping your own books and hiring an accountant to prepare year-end financial statements and tax forms. If you opt to keep your own books, make sure you invest in accounting software such as QuickBooks, www.quickbooks.com, or Quicken, www.quicken.com, because it is easy to use and makes bookkeeping almost enjoyable. Most accounting software also allows you to create invoices, track bank account balances and merchant account information, and keep track of accounts payable and receivable. If you are unsure about your bookkeeping abilities even with the aid of accounting software, you may wish to hire a bookkeeper to do your books on a monthly basis and a chartered accountant to audit the books quarterly and prepare year-end business statements and tax returns. If you are only washing windows on weekends to earn a few extra bucks, there is little need for accounting software or accountant services. Simply invest in a basic ledger and record all business costs and sales. You have to use a common-sense approach when calculating how much to invest in your business versus expected revenues and profits. Also remember to keep all business and tax records in a dry and secure place for up to seven years. This is the maximum amount of time the IRS and Revenue Canada can request past business revenue and expense information. To find an accountant or bookkeeper in your area, you can contact the United States Association of Chartered Accountants, ☎ (212) 334-2078, www.acaus.org, or the American Institute of Professional Bookkeepers, ☎ (800) 622-0121, www.aipb.com. In Canada, you can contact the Chartered Accountants of Canada, ☎ (416) 977-3222, www.cica.ca, or the Canadian Bookkeepers Association, ☎ (250) 334-2427, www.c-b-a-c.ca.

Accepting Cash, Checks, and Debit Cards

In today's super-competitive business environment, you must provide customers with many ways to pay, including cash, debit card, credit card, and electronic cash. There is a cost to provide these payment options—account fees, transaction fees, equipment rental, and merchant fees based on a percentage of the total sales value. But these expenses must be viewed as a cost of doing business in the 21st century. You can, however, reduce fees by shopping for the best service with the best prices. Not all banks, merchant accounts, and payment processing services are the same, and fees vary widely. Also check with small business associations such as the chamber of commerce to see if they offer member discounts, as it is not uncommon to save as much as 2 percent on credit card merchant fees, for example. Remember, consumers expect choices when it comes time to pay for their purchases, and if you elect not to provide these choices, expect fewer sales.

Cash is the first way to get paid, which is great because it is liquid and with no processing time required. As fast as the cash comes in, you can use it to pay bills and invest in business-building activities to increase revenues and profits. The major downside is that cash is risky because you could get robbed or lose it. In cases like that, collecting from your insurance company could prove difficult if there is no paper transaction as proof. Even if you prefer not to receive cash, there are people who will pay in cash, so get in the habit of making daily bank deposits during daylight hours. Also invest in a good-quality safe for cash storage for times when you cannot get to the bank.

Still the most popular way people pay for services is with a check. Needless to say, most entrepreneurs selling services will therefore have to become comfortable being paid with a check. You have to take a few precautions to ensure you don't get left holding a rubber check, especially when dealing with new clients. Ask to see a photo ID and write the customer's driver's license number on the back. If the amount of the check exceeds a few hundred dollars, ask the buyer to get the check certified or pay with a bank draft instead, especially if the client is new to your business. Also get in the habit of checking dates and dollar amounts to make sure they are right. I have been caught a few times with wrong dates and dollar amounts and it can be time-consuming to have to get a new check because of a simple error.

The debit card is another option, but will require you to buy or rent a debit card terminal to accept debit card payments. Most banks and credit unions offer business clients debit card equipment and services. The processing equipment will set you back about $40 per month for a terminal connected to a conventional telephone line and about $100 per month for a cellular terminal, plus the cost of the telephone line or cellular service. There is also a transaction fee charged by the bank and payable by you every time there is a debit card transaction, which ranges from 10 cents to 50 cents per transaction, based on variables such as dollar value and frequency of use. Accepting debit card payments will not be beneficial to all entrepreneurs selling services, but for those working from a fixed location such as a hair salon, or automotive detailing garage for example, accepting debit cards is very important.

Opening a Credit Card Merchant Account

Many consumers have replaced paper money altogether in favor of plastic for buying goods and services. In fact, giving your customers the option to pay for purchases with a credit card is often crucial to success. This is especially true if you plan to do business on the web because credit cards and electronic cash are used to complete almost all web sales and financial transactions. Therefore, most entrepreneurs will want to offer customers credit card payment options, and to do this you will need to open a credit card merchant account. Get started by visiting your bank or credit union, or by contacting a merchant account broker such as 1st American Card Service, www.1stamericancardservice.com, Cardservice International, www.cardservice.com, or Merchant Account Express, www.merchantexpress.com, to inquire about opening an account. Providing your credit is sound, you will run into few obstacles. If your credit is poor, you may have difficulties opening a merchant account, or have to provide a substantial security deposit. If you are still unsuccessful, the next best option is to open an account with an online payment service provider, which is discussed in the next section.

The advantages of opening a credit card merchant account enabling you to accept credit card payments are numerous. In fact, studies have proven that merchants who accept credit cards can increase sales by up to 50 percent. Not to mention that you can accept credit card payments online, over the telephone, by mail, and in person, as well as sell services on an installment basis by obtaining permission to charge your customer's credit card monthly, or per agreement. Of course, all these benefits come at a cost, especially when you consider you will have to pay an application fee, setup fee, purchase or rent processing equipment and software, pay administration and statement fees, and pay processing and transaction fees ranging from 2 to 8 percent on total sales volume. Once again, these fees must be viewed as the cost of doing business.

Online Payment Services

Online payment services allow people and businesses to exchange currency electronically over the internet. These services are very popular with consumers and merchants. PayPal, www.paypal.com, is one of the more popular online payment services with more than 40 million members in 45 countries, offering personal and business account services. Both types of accounts allow funds to be transferred electronically among members, but only the business account enables merchants to accept credit card payments for goods and services. Other popular online payment services include Yahoo Pay Direct, www.paydirect.yahoo.com, and Veri Sign Pay Flow, www.verisign.com. The advantages of online payment services are that they are quick, easy, and cheap to open, regardless of your credit rating or anticipated sales volumes, and you can receive payment from any customer with an e-mail account. You can have the funds deposited directly into your account, have a check issued and mailed, or leave funds in your account to draw on using your debit card. The only real disadvantage is that most services redirect your customers to their web site to complete the transaction. This can confuse people who in some cases will abandon the purchase. Nonetheless, the advantages of online payment services far outweigh any disadvantages.

Establishing Payment Terms

Every small business owner also needs to establish a payment-terms policy. Although you certainly want to standardize the way you get paid, at the same time you will also have to be flexible enough to meet clients' needs on an individual basis. Setting payment terms covers deposits, progress payments, and extending credit. It is important to remember that you want to establish clear, written payment terms with clients prior to providing services or delivering product. Your payment terms should be printed on your estimate forms, included in formal contracts and work orders, and printed on your final invoices and monthly account statements.

Securing Deposits

You have to get in the habit of asking clients for a deposit prior to providing services, especially if the work also involves product sales that have to be paid for by you in advance. In this case the deposit should be for at least the value of the materials. If you are supplying labor only, try to secure a deposit of at least one-third to one-half of the total value of the contract in advance of providing any services. Your order form or contract should have the deposit information clearly stated. Information on canceled orders or contracts and the amount of the deposit that will be refunded should also be on your forms. Securing a deposit is your best way of ensuring that, at minimum, basic out-of-pocket costs are covered should the customer cancel the job or contract.

Progress Payments

Progress payments are also a way to ensure that you do not leave yourself open to financial risk. The key to successfully securing progress payments is to prearrange your contract and payment terms. Agree on the amount that will be due at various stages of the project. You can use percentages to calculate the progress payments, such as 25 percent deposit, 25 percent upon delivery of any materials, 25 percent upon substantial completion, and the balance at completion or within 30 days of substantial completion. Or you may arrange for more concrete progress payments based on indicators that are relevant to the specific scope of work, the job, or the services provided. Regardless of the system you use, progress payments on larger jobs can dramatically lessen your exposure to financial risk.

Extending Credit

In most cases there is no need to extend credit to consumers unless you deliver a service such as pest control that is billed on a monthly schedule, or a major contract that is completed in stages. As a general rule, when a transaction is complete you should be paid in full. However, in the case of business-to-business sales, commercial clients will generally want some type of credit on a revolving-account basis, such as 30, 60, 90, or sometimes 120 days after delivery of the product or completion of the service. Ideally, you want to be paid as quickly as possible, so you might want to offer a 2 percent discount if invoices are paid within one week. And if you do extend credit, make sure to conduct a credit check first, especially when larger sums of money are at stake. There are three major credit-reporting agencies serving the United States and Canada—Trans Union, www.tuc.com; Equifax, www.equifax.com; and Experian, www.experian.com. All three credit bureaus compile and maintain credit files on just about every person, business, and organization that has ever applied for credit.

Debt Collection

No matter how careful you are when it comes to extending credit privileges to customers, once in a while you will not be paid on time, or at all. What can you do to get paid? The first rule of getting paid is to keep the lines of communication open with your delinquent client, and keep the pressure on to get paid through the use of nonthreatening telephone calls, letters, and personal visits. You cannot legally intimidate clients into paying you, but you can explain why it is in their best interest to pay you—namely, that you can hurt their credit rating or sue them in court if they do not pay. Another option is to hire a collection agency to collect the outstanding debt. Collection agencies generally charge a percentage of the total amount owed as their fee, which can range up to as much as 50 percent. The Association of Credit and Collection Professionals, www.acainternational.org, is a good starting point for finding a collection agency to work with. Your final option is to take the delinquent account to small-claims court, but remember that small-claims courts have limits as to how much you can sue for in your state or province, ranging from $1,500 to $25,000. Filing fees vary by state and province as well, and these must be paid upfront, but if you win, the fees are added to your award. As a rule of thumb, small business owners that take people to court for nonpayment generally represent themselves, as the amount of the potential award is usually small and does not justify lawyers' fees and expenses. Even if you win, you will not necessarily be paid the amount that you are awarded. You may win a judgment, but still have to chase the defendant through garnishment of income or seizure of assets to get paid. You can learn more about the small-claims court process and filing fees by contacting your local courthouse.

CHAPTER

3

BUSINESS AND MARKETING PLANNING

The importance of business and marketing planning cannot be overstated. It doesn't matter if you are going to launch a web design service with plans to go global and employ thousands, or if you are going to sell dog-grooming services from your home on weekends. You need to research and plan in order to minimize financial risks, while maximizing the potential for success and profitability. Depending on your venture, your business and marketing plans do not have to be highly sophisticated. Even a few well-researched and documented pages covering the basics are often sufficient to reveal the information you need to describe your business, identify your customers, present your service's beneficial advantages, develop your sales goals and marketing strategies, and create your action plan.

The purpose of this chapter is to help you research and plan your business and marketing strategies. To accomplish this goal, much of the information featured is in workbook format requiring you to answer critical business and marketing questions. You can then use your responses to develop a basic business and marketing plan—a suitable road map to help guide you from business idea to setup, to marketing, to sales, and ultimately to success. Do not feel intimidated by the business and marketing research and planning process. It is nothing more than collecting, analyzing, and recording the information that you need to know in order to start, operate, and prosper in business.

Similar to a business plan, information has been divided into four sections to enable you to easily tackle business and marketing planning exercises in a step-by-step format.

1. COMPANY
   - *Business description*
   - *Management team*
   - *Legal issues*
   - *Risks and contingencies*
2. MARKETING
   - *Marketplace*
   - *Target customer*
   - *Competition*
   - *Sales goals*
   - *Product, price, place, and promotion*
   - *Marketing budget*
   - *Action plan*
3. FINANCIAL
   - *Funding requirements*
   - *Funding sources*
   - *Balance sheet*
   - *Capital equipment and inventory list*
   - *Start-up costs worksheet*
   - *Monthly overhead worksheet*
4. APPENDIXES
   - *Personal documents*

- *Legal and financial documents*
- *Marketing documents*

If you need more specific information than is provided here, there are a multitude of goods books available that are dedicated solely to business and marketing planning, Barnes and Noble, www.barnesandnoble.com, and Amazon, www.amazon.com, both provide convenient online shopping for books. Equally, there are also lots of business plan software and templates available that can assist you in writing and formatting a business plan, including Palo Alto, www.paloalto.com, My Business Kit, www.mybusinesskit.com, and Plan Magic, www.planmagic.com. Most office and word processing software programs also include basic business plan templates and tutorials that can help novice entrepreneurs create and write a business plan.

Company

In the company section, you describe your business in detail, including the management team, legal issues, the potential risks your business faces, as well as contingency plans that can be activated in the event that *Plan A* does not come to fruition.

Business Description

Get started by providing an overview of the business that you have started, or the business start-up that you are considering, including business name, legal structure, location, and stage of development. (See Figure 3.1.)

FIGURE 3.1: Business Description Worksheet

A. What is your business name? ____________________

B. What services and/or products does your business sell? ____________________

____

C. What is the legal structure of your business? ____________________

❑ Sole proprietorship ❑ Partnership ❑ Limited liability corporation ❑ Corporation

D. Is your intention to incorporate a sole proprietorship or partnership in the near future, and if so, when? ____________________

____

FIGURE 3.1: Business Description Worksheet, continued

E. Where is your business located? ______________________

City ______________ State/Province ______________

F When did the business start, or when will the business be started? __________

____

G. If your business is already operational, list:

1) Its current stage of development. ______________________

____

____

2) Successes to date. ______________________

____

3) Challenges to date. ______________________

____

Management Team

Next you want to describe the management team (see Figure 3.2), including the owner(s) and key employees, as well as sales agents, professional service providers, and subcontractors. When describing the management team, think about what type of people your business needs to hire or align with, in order to operate the business and meet your business, marketing, and sales objectives.

FIGURE 3.2: Management Team Worksheet

A. List the owners of the business and describe their experience, training, and the duties each will perform.

1. ______________________

____

FIGURE 3.2: Management Team Worksheet, continued

2. ____

____

3. ____

____

B. List key employees and describe their experience, training, remuneration, and the duties each will perform.

1. ____

____

2. ____

____

3. ____

____

C. List professional service providers (lawyers, consultants, accountants, etc.), and describe the services they will provide.

1. ____

____

2. ____

____

3. ____

____

D. Will you contract with independent sales agents to sell your services? If so, describe their experience, the duties they will perform, and how they will be remunerated. __________

____

____

FIGURE 3.2: Management Team Worksheet, continued

E. Will you hire subcontractors to provide a portion or all of the services you sell? If so, describe their experience, the services they will provide, the guarantees they provide, and how they will be remunerated. ______________________________

____

____

Legal Issues

In this section you want to describe key legal issues having to do with setting up and operating your business. Break this information down into what registrations, permits, licenses, and other legal documents have been obtained to date, and what must still be obtained. Also, describe all insurance coverage needs, as well as any intellectual property information. (See Figure 3.3.)

FIGURE 3.3: Legal Issues Worksheet

A. Describe any legal issues specific to your business, in terms of regulations governing start-up and operations. ______________________________

____

B. Record the important licenses, permits, or registrations that are needed or that have been obtained, as well as the cost of each.

Needed	Obtained	Cost	Item
❑	❑	$ ________	Business license
❑	❑	$ ________	Employer identification number
❑	❑	$ ________	Vendor's permit
❑	❑	$ ________	Sales tax permits
❑	❑	$ ________	Import/export certificates
❑	❑	$ ________	Professional certificates
❑	❑	$ ________	Police clearance
❑	❑	$ ________	Zoning/building permits
❑	❑	$ ________	Fire safety/hazardous materials permits

FIGURE 3.3: Legal Issues Worksheet, continued

Needed	Obtained	Cost	Item
❑	❑	$ ________	Food safety permits
❑	❑	$ ________	Internet domain name registration

C. Describe your insurance requirements, such as fire insurance, general liability insurance, automotive, health, or business interruption insurance.

	Type of Insurance	Date Needed	Cost
1.	______________	________	$ ________
2.	______________	________	$ ________
3.	______________	________	$ ________

D. List and describe any intellectual properties such as trademarks, patents, or copyrights that the business owns, has applied for, or will be using under license from the property owner. Include the nature of these intellectual properties, and the advantages associated with ownership or right of use. ______________________________

____

____

____

____

Risks and Contingencies

It is also important to assess and discuss the risks associated with your business, services, marketing environment, and other aspects of your business, as well as a contingency or backup plan that will be implemented to deal with risks that may materialize (see Figure 3.4). For instance, a risk might be the loss of a key employee who brought specialized know-how to the business, as this loss could have a negative impact on your business. A contingency plan would be to identify two or three potential candidates in advance with the needed skills should you lose this key employee. Another risk might be a supplier going out of business. A contingency would be to identify additional supply sources that could be called upon if needed.

FIGURE 3.4: Risks and Contingenices Worksheet

Potential risk: ______________________________

Contingency plan: ______________________________

Potential risk: ______________________________

Contingency plan: ______________________________

Potential risk: ______________________________

Contingency plan: ______________________________

Marketing

For small businesses, marketing is of key importance. Based on your research and the information gleaned, you should be able to prove that there is sufficient demand for your service, that you can compete in the marketplace, and that the market is large enough to support your sales and marketing goals. In this section you want to describe the marketplace, target customers, competition, sales goals, the four Ps (product, price, place, promotion) , marketing budget, and your action plan. This information can then be used to market your services and any products, and guide your marketing decisions from where you are now to where you want to be in the future.

Marketplace

Describe the marketplace where you will be doing business (see Figure 3.5). The biggest benefit of conducting and recording marketplace information is that it enables you to greatly reduce your exposure to financial risk, increase your chances of capitalizing on marketplace opportunities, and prove that there is a big enough marketplace to support your anticipated sales.

FIGURE 3.5: Marketplace Worksheet

A. Describe the geographic trading area that your business will serve. ______________

____

____

FIGURE 3.5: Marketplace Worksheet, continued

B. How big is the current market? ____________________

____

____

C. How big is the potential market? ____________________

____

____

D. What is the current economic status of the market area? ____________________

____

____

Target Customer

Describe your target customers (see Figure 3.6), including information such as where they live, their age, their gender, what they do for a living, what they like to read, and what is important to them when they make buying decisions. This information enables you to aim your advertising, marketing, and sales activities directly at your target customers, saving you money and time by not targeting advertising and marketing activities where they will be ineffective.

FIGURE 3.6: Target Customer Worksheet

A. Where are your target customers geographically located? ____________________

____

____

B. What percentage of your target customers are male, and what is their age range? ____

____

____

FIGURE 3.6: Target Customer Worksheet, continued

C. What percentage of your target customers are female, and what is their age range?

D. What is the marital status of your target customers?

E. What level of education have your target customers reached?

F. What do your target customers do for a living?

G. What is most important to your target customers when making purchasing decisions: price, value, service, warranty, or quality?

H. What publications do your target customers like to read, and what radio stations and programs do they listen to?

Competition

You also need to know what other businesses are selling the same or similar services in the same area, and to the same target audience. You can use the information you gather and record to develop strategies to turn competitors' weaknesses to your advantage as well as to capitalize on marketplace opportunities (see Figure 3.7).

FIGURE 3.7: Competition Worksheet

A. List and describe your competitors.

1. ______________________________
2. ______________________________
3. ______________________________

B. What are your competitors' strengths?

1. ______________________________
2. ______________________________
3. ______________________________

C. What are your competitors' weaknesses?

1. ______________________________
2. ______________________________
3. ______________________________

D. What do your competitors do well that you should also be doing?

1. ______________________________
2. ______________________________
3. ______________________________

FIGURE 3.7: Competition Worksheet, continued

E. Strengths are the skills and resources you have that can be capitalized upon and used to your advantage to help you reach business and marketing objectives. Describe what strengths and resources your business has. ______

______

______

F. Describe how your company will be positioned in the marketplace, relative to competitors. Will you be known as the low-price leader, providing quality and service above all, or will you cater to the high-end segment of the market? ______

______

______

Sales Goals

Your sales goals should be defined in easily measured and quantifiable financial terms. If you are planning on utilizing more than one sales method, such as trade shows, internet, or salespeople, you will want to separate and list sales goals for each sales method individually. (See Figure 3.8.)

FIGURE 3.8: Sales Goals Worksheet

A. What are your first month sales goals? ______

______

______

B. What are your six-month sales goals? ______

______

______

FIGURE 3.8: Sales Goals Worksheet, continued

C. What are your first-year sales goals? ______________________________

____

____

D. What are your five-year sales goals? ______________________________

____

____

Product, Price, Place (Distribution), and Promotion

Developing your marketing strategy revolves around the four P's of marketing—product (the service you provide), price, place (distribution), and promotion. It is the combination of the four Ps that creates your marketing mix, which is, in effect, the entire marketing process. Essentially, the four Ps are about finding the right portions of each, enabling you to create the perfect marketing mix comprised of the marketing strategies that will allow you to meet or exceed your marketing objectives. (See Figure 3.9.)

FIGURE 3.9: Product, Price, Place, and Promotion Worksheet

Product

A. In detail, describe the service(s) you provide. ______________________________

____

____

B. What special features does your service have, and how do customers benefit by purchasing and using your service? ______________________________

____

____

FIGURE 3.9: Product, Price, Place, and Promotion Worksheet, continued

C. What advantages does your service provide over competitors' services? ______________

D. Describe your warranties and customer service guarantees. ______________

E. Describe any key product or service research and development initiatives underway or planned. ______________

Price

A. How much will you charge for your service(s), how did you arrive at your selling price, and what is your pricing strategy? ______________

B. How sensitive are your target customers to pricing issues, and why? ______________

C. How much do competitors charge for their service(s)? ______________

D. List the purchase payment options that you will provide to your customers—e.g., credit cards, debit cards, electronic transfers—and the benefits of providing these payment options, as well as the costs of providing each. ______________

FIGURE 3.9: Product, Price, Place, and Promotion Worksheet, continued

Place (Distribution)

A. Describe the primary method you will use to sell your services (e.g., from a retail storefront, office, homebased, trade shows, internet, etc.). ________________

____

____

B. Describe secondary methods you will use to sell your services. ________________

____

____

C. Describe any unique or proprietary systems that will be used in the delivery of services.

____

____

D. Describe the operations system you will use to manage sales, from initial order, to completion of service(s), to post-completion follow-up. ________________

____

____

Promotion

A. Describe what advertising media you will employ in the promotion of your services (newspaper, radio, television, Yellow Pages), as well as marketing materials such as fliers, signs, and business cards. ________________

____

____

B. Describe any direct sales tactics you will employ, including personal-contact selling, mail, telephone, and electronic approaches. ________________

____

____

FIGURE 3.9: Product, Price, Place, and Promotion Worksheet, continued

C. Describe how you will utilize public relations tools and mediums in the promotion of your business and services. ______________________________

____

____

D. Describe how you will use the internet to promote your services, including your web site and online marketing strategies. ______________________________

____

____

Marketing Budget

Use a ground-up approach (as in Figure 3.10) to calculate the cost of each marketing strategy and activity you intend to use to advertise, market, and sell your services. Break down each marketing activity by individual cost, and add them together to estimate your overall marketing budget.

FIGURE 3.10: Marketing Budget Worksheet

List your main marketing activities, the time period each covers, and the cost to implement.

	Marketing Activity	Time Period	Cost
1.	____________	____________	$ ________
2.	____________	____________	$ ________
3.	____________	____________	$ ________
4.	____________	____________	$ ________
5.	____________	____________	$ ________
6.	____________	____________	$ ________

Action Plan

The action plan section is really a big to-do list broken into categories and timetables (as shown in Figure 3.11), outlining when each promotional activity will be implemented and managed, as well as how and when you will measure the progress, success, or failure of each promotional activity implemented. By measuring results incrementally, you can make sure that the promotion is working and that you are on track to meet your marketing and sales objectives.

FIGURE 3.11: Action Plan Worksheet

A. Describe how each marketing strategy will be implemented. ______________________

____

____

B. Outline the timetable for implementation of each marketing strategy. ______________

____

____

C. Describe how you intend to manage each implemented marketing strategy. _________

____

____

D. Describe how you will track and measure the effectiveness of each marketing strategy.

____

____

E. Describe any contingency plans that you will use if any of these marketing strategies fail to meet sales goals and objectives. ______________________________

____

____

Financial

Many new entrepreneurs feel intimidated by financial planning because of a lack of experience. But remember, it only has to be as simple or as difficult as you want to make it. For a small business venture, you have to cover the basics—funding requirements, sources of funding, a balance sheet, equipment and inventory lists, start-up costs worksheet, and fixed monthly overhead worksheet, all of which are discussed in greater detail below.

Business plan software, such as Plan Magic, www.planmagic.com, and Palo Alto, www.paloalto.com, and accounting software such as QuickBooks, www.quickbooks.com, include customizable templates for financial forecasting and statements.

Funding Requirements

The first pieces of information that you want to include are the funding requirements for your new business. Specifically, you want to describe how much money is needed to start or grow the business, what it will be used for, and any future funding requirements (see Figure 3.12). Later in this section you will find a handy start-up costs worksheet to help calculate the total costs to start your business.

FIGURE 3.12: Funding Requirement Worksheet

A. Describe your current funding requirements. ______________________________

____

____

B. Describe what the money will be used for (e.g., purchasing tools and equipment, leasing a business location, obtaining business permits, etc.). ______________________________

____

____

C. Describe any future funding requirements and what the money will be used for (e.g., business expansion, equipment upgrades, etc.). ______________________________

____

____

Funding Sources

The next step is to identify and describe the source of your funding requirements (see Figure 3.13). In other words, this is the section where you describe where the money will come from to get started or grow the business—bank loan, private investors, or partnerships; how the money will be repaid (cash or equity); and where the money will come from to meet a repayment schedule (generally through the business revenues).

FIGURE 3.13: Funding Sources Worksheet

A. Describe how will you fund your business start-up investment. If you are going to fund the investment from more than one source, describe each. ______________________

____

____

____

B. If you are borrowing money to start your business, describe the terms and conditions including rate of interest and how the money will be repaid including the repayment schedule.

____

____

____

____

Balance Sheet

If your business is already operational, you will also want to create a balance sheet that lists your assets and liabilities, thus allowing you to determine your net equity position. Assets are items of value that your business owns, while liabilities are debts that your business owes—net equity is the difference between the two. Completing Figure 3.14 will enable you to generate a basic balance sheet. However, consult with your accountant to create a legal and audited balance sheet, which takes into account short- and long-term assets and liabilities, as well as depreciation on physical assets for tax or business valuation purposes.

FIGURE 3.14: Balance Sheet Worksheet

A. Calculate the value of current and fixed business assets.

Item	$ Value
Cash on hand	$ __________
Inventory	$ __________
Accounts receivable	$ __________
Loans receivable	$ __________
Investments	$ __________
Buildings and land	$ __________
Leasehold improvements	$ __________
Equipment and tools	$ __________
Transportation	$ __________
Deposits	$ __________
Miscellaneous assets	$ __________
Total assets	$ __________

B. Calculate liabilities

Accounts payable	$ __________
Mortgages	$ __________
Accrued expenses	$ __________
Loans	$ __________
Total liabilities	$ __________

C. Subtract your total liabilities from your total assets to calculate your net equity

Total assets	$ __________
Total liabilities	$ __________
Net equity	$ __________

Capital Equipment and Inventory Lists

Equipment and inventory lists should include what you currently have, what is needed in the short-term (less than 12 months), and what is needed for the long-term (more than 12 months). Additionally, you should include the number of units that are required, the cost of the items, and the date when the required items will be purchased. (See Figure 3.15.)

FIGURE 3.15: Capital Equipment and Inventory Lists Worksheet

Current Equipment

Equipment Description	# of Units	$ Unit Cost	Total Cost
		$	$
		$	$
		$	$
		$	$
		$	$

Needed Equipment

Equipment Description	# of Units	$ Unit Cost	Total Cost	Date Required
		$	$	
		$	$	
		$	$	
		$	$	
		$	$	

Current Inventory

Inventory Description	# of Units	$ Unit Cost	Total Cost
		$	$
		$	$
		$	$
		$	$
		$	$

Needed Inventory

Inventory Description	# of Units	$ Unit Cost	Total Cost	Date Required
		$	$	
		$	$	
		$	$	
		$	$	
		$	$	

Start-Up Costs Worksheet

Use this handy worksheet (Figure 3.16) to calculate how much money you will need to start your new business. Ignore items not relevant to your specific business start-up and add items as required.

FIGURE 3.16: Start-Up Costs Worksheet

A. Business Setup

Business registration	$ ________
Business license	$ ________
Vendor's permits	$ ________
Other permits	$ ________
Insurance	$ ________
Professional fees	$ ________
Training and education	$ ________
Bank account	$ ________
Merchant accounts	$ ________
Payment processing equipment	$ ________
Association fees	$ ________
Deposits	$ ________
Other ____________________	$ ________
Subtotal A	$ ________

B. Business Identity

Business cards	$ ________
Logo design	$ ________
Letterhead	$ ________
Envelopes	$ ________
Other ____________________	$ ________
Subtotal B	$ ________

C. Office/Storefront/Workshop

Rent deposit	$ ________
Damage deposit	$ ________
Communication equipment/devices	$ ________
Computer hardware	$ ________

FIGURE 3.16: Start-Up Costs Worksheet, continued

Software	$ ________
Furniture	$ ________
Other office equipment	$ ________
Office supplies	$ ________
Renovations and improvements	$ ________
Fixed tools and equipment	$ ________
Portable tools and equipment	$ ________
Other ____________________	$ ________
Subtotal C	$ ________
D. Transportation	
Upfront cost to buy/lease transportation	$ ________
Registration	$ ________
Insurance	$ ________
Special accessories	$ ________
Other ____________________	$ ________
Subtotal D	$ ________
E. Web Site	
Domain registration	$ ________
Site development fees	$ ________
Search engine and directory	$ ________
Equipment	$ ________
Software	$ ________
Content and web tools	$ ________
Hosting	$ ________
Other ____________________	$ ________
Subtotal E	$ ________
F. Marketing	
Research and planning costs	$ ________
Signs	$ ________
Brochures and fliers	$ ________
Catalogs	$ ________

FIGURE 3.16: Start-Up Costs Worksheet, continued

Initial advertising budget	$ ________
Initial online promotion budget	$ ________
Product samples	$ ________
Other ____________________	$ ________
Subtotal F	$ ________
G. Product Inventory (if applicable)	
# 1 ____________________	$ ________
# 2 ____________________	$ ________
# 3 ____________________	$ ________
# 4 ____________________	$ ________
# 5 ____________________	$ ________
Subtotal G	$ ________
Adding Up the Costs	
Business setup	$ ________
Business identity	$ ________
Office	$ ________
Transportation	$ ________
Web site	$ ________
Marketing	$ ________
Inventory	$ ________
Total start-up costs	$ ________
Working capital	$ ________
Total investment needed	$ ________

Monthly Overhead Costs Worksheet

You also need to know the total monthly cost of fixed overhead expenses. Use Figure 3.17 to calculate that amount. Complete only the items that are relevant to your particular business.

FIGURE 3.17: Monthly Overhead Costs Worksheet

A. General Office	
Rent or mortgage	$________
Utilities	$________
Loan and interest repayment	$________
Bank and merchant account fees	$________
Business taxes	$________
Business permits	$________
Insurance	$________
Workers' compensation	$________
Equipment leases, loans, and rentals	$________
Equipment maintenance	$________
Alarm monitoring	$________
Office supplies	$________
Postage	$________
Courier and delivery	$________
Cleaning and maintenance	$________
Other ________________	$________
Subtotal A	$________
B. Communications	
Telephone and fax lines	$________
Toll-free line	$________
Internet connection	$________
Cellular telephone	$________
Answering service	$________
Pager	$________
Two-way radio	$________
Communications equipment lease	$________
Other ________________	$________
Subtotal B	$________

FIGURE 3.17: Monthly Overhead Costs Worksheet, continued

C. Wages and Fees

Personal wages	$________
Employee wages	$________
Employee and management benefits	$________
Accounting fees	$________
Legal fees	$________
Consultant fees	$________
Business association fees	$________
Other ____________________	$________
Subtotal C	$________

D. Marketing

Yellow Pages	$________
Print advertising	$________
Broadcast advertising	$________
Outdoor advertising	$________
Fliers	$________
Direct mail and telemarketing	$________
Trade shows and seminars	$________
Public relations	$________
Contests	$________
Product samples	$________
Sponsorships	$________
Surveys, polls, and research	$________
Customer appreciation and gifts	$________
Graphic design and copy fees	$________
Other ____________________	$________
Subtotal D	$________

E. Web Site and E-Commerce

Hosting	$________
Maintenance	$________
Content and web-tool fees	$________
Internet advertising	$________

FIGURE 3.17: Monthly Overhead Costs Worksheet, continued

Search engine fees		$________
Paid placement fees		$________
Online payment system fees		$________
Other ____________________		$________
	Subtotal E	$________
F. Transportation		
Lease or loan payment		$________
Fuel		$________
Insurance		$________
Repairs		$________
Licensing		$________
Parking		$________
Cleaning		$________
Other ____________________		$________
	Subtotal F	$________
G. Miscellaneous		
Travel		$________
Entertainment		$________
Uniforms and dry cleaning		$________
Subscriptions		$________
Charitable donations		$________
Other ____________________		$________
	Subtotal G	$________
Adding Up the Costs		
General office		$________
Communications		$________
Wages and fees		$________
Marketing		$________
Web site and e-commerce		$________
Transportation		$________
Miscellaneous		$________
Fixed monthly overhead total		$________

Appendixes

If you create a business and marketing plan from the information provided in the three previous sections, you will need to include an appendix, which is the section reserved for supporting documents such as resumes for the principals, research surveys, market studies, financial forecasts, supplier and/or vendor agreements, and if your business is already established, things such as client testimonials. Think in terms of all documents that support your plans, activities, statistics, and forecasts, divided into three categories: personal documents, legal and financial documents, and marketing documents.

Supporting documents can be especially helpful if you are going to use your business plan as a tool to secure funds to start or grow your business. If your business and marketing plans are going to be used strictly as a road map to help guide your business, you will not need to create and include these documents. Nonetheless, it is still a good idea if for no other reason than to keep all important and relevant business documents together in one binding. If your intentions are to use your business plan to secure funds, make sure to include only copies of supporting documents, and not originals.

Personal Documents

The personal support documents should include resumes for all the main players in the business, including owner(s), managers, key employees, sales agents, and subcontractors, even if they are only simple one-page resumes highlighting experiences in bullet-list format. Copies of training certificates or specialized licenses held by the owner(s), managers, or key employees should also be included. And if the purpose of the business plan is to secure funding, you will need to include a personal asset statement for each of the people who are applying for the loan. The asset statement should list all assets, such as real estate, automobiles, equities, savings plans, and all personal liabilities, including property mortgages, personal loans, and credit cards.

Legal and Financial Documents

There are also legal and financial documents to include with your business plan, and depending on the purpose of your business plan, these documents, statements, and forecasts might include any or all of the following:

- Business registrations, incorporation papers, permits, and licenses
- Business insurance coverage documents
- Warranties and guarantees you provide
- Vendor, supplier, and/or subcontractor agreements in force

- Domain name registrations
- If applicable, patents, trademarks, and copyright documents
- Start-up cost estimates and fixed operating cost projections
- Break-even analysis, and short-term and long-term sales projections
- Equipment and inventory projections, estimates, and lists

Marketing Documents

Documents supporting your marketing research and statements within your business and marketing plan should be included. Any or all of the following would qualify as marketing support documents:

- Research documents, including surveys, questionnaires, and focus group results
- Target customer profile
- PEST (Political, Economic, Social, and Technical) and SWOT (Strengths, Weaknesses, Opportunities, and Threats) analyses
- Business marketing materials, including brochures, product photographs, catalogs, price lists, and print advertisements
- Press clippings
- Client testimonials and company, individual, or organizational endorsements
- Competitor brochures, price lists, warranties, and print advertisements, and Better Business Bureau reports, if available
- Marketing budgets and projections

CHAPTER

4

SETTING UP SHOP

In order to sell services, you need a base of operations to work from; you need to set up shop. Setting up shop goes far beyond a business location and includes equipping your office with furniture, technology, and communication devices, and taking your business online with a web site so that you can sell your services to a worldwide audience. Setting up shop also means that you must build a team to help operate your business to maximize the potential for success and profitability. Your business team can include family members, friends, employees, professional services, suppliers, subcontractors, and business alliances. You also have to create a business image, one that over time and with consistent use, people will start to visually identify with your business and the services you sell (referred to as branding). This chapter covers some of the more important bases when it comes time to physically set up your business.

Choosing a Business Location

Choosing a location for your business will depend on a number of factors, such as the types of services you plan to sell, office space requirements, budget, workshop space requirements, whether you will have client visits, and if you require high-visibility street exposure to attract walk-in business. Another business location is the internet, which is discussed later in this chapter.

Many businesses, especially those selling services, can also be operated on a mobile basis, such as car-detailing, dog-walking, personal chef service, and marketing consultant. For entrepreneurs providing these types of services, suitable and reliable transportation will be of greater importance than a physical business location. But regardless of whether you operate your business on a mobile or stationary basis, you will still need to establish some base of operation, probably in your home. This section covers information on three basic operating locations—homebased, office, and storefront. It is worth noting that, excluding your home, more times than not business owners are better off renting a business location rather than buying a location, at least until the business proves stable and profitable.

Homebased

If you plan on setting up shop at home, the first issue to tackle is: Can you legally operate a business from your home? Chances are you can, although probably with some restrictions. There is no standard, across-the-board set of rules, and each community in the United States and Canada has its own home business zoning regulations and specific usage guidelines. The majority of municipalities do allow businesses to operate from a residence, providing the business activities do not negatively impact neighbors and the neighborhood in general. From a zoning standpoint, the potential issues include exterior signage, parking, noise, fire, storage of hazardous substances, deliveries and shipping, nonfamily employees working from your home, and customers visiting your home. Long before you decide to start to operate your business from home, you need to check zoning rules, regulations, and restrictions. I suggest that you visit your city or municipal planning department or bylaws office for further information.

The second issue is determining what space in your home will best suit your business needs. Homebased workspace options range from any room of the house to a separate outside structure. I have used a converted garage, a den, a living room, a basement, and a spare bedroom for various home business ventures over the years, and each has advantages and disadvantages. Careful consideration must be given to the needs of your family and how space in the home is currently being utilized for day-to-day living, special occasions, seasonal activities, and guests. Because setting up a home workspace requires balancing the needs of your business with the needs of your family, compromises will probably have to be made on both fronts.

If you will have no (or few) clients coming to your home, workspace issues are not as important, but there are still a few things to consider. First off, if money is tight, select a room that will require the fewest alterations and preferably one with a door that shuts to keep business in, and family, friends, and pets out when necessary. But at the same time make sure your workspace is large enough to operate your business. Working out of two or three separate areas of the home is far less productive than working from one. Also, try to make your workspace a single-use area. Ideally, the room should not double as the dining room at night or the children's playroom. If you will be having numerous clients visiting your home, workspace issues are much more important, such as a separate entrance for clients, washroom facilities, and parking. Another consideration is the appearance of your home. Peeling paint, threadbare carpets, and broken porch boards send customers the wrong signals about your business. If your home needs a spruce-up, then do it before you get started.

Whether you have customers coming to your home or not, you will also need storage space for equipment, possibly inventory, and business records. Provided you have enough storage space to meet your needs, the space you use will also need to be easily accessible, dry, and free of critters. It must also be secure so there is no risk that valuable business equipment, inventory, and records will be stolen. If you do not have suitable storage space, is there storage for rent close-by with good access, and how much does it cost? There is more to know about operating a business at home than space permits here. Consequently, you might want to sign out a copy of 📖 *Entrepreneur Magazine's Ultimate Homebased Business Handbook* (Entrepreneur Press, 2004) from your local library, or purchase one from retail booksellers nationwide and online. The book is an *A* to *Z* explanation of everything you need to know about starting and operating a homebased business.

Office

A second option is to rent commercial office space in a strip plaza, mall, office tower, or low-rise building. The space you rent could be on a month-to-month basis, but the majority of landlords prefer to lease space for a set amount of time, generally no fewer than 12 months and commonly as long as ten years. An alternative to a long-term lease agreement is to rent space in a shared office space environment, otherwise known as an executive office suite. There are many benefits to shared office facilities, such as having your own individual office, along with access to extended office facilities and services for the use of all tenants. An executive office suite can give you everything you need at a fraction of what you would normally pay to rent, equip, and staff a traditional office space. These facilities and services can be included in your rent or billed on a user basis, depending on your rental agreement. The benefits of shared office space include things such as boardroom space, centralized reception, answering service and toll-free options, fax service, internet and e-mail accounts, web site hosting and maintenance, shipping and receiving options, mailboxes, word processing, database management, centralized client waiting rooms, and notary and paralegal services. Executive office space is a great choice for small businesses just getting off the ground because most come fully furnished, there are no long-term lease agreements, and as a rule of thumb, rents are very reasonable.

If you need your own traditional office for space or business image reasons, issues that need to be addressed before signing the lease agreement include:

- Budget
- Lease term
- Leasehold improvement requirements
- Parking and access to transit
- Street visibility, if necessary
- Proximity to your target audience or current customers
- Washroom, kitchen, and boardroom facilities
- Cleaning, maintenance, and security issues

Storefront

The third location option is a retail storefront, which will be necessary if your business depends on walk-in traffic to generate new sales. Potential storefront locations include a shopping center, a freestanding commercial building, in the downtown core, or in a strip plaza. Like any business that relies on walk-in traffic, location is the critical success factor, and without the right location your chances of business failure increase exponentially. Consequently, your storefront location needs to be in proximity to the largest population of your target audience, and it must also have excellent visibility to your target audience. Choosing a less visible space to save $1,000 per month on rent is a waste of money, because you will spend an additional $2,000 to reach your target audience through advertising and promotion just to inform them where your business is located. On that note, you might want to get a copy of *Location, Location, Location*, by Luigi Salvanenschi, (Entrepreneur Press, 2002). Though meant primarily for product retailers, the book is full of excellent advice for any business that needs to select the right location to benefit from walk-in business.

I have compiled a handy location checklist (See Figure 4.1) to aid in the selection of the right storefront location for your business.

FIGURE 4.1: Location Checklist

Yes	No	
❑	❑	Is the location large enough for your current needs and is there the potential to expand inside or outside to accommodate future growth?
❑	❑	Are the exterior and interior of the building in a good state of repair?
❑	❑	Does the location meet zoning, fire, and handicapped-accessibility regulations?
❑	❑	Is the rent within your budget, and are the lease terms favorable?
❑	❑	Does the location require an unusually large amount of leasehold improvements?
❑	❑	Are mechanical requirements such as electrical, heating, plumbing, and communications suitable for your type of business?
❑	❑	Does the exterior of the building have "curb appeal" that is consistent with the business image you want to project?
❑	❑	Is there suitable parking, and is it free or paid, and does this impact on your business?
❑	❑	If applicable, is there good access to public transit?
❑	❑	Does the store have the type of visibility that you want or require?
❑	❑	Will the competition in the area enhance or detract from your business?
❑	❑	Is your business compatible with the other businesses in the general area?
❑	❑	Is there suitable space for exterior and interior signage, and will local ordinance permit the type of signage you want to install?
❑	❑	Do pedestrian and passing motorist traffic counts meet your requirements?
❑	❑	Are there any restrictive covenants in place preventing you from marketing and promoting your business in the style that you want to?
❑	❑	Is the store located in an area that is comprised mainly of your target audience?

Equipping Your Office

The need for office equipment, furniture, technology, and communication devices will vary depending on your business location and the types of services you sell. Of course, every business will need the basics such as a desk, computer station, and telephone, which are discussed in greater detail below. Budget will also come into play when you are equipping your office, and for the *financially challenged entrepreneur* there are a few ways to equip an office on a shoestring budget, or at least substantially reduce the amount of money you need upfront.

The first way to reduce equipment costs is to barter or trade for what you need. For instance, if you operate a catering service, ask the local sign shop if they would be interested in trading catering services for new signs. You can also join a local barter club and trade your services with members who sell office equipment. You can visit Barter News, www.barternews.com, which is an online magazine dedicated to the world of business barter clubs, organizations, and industry information to track down a barter club in your area.

Another way to save money on office equipment is to purchase secondhand, factory seconds, or floor models. Scan classified and auction listings in your local newspaper for secondhand office furniture and equipment. Generally you'll save as much as 75 percent off new costs by buying used. Also call around to your local office outfitters and inquire about factory seconds and the floor models they have available. Purchasing seconds or floor models with slight blemishes will often save you as much as 25 percent off the retail price.

Likewise, you can also take the no-money-down route and lease brand-new office furniture, equipment, and computers for your business, or rent these items. You will have to pay for these items monthly, but you will not be tying up precious marketing cash buying them. Keep in mind too that lease and rent payments are 100 percent deductible business expenses.

Furniture

If clients will be visiting your office, your furniture, equipment, and décor will need to reflect this, both in appearance and function. If clients are not visiting your office, you will have more leeway, because it won't really matter if furniture colors and styles are mismatched or if you purchased a secondhand desk. All that really matters is that your furniture and equipment are reliable and comfortable. So what are the basics that every office needs, regardless of the types of services you sell?

DESK

You will need a desk large enough for a computer monitor with tower storage underneath, a printer, and a telephone/fax machine. By having a desk large enough for basic equipment, you can be more productive by not having to get up from the desk to answer the telephone or move to a separate computer workstation.

Comfortable Chair

If you can only splurge on one piece of office furniture, a comfortable and ergonomically correct chair should be that luxury item, especially if your business keeps you in front of the computer or on the telephone for long periods of time. Key features to look for are distance from the seat to floor, adjustable armrests, and adjustable seating positions.

File Storage

Business and client records are important, so investing in a good-quality file storage system is money well spent. Purchase a file cabinet with a locking mechanism and complete with hangers and folders large enough to suit your business at the present and for future growth, because the difference is only about $50.

Bookshelf and Worktable

Bookshelves and worktables are also indispensable items for the office. Bookshelves can be used to organize and store books, product catalogs, office supplies, and computer software and disks. Worktables separate from your desk are also big timesavers because they can be used for working on lower-priority jobs, opening and sorting mail, book and record-keeping duties, and much more.

Technology

Like office furniture, there is basic technology that every business needs to operate, including a computer, operating system, software, monitor, modem, and printer. Depending on the services you sell, you may not need the latest technology, but your equipment must be reliable and the software you use must enable you to be efficient and productive.

Computer

Assuming you know how to use a computer (if not, waste no time signing up for computer training ASAP), the main considerations are processing speed and data storage capabilities. Both change on a daily basis, so I won't talk about the basics other than to advise you to get as much speed and memory as you can afford. Desktop computers range from a low of $600 to as much as $3,000 for a top-of-the-line computer used by web developers and designers. Additionally, if your business takes you on the road a lot, you should purchase a notebook computer, again with as much speed and memory capacity as you can afford. Expect to pay in the range of $1,500 to $4,000.

MONITOR

A computer monitor is another essential piece of equipment. You can purchase a standard monitor, a flat screen monitor, or a flat panel LCD monitor, which is the best choice if desk space is limited. New 17-inch monitors start at about $150, and can go as high as $1,500 for a 21-inch LCD that would be suitable for professional desktop publishing.

KEYBOARD AND MOUSE

Basic keyboard and mouse sets are very inexpensive, only about $50. But if you are like me and dislike wires cluttering your desktop, consider spending an extra $100 to upgrade to a wireless keyboard and mouse set; it frees space on your desk and prevents wires from getting wrapped around everything.

MODEM

Most computers come with a standard 56K modem, which is needed to connect to the internet. You can also opt for a more expensive modem, giving you the ability to connect to high-speed cable internet (if available in your area), which allows you to download files up to 20 times faster than a standard dial-up internet connection.

PRINTER

An inkjet printer starts at about $50, while a laser printer costs in the range of $200 to $1,000, depending on features, color option, and print speed. But I suggest that you buy a laser printer if you are going to be doing a lot of printing because on average each printed page will cost half as much as what it would cost to print a page with an inkjet printer.

DIGITAL CAMERA

A digital camera is an indispensable piece of equipment for business owners. You can take pictures of products, clients, and completed jobs, and because the images (photographs) use digital technology, they are easily transferred to your web site, e-mails, or desktop publishing programs. It enables you to easily create brochures, presentations, catalogs, and fliers, inhouse and for a fraction of what it costs to have these items created at a print shop.

COMMUNICATIONS

The proliferation of high-tech communication devices in the last few years makes it very easy to spend a whole lot of money in a very short time. But, once again, if you can get by with just the basic communication devices at first, you have the potential to upgrade to new and better equipment using future profits.

TELEPHONE

One of the first communication devices you should purchase and install is the good old desktop telephone. Ideally, this telephone will have business features and functions such as on-hold, conferencing, redial, speakerphone, broadcast, and message storage capabilities.

FAX MACHINE

Although fax transmissions have greatly declined in the last few years because of the increased use of e-mail, a fax machine will still be needed to operate your business. Most contracts and agreements that need to be signed are legal when faxed if both parties agree in the contract. If you do not want to purchase a separate fax machine, you might consider purchasing an all-in-one office document center, which usually includes a telephone, fax, scanner, and copier in one machine.

CELLULAR TELEPHONE

A cellular telephone is now a must for all business people. Not only do they enable you to take incoming calls from almost anywhere, but they also enable you to stay in constant contact with your best customers and hottest prospects. Cellular telephone service plans are now very inexpensive: for less than $50 per month, you can have nearly unlimited access to as many minutes as you want. Consider purchasing a cell phone with internet features that give you the ability to check e-mail when you are away from your computer.

TELEPHONE HEADSET

If your business keeps you working at a computer all day or in your car, a headset will be a definite need. It leaves your hands free to work on the computer as you talk on the phone, or to drive your car in relative safety. Headsets, both wired and wireless, are available for both your desktop phone and your cellular phone. Count on spending in the range of $25 to $75 for each.

INTERNET CONNECTION

You will also need an internet connection that enables you to access the web and send and receive e-mails. Unlimited dial-up access generally costs in the range of $15 per month; high-speed access generally runs in the range of $20 to $50 per month, but you will also need to upgrade your modem at an additional cost if you choose high-speed.

Office Equipment and Supplies Checklist

Setting up a new office is complex because there are so many pieces of furniture, equipment, and basic supplies needed to create an efficient office ready for maximum productivity. It helps to have a checklist (see Figure 4.2), which can be used as a yardstick to keep track of the items you need.

FIGURE 4.2: Office Furniture, Equipment, and Supplies Checklist

Office Furniture and Equipment

- ❑ Desk
- ❑ Comfortable chair
- ❑ File cabinets
- ❑ Overhead and work lighting
- ❑ Client seating
- ❑ Fireproof safe
- ❑ Desktop and pocket calculators
- ❑ Bookcases
- ❑ Postage meter
- ❑ Worktable(s)
- ❑ Office decorations
- ❑ Labeling machine
- ❑ Wall whiteboard and markers
- ❑ Radio
- ❑ Paper shredder
- ❑ Photocopier
- ❑ Wastebasket
- ❑ Recycling bin
- ❑ Alarm system
- ❑ Fire extinguisher
- ❑ First-aid kit

Computer Hardware and Accessories

- ❑ Desktop computer and monitor
- ❑ Keyboard and mouse
- ❑ Printer
- ❑ Modem
- ❑ Notebook computer
- ❑ CD writer
- ❑ PowerPoint projector
- ❑ Digital camera
- ❑ Palm organizer
- ❑ Surge protector
- ❑ Computer locks
- ❑ Scanner

Computer Software

- ❑ Word processing program
- ❑ Virus protection software
- ❑ Accounting software
- ❑ Desktop publishing software
- ❑ Contact management software
- ❑ Web site building and maintenance software
- ❑ Payment processing software
- ❑ E-commerce software
- ❑ Inventory management software

Communications

- ❑ Telephone line
- ❑ Internet connection
- ❑ Toll-free line
- ❑ Desk telephone
- ❑ Fax machine
- ❑ Cordless telephone
- ❑ Answering machine/service
- ❑ Cordless headset
- ❑ Speakerphone
- ❑ Pager
- ❑ Tape recorder
- ❑ Cellular telephone with internet features

FIGURE 4.2: Office Furniture, Equipment, and Supplies Checklist, continued

General Office Supplies

❑ Business cards	❑ Envelopes	❑ Stationery
❑ Imprinted advertising specialties	❑ Postage stamps	❑ Printer cartridges
❑ CD and floppy disks	❑ Pencils and pens	❑ Printer paper
❑ Cleaning supplies	❑ Fax paper	❑ Notepads
❑ File folders	❑ Stapler	❑ Scissors

Building Your Business Team

Building your business team is just as important as any other piece of the business puzzle, and depending on your business structure and the services you sell, your business team might include family members, employees, sales agents, subcontractors, suppliers, professional service providers, and other team players such as business associates. As you can see, your business team has the potential to be very comprehensive. Consequently, a plan must be developed to build your business team for the present and for future growth.

Family Members

Family members make up the first part of your business team, especially the ones who will also be working in the business. Even family members who do not work in the business will be affected by the business as well as the business decisions you make. The business will have an effect on your family, and your family will have an effect on your business—it is inevitable. Consequently, one goal of business owners is to gain family support for the venture; the family must understand why you want to start a business. Don't be upset if your family members do not share your level of enthusiasm for your new business. Remember that in most cases, the new business will be your dream, not theirs. As in any new business venture, there are inherent financial risks, which may make some family members nervous. But more important, do not view your family members as a pool of temporary help when you get busy. The decision of whether or not to work in the "family business" must be left up to each family member. With that said, however, many small family businesses have flourished and grown into multinational corporations.

Employees

Depending on the services you sell and your business goals, you may or may not need to hire employees. Employing people does add lots of additional administrative and management work, but if your plans are to grow your business, at some point you will need to hire employees. The trick is, of course, to hire the right people the first time around, because poor customer service practices will alienate customers, and salespeople who prefer to talk when they should be listening can drive business to the competition faster than a speeding bullet. Unfortunately, discovering that you have hired the wrong person for the job generally comes too late, long after the damage has occurred. So what are the characteristics of a good employee? Good employees are productive, project a professional image, are honest, loyal, confident, punctual, and can work with minimal supervision. Hiring good employees is only part of the equation, because to attract good employees you need to be able to offer and provide them with a fair salary, opportunities for advancement, job security, new challenges, and above all, recognition. Additional features such as heath care and dental plans, profit-sharing plans, and flexible work schedules will also go a long way toward attracting and retaining top talent.

There are other than hiring full-time employees, such as hiring temporary workers on an as-needed basis, and hiring sales agents and subcontractors. Sales agents and subcontractors are discussed further along in this section. Employing temp workers to meet your short-term labor requirements is one of the better alternatives. The cost is generally 25 percent more expensive per hour on average than you would have to pay if you hired an employee, but when you factor in the time saved by not having to run help wanted ads, interview candidates, and check work references, the difference is negligible.

If you decide that hiring employees is the best option, you will have to comply with laws and regulations governing employment practices, including, but not limited to, labor laws, minimum wages, health and safety workplace issues, work hours, and workers' compensation insurance coverage. As an employer, you will need to obtain an Employer Identification Number (EIN), and you are also required to withhold and remit employee income tax and Social Security Insurance. Labor laws may be researched in the United States by contacting the Department of Labor, ☎ (877) 889-5627, ✐ www.dol.gov; in Canada, you can contact Human Resources Development Canada, ☎ (800) 567-6866, ✐ www.hrdc-drhc.gc.ca. To obtain an Employer Identification Number in the United States, visit your local Internal Revenue Service office or visit the IRS web site, ✐ www.irs.gov, to download the EIN form. In Canada, you can visit local Canada Customs and Revenue Agency offices or visit the CCRA web site, ✐ www.ccra-adrc.gc.ca, to download the EIN form.

Sales Agents

An alternative to hiring salespeople to sell your services is to contract with a freelance sales agent(s). This can be a very good alternative for small business owners operating a sales driven business, such as home improvement services, consulting services, and internet technology services, for several reasons. First, the majority of sales agents (also known as independent or freelance sales consultants) prefer to work on a contract basis for tax reasons and to maintain the ability to represent more than one business client at a time. This saves extra paperwork and you do not have to worry about providing employee benefits, because freelance sales agents are self-employed. Second, sales agents generally are armed with the tools they need to sell—transportation, computer hardware and software, cell phones, and other tools of the trade, saving you money by not having to purchase these items. Third, and perhaps the biggest benefit of contracting with sales agents, is the fact that they bring two big assets to the table—the ability to prospect effectively for new business, and in most cases, an existing customer and contact base that can be capitalized on immediately. Almost all sales agents prefer to work on a performance-based fee system, retaining a portion of their total sales as a commission. Depending on what is being sold and the costs associated with selling the service, gross commissions can range from 5 to 30 percent of the total sales value.

Subcontractors

It is also common practice for small business owners to subcontract all or some of their work to other qualified individuals and businesses. For instance, general contractors will subcontract various segments of a renovation contract to different sub-trades—framing crews, roofers, painters, and electricians. A desktop publishing service might subcontract various tasks such as printing, proofreading, and graphic design to qualified businesses in fulfilling a client's contract. Depending on how you structure your business and fulfill contracts, you might also find that you need to hire subcontractors to complete all of the work for some clients. When hiring or contracting with subcontractors, you do have to take some precautions because your subcontractor's work or performance is viewed as your work or performance in the eyes of your customers. After all, your client contracted with you for the job, not your subcontractors. Likewise, you will need to make sure your subcontractors are reliable and fully insured. You will also need to know that they warranty or guarantee their work. Additionally, always work from a written and binding contract that spells out all the details, including payment, performance, and liability issues between the two parties.

Suppliers

Suppliers from whom you purchase products and services for the operation of your business are also important members of your business team. Suppliers can play a major role in your ultimate success or failure. Consequently, these relationships need to be carefully developed and managed. Decisions to select and work with one supplier over another cannot be based solely on who offers the lowest price; you also have to factor in many other influences, such as payment terms, warranties and guarantees, and reliability. Remember that your supplier's promises to you are your promises to your customers. If your supplier lets you down, you in turn let your customers down. Find out what tools, equipment, or marketing materials your suppliers offer for free or at greatly reduced costs to help their vendors. Many have programs in place in which they offer their trade accounts valuable equipment, marketing materials, and cooperative advertising opportunities that will help businesses to be more efficient, productive, and profitable. Items that you might be able to tap your suppliers for include:

- Ongoing specialized training
- Advertising specialties such as pens, notepads, and hats
- Product samples, displays, and brochures
- Contest prizes, management, and support
- Store, job site, and vehicle signs
- Special-event signs, posters, banners, and table tents
- Technical support and customer service assistance
- Computer hardware and software
- Specialized tools and equipment

Working with Professional Services

Professional service providers such as lawyers, bankers, accountants, and consultants are also important business team members. When selecting professional service providers, it is imperative to keep in mind that often it is the professional's experience, knowledge, and advice that you will be leveraging to stay in business, to grow your business, to keep you out of trouble, and to help you with a whole host of other issues pertaining to the setup and management of your business.

LAWYER

Anyone who has ever been in business knows that operating a business and having access to good legal advice go hand in hand. I can't imagine trying to take a business from start-up to full operation without legal advice. Competent lawyers with small-business experience will be able to advise you on which legal business structure best meets your needs, insurance and liability issues, drafting of legal documents, money collection and small-claims court matters, estate planning and continuation of your business, and other contracts. To find a lawyer in the United States, you can contact the American Bar Association, ☎ (202) 662-1000, www.abanet.org, and in Canada, the Canadian Bar Association,

☎ (800) 267-8860, ✐ www.cba.org. These associations will help you locate a lawyer in your area who specializes in small business legal matters.

Banker

Establishing a business relationship with a banker includes all employees at the bank where you open your business accounts—manager, loan officers, and tellers. Having a good working relationship with a bank or credit union is a critical success factor for small businesses. You never know when you will need to borrow working capital or growth capital, or secure a quick loan to get you through the next 60 days until a client contract is completed, billed, and collected.

Accountant

Even with the proliferation of accounting and bookkeeping software, hiring an accountant to take care of more complicated money matters is wise. Accountants pride themselves on the fact that they do not cost you money, but rather make you money by discovering items overlooked on tax returns, by identifying business deductions you never knew existed, and by creating financial plans. Contact the Association of Chartered Accountants in the United States, ☎ (212) 334-2078, ✐ www.acaus.org, to find a small business CPA in your area; in Canada contact the Chartered Accountants of Canada, ☎ (416) 977-3222, ✐ www.cica.ca.

Consultants

Professional consultants have long played a role in helping small business owners meet and exceed their business and marketing objectives through coaching, planning, new business development, and training strategies. Consulting experts are available in just about every business discipline imaginable, including small business, logistics, marketing, sales, employee and management training, computer, internet technologies, franchising, advertising, and public relations. The first step in hiring a business consultant is to define your objective. What do you want to fix, improve, or venture into? Once you know your objective(s), then you can select and interview a few potential candidates for the job. There are a number of online consultant directories such as The Training Registry, ✐ www.training registry.com, which lists consultants by specialty and is indexed geographically. Elance Online, ✐ www.elanceonline.com, is also a great place to find expert consulting services.

Other Team Players

There are also other businesses, associations, and organizations that you will want to build relationships with to enable you to operate your business more productively, promote your services more efficiently, and gain valuable insights into your business, industry, and customers. Ideally, all this and more will be achieved. Not as crucial as some of the more frontline members of your business team, other players nonetheless can play a major role in contributing to the success and profitability of your business.

Business, Industry, and Professionals Associations

Joining business, industry, or professional associations relevant to your business, the services you sell, or the community where you do business can become a gold mine of valuable information, assistance, and business-building opportunities. Joining means that you can have access to member discounts on products and services used to operate your business, as well as networking opportunities, new business alliances, advertising opportunities, and learning and education opportunities through seminars and workshops. The largest small business association in North America is the chamber of commerce. To find a chamber near you in the United States, visit, www.uschamber.com, and in Canada visit www.chamber.ca.

Cross-Promotional Partners

Building cross-promotional partnerships with other businesses in your community can also prove very beneficial and profitable, mainly because you can capitalize on each partner's experiences, resources, and customer base. Cross-promotional activities should be developed so they increase brand awareness, have the ability to reach a broader audience, and attract new business to you while driving down the cost for each partner to market and promote their respective businesses, goods, and services. Basically, cross-promotional activities enable entrepreneurs who share similar goals and objectives to band together to minimize financial risk while maximizing potential profits.

Schools

It is also wise to bring local schools and educational institutions aboard as team players, because many have cooperative work programs in place that are designed to bring community businesses and young people together. Students can receive much-needed, hands-on work experience, and businesses can benefit from the students' fresh ideas and creativity. Students can also be great teachers, helping small business owners with computer hardware and software training, as well as marketing research and planning. Don't forget that building business relationships with schools also gives you access to a pool of eager part-time, seasonal, or temporary help.

Competitors

Competitors can also make up part of your business team, especially if you join forces with those competitors who operate outside of your geographical trading area to build strong business coalitions. Banding together with competitors may enable you to negotiate lower supply costs based on increased purchasing power. And as part of a larger coalition, you may find that you are able to bid on and secure goods and service supply contracts that would normally be too large for just your business to handle alone. You will be able to identify and overcome marketing and business challenges facing the industry through collective brainstorming and the planning process, not to mention offering to assist one another with overflow work during busy times.

Creating a Business Image

When setting up your business, you will also need to create a business image to help brand your business and services and project a positive image. This is especially important for service providers because most do not have the advantage of elaborate offices or elegant storefronts to impress prospects and customers. Instead, they must rely on imagination, creativity, and paying attention to the smallest detail when creating and maintaining a professional business image.

Logos and Slogans

The first consideration is an attention-grabbing logo and memorable slogan to help build consumer awareness of the services you sell and project a positive business image. Business logos and promotional slogans play a major role in branding, especially logos because of their visual recognition qualities—consumers see instantly that it is a brand they know, like, and trust. To develop a slogan simply think about the biggest benefit that people receive from buying your service, and create a brief yet powerful slogan around that benefit. Logos, however, can be a little trickier to create unless you have design experience and a creative flair. But if these are skills you lack, there are many logo design services such as The Logo Company, www.thelogocompany.com, and Logo Bee, www.logobee.com that can help you create a professional logo for your business, with prices for basic design services starting at less than $100. Keep in mind, however, that once you have decided on a logo and a promotional slogan, you must consistently incorporate them into every area of your business, including stationery, signage, promotional materials, uniforms, and advertising. The more often consumers are exposed to your brand through the consistent use of logos and slogans, the more they will remember it, giving you brand recognition.

Print Identity Package

An identity package is comprised of the various print elements that you use daily in the course of operating your business—business cards, stationery, receipts, envelopes, estimate forms, presentation folders, marketing brochures, catalogs, fliers, and account statements. Key to a great print identity package is consistency throughout the entire package, just as in your entire marketing program. You want to develop a standard color scheme and font and combine these with your logo and slogan for consistent use so that customers and prospects begin to visually link your business with your identity program. Remember to obtain three quotes for all your printing needs, and do not necessarily buy based only on price. Instead, base your purchasing decision on quality, value, reputation, and turnaround time. In addition to your community printer, there are also many printers doing business online such as Print USA, www.printusa.com, which offer free quotes on a wide variety of products.

Uniforms

Top businesspeople have long understood the benefits associated with uniforms emblazoned with their business name and logo. These benefits include branding the business name and products, projecting a professional image, and helping to distinguish employees from customers. Uniforms also happen to be terrific advertising and promotional tools. Great-looking uniforms do not have to be expensive; for as little as $20 each you can purchase smart casual golf shirts silkscreened or embroidered with your business name and logo. Hats start at $10 each, jackets at about $50. T-shirts that you can give away to customers and use in special promotions cost about $10 each. All of which is money wisely spent to project a professional image and advertise your business.

Selling Your Services Online

If you are excited about the idea of selling your services online, you should be. American consumers spent more than $95 billion on online purchases in 2003; that figure is expected to reach $230 billion by 2008! Granted, products do account for the larger portion of online sales, but many entrepreneurs sell their services online and make incredible profits in the process. There is a lot to know and learn about taking your business online and selling your services to consumers around the globe. Needless to say, space restrictions do not allow for an in-depth explanation of everything you need to know about doing business online, but the following information covers the important basics. These are: developing a web site, selecting a domain name, registering your site with search engines, and optimizing your keywords.

Developing a Web Site

Not every service is suitable for selling online. So your first decision will be to determine if you need a web site. Even if you are not planning to sell your services online, a site can still be a very effective communication tool and useful for gathering information captured from visitors for research and planning purposes. Ultimately, you will have to decide if the time and money spent to develop, maintain, and market a web site will be a wise investment and help you to meet your business objectives. If you do decide to sell your services online, the advantages are apparent—the ability to sell 24 hours a day, communicate with prospects and customers quickly and cheaply, update your marketing message and special promotions almost instantly, and be able to sell to consumers around the globe.

Once you have made the decision to build a web site, there are many decisions to be made: How much will it cost to create a web site? Who will build it? Who will maintain it? Who will host your site? What purchase payment options will you provide customers? And how will the site be promoted? The first option is to design, build, and maintain your own web site. Fortunately, there are numerous good web site building programs available that enable novices to build and maintain their own sites, but you will still need to be familiar with computers and the internet if you go this route. Hosting and maintenance costs will vary depending on the services you select—e-commerce shopping carts, payment systems, order tracking, content, web tools, site statistics, and database storage options. Expect to pay a minimum of $50 per month for basic business web site hosting and about $250 per month for premium services.

The second option is to hire a professional to design and build your web site. Costs here have dramatically decreased in the past few years. In fact, for less than $1,000, you can have a complete, fully functional web site built with e-commerce, visitor interaction, and database marketing options. Consult your local Yellow Pages for web developers in your community.

Selecting a Domain Name

Selecting a domain name for your new web site requires careful consideration because the domain name you select must be suited to the services you sell, which is easier said than done. Good dotcom designations are becoming increasingly difficult to acquire. The domain name that you choose should also be short, easily remembered, and easily spelled. Start the process of choosing a domain name right away, and register a few variations as soon as you have compiled a short list. Good names are hard to get, and the ones that do become available go fast. Domain name registration fees vary depending on the name and the registration service you choose, but expect to pay from a low of $10 per year for a budget registrar, to as much as $75 per year with a full-service registration company. Most registrars also offer discounts if you register a name for a longer period—up to ten years. The majority of domain registration services also provide various additional internet and e-commerce services and packages, ranging from web site design to shopping carts, hosting and maintenance services, and web site promotional services. A few of the more popular domain name registration services include Domain Direct, ✐ www.domaindirect.com, Register, ✐ www.register.com, and Network Solutions, ✐ www.networksolutions.com.

Registering Your Site with Search Engines

Because you don't know which search engine or directory people will use when looking for products and services online, you will need to register your web site and pages with numerous engines and directories to ensure maximum exposure. But before you start registering, you should know the basics. Search engines are indexed by bots or spiders, which extract specific information and keywords from web site pages, which are then used for indexing. Search directories use people referred to as directory editors who compile the information by hand, which is generally indexed and grouped based on relevance to the submitted search. However, the line between search engine and search directory is increasingly blurred. Most major search engines and directories use both mechanical and human power to build and index information or supplement each other's services, so you need to register with both.

Registering with engines and directories can be very frustrating and time-consuming because there are no standard guidelines, as most searches engines and directories have individual submission policies. There are search engine and directory submission services that will automatically submit or register your web site to all major search engines and directories, which is a wise choice for entrepreneurs on a tight time schedule. Most of these services require that you only complete one relatively basic form, and they will do the rest. Some submission services are free, but the majority charge fees if you want quick listings, regular maintenance, and other premium listing services. These services allow small business owners with limited time to optimize their web sites for the best search-rank results—a great value for a relatively small fee. The more popular submission services include Add Me, ✐ www.addme.com, Submit It, ✐ www.submit-it.com, and Submit Express, ✐ www.submitexpress.com. Google, ✐ www.google.com remains the most widely known search engine, while Yahoo, ✐ www.yahoo.com is the most widely known search directory.

Optimizing Your Keyword

The majority of internet users conduct searches for products, services, and information by using keywords and keyword phrases. Therefore, you will definitely need to optimize your web site for keyword searches. Most online marketing specialists suggest a keyword density of about 5 percent. This means that keywords will comprise 5 out of every 100 words of site content, and will appear in page titles, headers, meta tags, and hyperlinks. Each web page is unique in terms of the information featured and its marketing objective, so be sure to select different keywords relevant to each page. Also be descriptive when selecting keywords and phrases, and combine multiple keywords into short descriptive phrases, because few people type in single search words. A good starting point is to make lists of words describing your services and conduct search engine and directory searches using these words. The top ten results will help you pinpoint the best and most descriptive keywords to use when optimizing your own keywords for your web pages. There are also keyword generators and even keyword creation services that will optimize your keyword selection for a fee, such as Word Tracker, www.wordtracker.com. A final note, always include the maximum number of keywords the search engines allow, but keep in mind that directories base ranking more on the quality of the content than just on keywords. So concentrate on quality content as well to improve search results.

CHAPTER

5

EVERYTHING ELSE YOU NEED TO KNOW TO OPERATE YOUR BUSINESS

This chapter will provide a brief yet informative rundown on a few of the more important business topics and issues that have not been discussed thus far, which I like to refer to as "everything else you need to know to operate your business so you can sell your services for big profits." You will learn the importance of providing great customer service, how to price your service for profitability, how to effectively advertise your business and services, great public relations tools that you can put to work for your business, event marketing secrets that get results, super productive selling and closing techniques, options for growing your business, and a host of additional helpful information, ideas, and tips that have been specifically developed to put you on the path to long-term business success and profitability.

Keeping Your Customers Happy

In business, often what separates winners from losers is simply the ability to keep customers happy—and coming back for more. Your ability to survive in business and be financially viable will be based on many factors, but one of the biggest contributing factors will be your ability to retain customers and foster long-term and profitable selling relationships. According to the U.S. Small Business Administration, 65 percent of people stop buying from a business because of poor customer service. This is a startling statistic, especially when you consider that it costs ten times as much to find a new customer as it does to keep a customer you already have.

The best way to provide great customer service is to treat your customers the way that you like to be treated when you trade your hard-earned money for goods and services at other businesses. How do you keep your customers happy? It is a combination of many things, including providing great customer service, appreciating your customers, and giving them peace of mind in the knowledge that they are protected via ironclad warranties, all of which are discussed in greater detail below.

Serving Up Great Customer Service

One of the easiest customer service concepts to grasp is the simple fact that people like to do business with people they like. It stands to reason that you should go out of your way to be likeable—smile, take an interest in your customers, treat them fairly, and thank them for their patronage; that's about all it takes. The second easiest customer service concept to master is to always fix the customer's problem first. When you have an unhappy customer, regardless of the source of the complaint, always look for ways to fix his or her problem first, quickly, and without hesitation. Once this has been achieved, turn your attention to the source of the problem or complaint. Excuses like "I'll get back to you" or "That's a manufacturer's problem" just don't cut it in today's highly competitive business environment.

In addition to being someone with whom people like to do business, and always going out of your way to fix the customer first when faced with a challenge, there are four other important components to providing great customer service. These include eliminating the potential for mismatched expectations, being reliable, being flexible, and staying in contact with customers.

Eliminate the Potential for Mismatched Expectations

The vast majority of customer service complaints arise from mismatched expectations, usually caused by faulty communication or the way that a product or service was described and understood. The cost resulting from mismatched expectations is enormous, especially when you factor in lost customers and the amount of time required to fix the problem. It makes sense to reduce the potential for mismatched expectations between you and customers by reviewing all details of the sale prior to installation of the product or delivery of the service. Review the price, the scope of work, the start and completion dates, the payment method, and the guarantees; ask specific questions about what the customer expects the service to do for his or her business.

Be Reliable

All business owners, and especially service providers, should be 100 percent reliable. If you say you'll be there at ten, arrive five minutes early. If you guarantee your work, then fix it if something goes wrong, no questions asked. Reliability is one of the common denominators that all successful businesses share, especially businesses that provide services, because your track record of happy clients is one of your most important marketing tools, and often the only one that carries any weight. No one wants services they have paid for not to live up to promises. We all want to know that when we purchase a service, the company that sells it is reliable and will be there for us in the future should something go haywire.

Be Flexible

Recognize that customers are not all the same and they want and need different things. Each customer must be viewed as an individual, not merely as part of a group. Be flexible and willing to bend the rules once in a while when your customers need you to, even if it is an inconvenience to you and your business. Ask customers what they want, and develop solutions to meet each individual's needs. Going the extra mile for customers almost always means price will be less of a factor in buying decisions. When you are flexible and go out of your way to treat people in a special way, you no longer have to work as hard to persuade them to your way of thinking. When was the last time that you stopped shopping at a particular business because you received exceptional treatment?

Stay in Contact with Customers

Another important component of providing great customer service is contact. In business it is very easy to become complacent about longtime customers for two reasons. One, because they are good customers, you just expect that they will always be there. Two, we become engrossed in always looking for new customers and forget about the customers we already have. Over time, if customers do not feel that they are appreciated or that you value their business, they will take their business elsewhere. Stay in constant contact with all your customers by sending them e-mails, writing letters, calling them, or by making personal visits. The more you stay in contact with your customers, the better you will be able to serve them, which greatly diminishes the potential for them to take their business elsewhere.

Customer Appreciation

A large part of what makes up great customer service is how you show your customers that you appreciate them and their support of your business. It is no secret that when your customers feel that you truly appreciate their business, they will go out of their way to refer your business to others. So how can you show your customers your gratitude for their continued support? In addition to sending them greeting cards on holidays, birthdays, and other important occasions, here are a few great ideas:

- Host an annual customer appreciation party and invite your best customers and hottest prospects. The party can be held at a local restaurant or, if your budget is tight, host the party right at your home, perhaps a backyard barbecue if weather permits.
- Find out what newspapers or magazines your customers like to read and buy them a monthly subscription. Every time they receive and read it, they will instantly think of your business and services.
- Find out what hobbies your customers like, and armed with this information, you can purchase gifts for them that are relevant to their hobbies or interests—sports or theater tickets, artwork, or gourmet foods are examples.
- If your customers are business owners, professionals, or salespeople, work hard to send them a new referral every day, week, or month.
- Give customers key chains, pens, notepads, calendars, coffee mugs, travel mugs, clocks, mouse pads, or T-shirts emblazoned with your business name and logo, and be sure to send along extras so they can give them to their friends and family members.
- Every once in a while, completely out of the blue, give your best customers a "most valued customer discount." It does not have to be large—even 5 percent is enough to clearly get the message across that you appreciate their business.

Ironclad Warranty

Another important element of providing great customer service is to put your money where your mouth is and back up your claims of excellence by providing an ironclad workmanship warranty. Not only will an ironclad workmanship warranty back up and support your marketing claims, you can also use your warranty to distinguish your business from competitors. For instance, if your competitor's workmanship warranty is for one year, make your warranty two; if theirs is five years, make yours seven. If the competition's workmanship warranty is loaded with small print that does not have the consumer's best interests in mind, then be sure to zap the small print from your warranty. And if your competitor's warranty is nontransferable, make yours fully transferable and without cost.

Customers want to know that, should problems arise after the sale, and after the service has been performed and paid for, that they will have an ironclad workmanship warranty from your business. The warranty clearly states that you will stand behind your work, and if problems should arise, they will be corrected within a reasonable time frame, at no cost for the duration of the warranty period. Yes, depending on the services you sell, there must be terms and conditions for workmanship warranties, ones that will protect your business. But every business that sells services should develop the best workmanship warranty possible. After all, you know the quality of the service you provide best, and if you are not prepared to back it up with an ironclad warranty, then in all probability you are not providing a quality service at all.

Determining Your Pricing Strategy

Pricing is a very important element of the marketing mix and your marketing strategy. If your prices are too high, you will probably meet with resistance as you try to sell your services. If your prices are too low, you may also meet resistance to your services because of perceived quality issues, or you may lose money on each transaction. Factors influencing pricing formulas and strategies include costs associated with the delivery of services, fixed operating overhead, marketplace economic conditions, primary and secondary competition in the marketplace, consumer demand, seasonal pressures, political conditions, psychological factors, and how you want to position your services in the marketplace.

A significant pricing concept to keep in mind when devising pricing strategies is that consumers see prices in very clearly defined terms—the price that you charge for your service compared to how much the service will fill their needs and give value. When your pricing is correct, consumers don't think twice because they feel the price is commensurate with the value and benefits derived from the service. However, as soon as your price goes below or above the threshold of what consumers feel is in the fair range for your services, you will meet resistance to the purchase. At this point, consumers must begin to justify why they will make the purchase, and you never want your target audience to have to convince themselves to buy. That is always your job and is achieved through proper pricing, promotion, and positioning strategies.

Setting your prices or determining your pricing strategy has much to do with positioning your business and the services you sell in the marketplace and with external factors that can potentially influence the prices you charge. You can position yourself and become known for low prices, moderate prices, or prestige prices. Your positioning strategy answers two vital questions: "Where do your services fit into the market?" and "How does your target audience view your services in relation to your competitors' services?"

Low-Pricing Strategy

Selecting a low-price strategy means that you strive to sell your services at the lowest or near-lowest price in the marketplace. Generally, you have to sell a greater volume of services than you would at higher prices to produce an equivalent profit margin. The majority of small business owners wisely choose not to compete or position their business in the marketplace based on low prices. Many national corporations and franchisees that provide services have already adopted a low-price strategy, making it difficult for the small independent business to compete on this level.

Moderate-Pricing Strategy

A moderate-pricing strategy means a good-quality service delivered to consumers at a fair price. This is the pricing strategy that the majority of small business owners wisely choose. It leaves you enough financial leeway for competitive advantages to be developed and introduced, such as 24-hour service or a stronger warranty program. The moderate-pricing strategy gives small business owners the most flexibility by combining value and good service at a fair price, which is difficult to achieve if you adopt a low-price strategy.

Prestige-Pricing Strategy

A prestige-pricing strategy is generally used to deliver a high-quality service in an upscale or exclusive environment, although the quality or delivery of the service is not necessarily always superior; sometimes it is only perceived to be better by consumers. Prestige pricing can be a deliberate pricing tactic in which you set your prices higher to separate your services from competitors by projecting an image of quality and exclusivity. If you are selling a niche service to a very small target audience, a prestige pricing strategy can work, and work extremely well. But if you are selling a common service, it can be difficult to create persuasive competitive advantages.

Competitive Strategy

A competitive pricing strategy means that you find out how much your competitors are charging for their services, and you charge more or less, depending on how you want to position your services in the marketplace. The downside to a competitive pricing strategy is that it is not scientific. Your variable and fixed costs may be more or less than your competitors' costs, and what may be a profitable price point for one business may not be for another charging the same price. You can find out how much your competition is charging by mystery-shopping their businesses, becoming a customer, asking pricing questions, checking out advertisements, price lists, and information posted on their web sites, and by subscribing to newsletters and catalogs. If you adopt this pricing strategy, it is in your best interest to create unique competitive advantages to separate your services from competitors' services.

Performance-Based Strategy

Another pricing strategy used by service providers is performance pricing, which means that you are paid for your service based on your performance. For instance, an expense reduction consultant might work on a performance basis, retaining 50 percent of the total amount of money that she saves a client by reducing overall operational expenditures. Or, a freelance sales consultant might retain 10 percent of the total value of the goods and services he sells for his client, and if no sales are made, no commission is earned. The risk with performance pricing is that you do not get paid, while still accruing expenses, unless you generate the results anticipated.

Cost-Plus Pricing

Regardless of the pricing strategy you adopt, you still need to cover all costs associated with operating your business, as well as generate a profit. Consequently, you have to figure out your fixed operating costs, your variable costs associated with the delivery of services, and add a profit. The formula, therefore, is:

variable costs + fixed costs + profit = selling price.

As a rule of thumb, labor costs generally represent the largest share of expenses for service providers. So the first step is to figure out how much you want to earn per hour. I would suggest that you base your decision on three factors: (1) how much money you need to earn to pay your personal and family expenses; (2) the industry average for the job; and (3) a premium if the service you provide is highly specialized or risky. Once you have determined how much per hour you want to earn, the next step is to calculate your fixed costs, which are business expenses (that do not fluctuate regardless of the amount of sales you make), such as telephone, rent, and insurance. In Chapter 3, you will find a handy monthly overhead costs worksheet that you can use to determine your fixed operating costs.

The next step is to determine the costs incurred in the delivery of the service, which are referred to as variable costs. For instance, if you operated a roofing repair service, the costs to purchase shingles and nails for a specific repair would be variable costs. The next step is to calculate and add a profit to all jobs. Every business needs to generate a profit in order to stay in business and remain competitive in the marketplace. Most small business owners use a percentage to calculate a profit on each job, such as total costs plus 20 percent.

The final step is to tie it all together. The formula used to arrive at a selling price is:

labor x the number of hours to complete the job + fixed expenses
then the number of hours to complete the job ÷ by fixed expenses
+ variable expenses X profit = selling price.

In the example below, we will assume that fixed business expenses are $1,000 per month, and there are 160 billable work hours each month,

$1,000 ÷ by 160 hours = $6.25 per hour fixed expenses
resulting in the total job requiring $25 hours to complete.

Labor rate, $20 per hour x 25 hours	= $500.00
Fixed expenses, $6.25 per hour x 25 hours	= $156.25
Variable expenses for the job	= $150.00
Total	= $806.25
Profit 20%	= $161.25
Selling price	= $967.50

Another factor that should be considered when determining pricing formulas is your client's budget. Service providers should remain flexible and open to the possibilities, which means if your client's budget is $1,000 for a project and you have quoted $2,000 to complete the job, do not view this as a totally lost cause. Instead, identify what services you can provide to meet your client's budget by prioritizing the details (goals) of the job and eliminating low-priority aspects.

Advertising Your Services

Advertising is a tool that when used correctly can drive a multitude of well-qualified prospects to your business to buy your services. Conversely, advertising can be a complete waste of time and money reaping little, if any, sales. Consequently, you have to make well-researched and informed decisions when it comes to allocating your precious advertising money. You can, providing you follow the Golden Rule of Advertising for small business owners: You do not need to spend a bundle advertising your services. Just make sure the money you do spend reaches your target audience. You will need to create a system for tracking your advertising activities so you can determine the effectiveness of each. This is important because it allows you to allocate your advertising dollars where they have the greatest impact in reaching your target audience and generating the most revenue. This section covers the advertising basics—writing great copy, newspapers, magazines, Yellow Pages, radio, promotional fliers, and signs.

Writing Great Copy

Great advertising copy grabs the attention of your target audience, creates interest in your message, builds desire for what you have to sell, and compels people to take action and buy. This is referred to as the AIDA advertising formula—attention, interest, desire, and action. Even if you plan to do little in the way of traditional advertising, you still need the ability to create great copy for use in sales letters, presentations, fliers, newsletters, and web site content, for instance.

Because you only have a brief moment to grab your target audience's attention and pull them in to your message, the starting point of all great copy is a powerful headline. "Lose ten pounds in three weeks, guaranteed," is an example of a powerful headline that grabs readers' attention and pulls them into the message. Clever copy also appeals to people on an emotional level, utilizing emotional triggers to spark basic human feelings such as the need for friendship, the longing for security, and the desire to achieve. When used properly, emotional triggers can double and even triple ad response rates.

Arguably, the most important aspect of creating great copy is to always ask for the sale. You can have the best attention-grabbing headline, a wow sales pitch, and an unbeatable offer, and all will be for naught unless you ask your audience to buy, giving compelling reasons to do so and providing the tools they need to take action—namely how they can reach you right away. Unlike multinational corporations with bottomless money pits for brand-building advertising, small business owners have to ask for the sale in every advertisement, regardless of the medium.

Newspapers

The best advice that I can pass along about newspaper advertising, especially display ads, is to always purchase newspaper advertising based on your marketing plan, advertising budget, and the publication's ability to reach your target audience. Never let yourself be lured in by huge circulation numbers, critical placement promises, and frequency discounts. That aside, there is a great variety of newspapers—national, regional, daily, community weeklies, penny-saver types, school, association and clubs, and electronic. And one of the best ways to research newspapers for advertising purposes is to go online and visit newspaper directories such as News Link, www.newslink.org, and News Directory, www.newsdirectory.com. Both list thousands of publications indexed geographically.

There are basically two types of newspaper advertising options—display ads and classified ads. For the majority of small business owners, display advertising in national and regional newspapers is not effective; community papers can be somewhat effective for major sales or events, but must be approached with caution. In the first place, large display ads tend to be very expensive, and placing ads only occasionally because of a limited budget does not work. Generally, outside of special sales or promotional events, you need repetition to build long-term beneficial awareness of your business and services. Also, most newspapers, regardless of size, are crammed with display advertisements. That leaves the advertiser competing with hundreds of other ads to capture the readers' attention. Display advertising can work, but there are certain steps to follow, starting with getting the media kit or card for newspapers you are considering. The media kit will tell you all about the newspaper's readership base—who they are, where they come from, what they do for a living, their level of education, and how much money they make. That information can then be used to determine if the newspaper's target audience is your target audience. If not, move on until you find a match.

Classified advertising, on the other hand, is unquestionably one of the service providers' best friends. Not only are these ads easy to create and cheap to run, but they almost always have a higher response rate than display advertisements because people generally read the classifieds looking for a specific service to buy, not for entertainment, as in other sections of the newspaper. This is especially true of businesses that provide services such as home repair, home maintenance, automobile maintenance, and computer specialties. Once again, pick publications that are read by your target audience, and choose a classified heading that people are most likely to read. Because classified advertisements are cheap and quick to post, continually look for ways to improve your results by testing new ads in various publications. Test your headline, your main sales message, and your special offers on a regular basis. Classified advertising costs vary by publication, number of words, number of insertions, and other factors such as the use of icons and photographs, which, by the way, almost always increase response rates, making the few extra dollars they cost a very worthwhile investment.

Magazines

Magazine ads have a definite edge over many other types of advertising, mainly because they have a tendency to be around for a while—on a desk, in a waiting room, in a lunchroom, or on a coffee table. Because magazines have a longer shelf life than newspapers, newsletters, coupons, and fliers, the advertisements also tend to be seen by the same reader more than once. Most advertising gurus agree that next to radio, magazine advertising offers small business owners the best opportunity to reach a very select target audience in a relativity cost-efficient manner. But keep in mind that unlike your experience with classified advertisements and coupons, you cannot expect immediate results from magazine advertisements. It takes continuous and consistent exposure to your target audience before results will begin to surface. Therefore, you must be patient and not too quick to pull the advertising plug if the telephone doesn't start ringing the day after the magazine hits newsstands.

Magazines are unquestionably one of the best advertising mediums for reaching a specific audience, because magazines have a tendency to cater to one specific portion of the population, based on geographic, demographic, and psychographic profiling, or a combination of market segmenting. The first place to find out more about a magazine's particular target audience is through the publisher's media kit or fact sheet. In the kit you will find information about who reads the magazine, number of subscribers, the subscribers' average incomes, their hobbies, education, and income levels. Magazine publishers go to great lengths to compile information about their readers because this is the crucial data that sells advertising space. Therefore, before jumping in and signing up for a year's worth of full-page magazine ads, carefully research the publication's readership to determine if these people meet your target audience requirements. To locate magazines and other publications that cater to a specific audience, visit Pub List, www.publist.com, which is a free-to-use directory, listing in excess of 150,000 domestic and international print and electronic publications.

There is also much debate as to which size display advertisement is the best—full-page, half-page, third-page, quarter-page, and so forth. All have their pros and cons. Full-page advertisements can be costly, but on the flip side you get great exposure. While quarter-page ads are much cheaper, they are often featured near the back of the magazine with one or more other advertisements on the same page. You also have to consider frequency, which refers to the number of times that your target audience is exposed to your advertisement in the same magazine. Most advertising experts agree that there should be a minimum of three times, but preferably six to twelve times consecutively, for an ad to have real impact on your business.

Yellow Pages

Not all service providers need to advertise in the Yellow Pages, especially when you consider that full-page ads can easily cost $1,000 per month, and more. There are really three levels to consider, one of which your business will fall in to. The first level is services that people need in a hurry, such as a roofer to fix a leaky roof, a plumber to fix a burst pipe, and a notary public to notarize and witness time-sensitive documents. The second level includes services that people need only occasionally, and because of this they generally do not have a service provider in mind and rely mainly on the Yellow Pages to find one. These include service providers such as movers, house inspectors, caterers, and carpet cleaners. At the third level are highly specialized services that only a small percentage of the population will ever need; examples include information researchers, image consultants, and home office planners. As you can imagine, advertising in the Yellow Pages is extremely beneficial for the first level of service providers, and calls for the biggest ad the budget will allow. The second level of service providers can benefit from being in the Yellow Pages, yet they have other advertising options that can generate equal, if not better, results. The third level of service provider is so highly specialized that Yellow Pages advertising will be of little benefit.

If you decide that Yellow Pages advertising is right for your business, use the following helpful tips to increase the effectiveness of your ad.

- Design your advertisement from your customers' perspective so it will speak directly to and appeal to the majority of your target audience. Why do they do business with you, and what do they like best about your business and services? What is your competitive advantage? Is it best quality? Is it convenient 24-hour service? Is it lowest prices, guaranteed? Or are you the most qualified to handle the job in the area? Research has also shown that ads with photographs or illustrations greatly outperform ads without them.
- Statistically speaking, size matters. The larger your ad, the more people you can expect to call you. Buy the biggest, boldest advertisement you can afford. It positions you closer to the beginning of each new alphabetical heading and ahead of competitors with smaller advertisements, especially if you fall into the first level of service providers.
- Yellow Pages display advertising is one of the rare advertising occasions when you want to list as much information as possible. List all services you provide, including specialized services or authorized services; all the ways that people can pay, including credit cards and financing options; credentials and special training that you have; and special information such as liability insurance coverage, bonding, special certificates or permits, and professional association memberships.

- Motivate people to call by using phrases like, "Call now for a free estimate." Give them lots of ways to contact you—telephone number, toll-free number, fax number, cell number, e-mail and web site addresses, and after-hours contact information.

Radio

Radio speaks to your target audience on a more intimate one-on-one basis—in their cars, at the office, or at home. For that reason, radio has long been a favorite advertising medium for small business owners. The key to successful radio advertising is repetition, which in radio advertising terms is referred to as *frequency*, the number of times the audience is exposed to your message. The more they hear your ad, the more they will recall your business and services when it comes time to buy. Also keep in mind that you are buying the audience, never the station. You need to match the image you want to project for your business to the appropriate radio station. For example, if your target audience is people over 50, try talk radio and easy listening formats. If you are not effectively reaching your target audience, your ads will simply not be productive, regardless of how frequently they are broadcast.

When writing copy for your radio ads, you have to think and create visually. You must paint an exact visual portrait of how your service works and how users benefit, so listeners can fully understand and appreciate what you have to sell. Also, purchase 30-second commercial spots rather than 15-second spots. The latter seldom allow enough time to create a lasting and memorable impression. Thirty seconds will enable you to get across about 50 to 75 words comfortably, along with a simple jingle or memorable audio hook such as a drumbeat or lion's roar. Ideally, you will want to have the same time slot day in, day out. Most marketers find the morning 6 A.M. to 10 A.M., or afternoon 3 P.M. to 7 P.M. drive slots are the best. Radio audiences are extremely loyal to their favorite stations, on-air personalities, and on-air programs. Therefore, once you have identified your target audience and the station and programs they listen to, stick like glue to that station, time slot, and program. You want these listeners to feel the same loyalty to your brand, and through repeated exposure, to your marketing message.

Promotional Fliers

Promotional fliers represent one of the best advertising vehicles and values available to small business owners, because they are a fast and frugal yet highly effective way to promote your services. Commercial printers charge $50 to $80 per hour to design marketing materials like fliers, brochures, and newsletters, so you can save a lot of money if you take the time to learn basic design skills to create high-impact, printed promotional fliers inhouse on your own computer. In addition to computer hardware, you will also need design software, and the most popular desktop publishing software comes from Adobe, ♂ www.adobe.com, and Corel, ♂ www.corel.com.

In addition to saving money, by having the ability to create your own fliers you will also save time, because you can create promotional materials and be ready to use them within a day, instead of waiting days or weeks working around a printer's schedule. Once your fliers been have created and printed, they can be copied in bulk for as little as two cents each at your local copy center, or you can invest in a high-speed laser printer for about $350 and keep the printing inhouse.

The great benefit of printed promotional fliers is that they can be used everywhere and for everything, even as a replacement in most cases for your business cards. Hand them out at seminars, trade shows, and networking meetings. Hire students to canvas busy parking lots, tucking fliers underneath windshield wipers, and leave them in public transit areas such as buses, subway cars, and train stations for riders to read and take home. You can also stock a supply of promotional fliers and thumbtacks in your car so you can make a weekly run, posting your new fliers on every community bulletin board in your area—at supermarkets, libraries, schools, community centers, laundries, fitness clubs, churches, and gas stations.

Signage for Service Providers

Like fliers, signs represent incredible advertising value for service providers, mainly because they work to promote your business 24 hours a day, 365 days a year, virtually for free once purchased. Depending on the services you sell and your business location, there is a wide range of signs to be considered, but the basics for the majority of small businesses will include storefront or office signs, homebased business signs, job site signs, and vehicle signs.

STOREFRONT OR OFFICE SIGNS

At a glance, your signs tells people your business name, what you sell, why they should contact you, and the information needed to contact you. Therefore, your signs must be professionally designed, built, installed, and in keeping with the image that you want to project. Because you want to always make a positive first impression, keep all your signage in tip-top condition. Faded signs, peeling paint, torn banners, or signs that require maintenance in general send out negative messages about your business. Also use attention-grabbing design elements, colors, graphics, and pictures in your signs to lend visual description.

Homebased Business Signs

As with storefront and office signs, there are also local bylaws governing homebased business signs, which for the most part are much more stringent than commercial zoning signs. These bylaws will let you know if signage is allowed at your home, as well as the size of the sign, placement, and style. There is no one set of regulations for home business signage. Each municipality has its own regulations. A call to the planning department or city hall will be required to find out the local bylaws. Even if signage is allowed, consult with your immediate neighbors to find out their feelings on the issue and get their input on the signs. The last thing you want to do is alienate neighbors over business signs. Like you, their home is probably their biggest investment, and they do not want that investment to be devalued in any way. In fact, if clients are not coming to your home, you are better off not having signs at all. If you will be having clients coming to your home, keep your signs in open view, make them tasteful to match your home and streetscape—perhaps carved wood or brass on stone—and keep lighting to a minimum unless you can incorporate your sign into your exterior house light or motion lighting.

Job Site Signs

If you install products or provide services at your customers' homes and offices, you should definitely invest in professional, attention-grabbing job site signage, especially if jobs last more than a few days. Job site signs come in all sizes and are priced to fit all budgets. Some are metal with metal stands, while others are Coroplast®, or even simple plastic sleeves, similar to political yard signs but emblazoned with your business name, logo, and promotional message. The plastic sleeve-style fits over preformed wire stands, which push easily into the ground, making for very fast installation and pickup at a later date. Purchased in bulk, the plastic sleeve style signs are very inexpensive, less than $5 each, and can be reused many times. Business Signs Online, www.businesssigns.com, sells metal and Coroplast® made-to-order job site signs in various sizes, while Political Lawn Signs, www.politicallawnsigns.com, manufactures lightweight plastic job site and lawn signs.

Vehicle Signs

If you are going to use your vehicle for business my advice is to sign it; even if you only use it for business occasionally, you can still use magnetic signs that can be quickly installed or removed and stored in the trunk when using your car for family activities. I would not only sign the vehicle, I would also be sure to park in highly visible and high-traffic locations even if this means feeding parking meters.

Always think about maximizing the marketing value of these rolling billboards. Like store signs, at a glance, vehicle signs tell people your business name, a brief promotional message that best describes your services, and contact information, including telephone numbers and web site.

Advertising Online

There are many ways to promote your business and advertise your services online, but space limits us to discussing the basics—banners, e-publications, and pay-per-click programs.

Banners

Advertising banners are a popular way to promote your services and drive traffic to your web site. Costs range from a few dollars to a few hundred dollars per thousand impressions, depending on the target audience you want to reach. The idea of cheap banner advertising might be alluring, but your results can suffer dramatically if you don't present your advertising message to your primary target audience. Bigger is not always better. Mega web sites may attract untold numbers of visitors, but that does not necessarily mean they are comprised of your target audience.

E-Publications

Many service providers have found advertising in electronic publications to be a highly effective way to reach their target audience at a very modest cost, and with an estimated 100,000 electronic publications distributed monthly to choose from, you can definitely find one that reaches your target audience. Before committing to advertising, though, find out audience size, demographics, and advertising costs. Once again, bigger is not necessarily better, because these publications often contain more advertisements. Your main consideration should always be how to reach your target audience. Ezine Listings, www.ezinelistings.com, list thousands of electronic publications indexed by subject.

Pay-per-Click

Pay-per-click programs are another highly effective form of online advertising, which involves bidding on priority keywords that you believe your target audience will use to search for the services you sell. The big players are Google's AdWords, www.adwords.google.com, and Overture's Pay-For-Performance, www.overture.com. Although each pay-per-click program has different requirements and rules for keyword selection, both programs are similar in the way you bid for keywords. For instance, you can bid one dollar for a specific keyword. If yours is the highest bid, you win and get top search results rankings. On the other hand, if you bid 20 cents and someone bids more for the same keywords, your ranking will be greatly reduced.

Public Relations

Small business owners tend to shy away from trying to obtain publicity for their business, products or services, or special events. But why, when the potential to reach thousands, even millions, of people for free is a real possibility? Why not go for it? The answer is simple. Most don't realize they could easily create some publicity buzz around the services they sell. Look at their unique user benefits, interesting facts or statistics, success stories, or competitive advantages—it just takes a bit of imagination. To help get your creative ideas flowing, explained below are five simple yet highly effective publicity tools. These include press releases, articles, talk radio, and community publicity.

Press Releases

The quickest and easiest way to let people know about the benefits of the services you sell is to create a press release outlining the details and send it to the appropriate media outlets. Few forms of advertising or other marketing activities can match the effectiveness and credibility of the news media; our daily lives revolve around the news distributed in all formats—broadcast, print, and internet. We read newspapers, watch television, surf the internet, and listen to the radio, and we do so because we want to be entertained and informed. A great review in your local newspaper about a new music CD is more likely to pull customers into the store than any advertisement ever will. Publicity works because it grabs your consumer's attention, spells out the basic details, creates interest and desire, and inspires them to take action. If you are new to writing press releases, read a few first to get an idea about how to angle your story to attract readers, what type of information to include, formatting tips, and to whom to send it. A good place to read real press releases online is at PR Web, www.prweb.com. There you can browse through thousands of press releases for free, which can help you to write your own.

Articles

One of the best ways to secure valuable publicity is to write informative articles on your area of expertise. In other words, share your wealth of information, because the value of it increases as more people are exposed to it, and benefit because of it. One little-known fact is that every small business owner has important information that can be offered to the media in exchange for free publicity. For example, if you operate a handyperson service, offer to write a weekly article for your community paper about home repair tips. The key to successfully securing exposure in print is to develop a news or story angle that will appeal to a large segment of the newspaper's target audience. When I say newspaper, depending on the services you provide and the audience you want to reach, this can include local and national papers, community newsletters, trade journals, association newspapers, e-newspapers, magazines, and school papers. The media love to get informative articles because they typically do not pay for them and they appeal to and benefit their target audiences. All media outlets need good news, information, and activities to fill their publications.

Talk Radio

Talk radio represents a potential publicity windfall for small business owners who take the time to develop a strategy for being featured on these programs. Get started by conducting research on the show you would like to be featured on, learning about the show's format, style, and target audience. Next, develop a story idea revolving around something that would be relevant to the program and interesting to the show's audience. For instance, if you restore antiques, develop a show idea around teaching listeners about what to look for when buying antiques that need to be restored. Once you have developed your idea, send the program producer a professional business letter detailing your story, how it benefits his or her audience, and why you should be invited to discuss the topic on air. Also send a background sheet highlighting your qualifications and expertise on the topic. If you have written books, articles, or taught classes on the subject matter, be sure to include this information in your letter. To find suitable talk radio programs, visit Radio Locator, www.radio-locator.com, which has links to more than 10,000 radio stations.

Community Publicity

Getting involved in the community where you live and do business is also a great way to inform and keep the public up-to-date on the services you sell. It's obvious that people like to do business with people they know and like, and to refer friends, family, and associates to these businesses. So it makes sense to get active in your community—clubs, churches, charities, and business and social functions are all great places to meet new people, help out, hand out business cards, and talk about your business and the services you provide. Sponsorships are also a fantastic way to help out in the community and publicize your business at the same time. You can sponsor a Little League team, a charity event, or any number of community events. Or if you are really ambitious you could develop, sponsor, and manage your own special event for the benefit of the community, such as "(your business name here) clean up the beach day," sponsored by and named after your business.

Event Marketing

For decades, business owners and professionals have benefited from participating in various event-marketing activities, such as trade shows, seminars, contests, and personal contact networking. In this section you will learn a few secrets about each of these event-marketing activities, and how you can use them to help grow your business and sell your services.

Trade and Consumer Shows

The only difference between trade shows and consumer shows is that trade shows are generally for business-to-business interaction and transactions, while consumer shows are for the general public to attend, browse, and seek out information, products, and services they want and need. For service providers, few marketing activities can match the effectiveness of trade and consumer shows as a way to showcase and sell their services to a large audience at one time, in one place, and in a cost-effective manner. Over the course of the show, you can make personal contact with hundreds, if not thousands, of qualified prospects, affording you tremendous opportunities to generate sales leads or sell your services.

These days, there is a trade or consumer show that is suitable for every type of service provider—home and garden, construction, business, food, industry-specific, sports and recreation, computer, software, publishing, pet, car, real estate, financial investment shows, and the list goes on and on. In fact, there are in excess of 10,000 trade and consumer shows annually in North America. Fortunately, you can click through hundreds of show listings online, and in no time gain valuable insights into each. More importantly, you'll learn about the people who attend to make sure they match your target audience. Like other types of event marketing, considerations for selecting the right show include costs, competition, audience, duration, and geographic location. One online show directory is Trade Shows Online, www.tradeshows.com, which lists trade and consumer shows, conferences, and expos, geographically and by industry. Before making the commitment to exhibit, I strongly suggest that you attend shows first to get a feel for the types of exhibitors, the show's management, and the audience to make sure they are all compatible with your overall marketing objectives and goals.

When designing your booth and displays, keep in mind that booths alive with exciting service demonstrations draw considerably more interest and larger crowds than static booths. The show pace can be fast and furious, and time is a commodity that is always in short supply. So it is important to have an effective and well-rehearsed sales plan ready to put into action. Your sales plan should revolve around four key elements—engaging prospects, qualifying prospects, presenting your services, and closing the sale or generating a sales lead. Consult your Yellow Pages to source businesses that sell or rent trade show displays in your area, or visit Trade Show Exhibits Sales & Rentals, www.trade-shows.org, which offers free online quotes for display and exhibit sales and rentals.

Seminars and Workshops

Much like trade and consumer shows, seminars and workshops are also great forums for entrepreneurs to showcase their expertise to a captive audience of qualified prospects, which in turn can provide numerous business-building opportunities, such as selling services, prospecting for new business, generating publicity, generating sales leads, building a valuable contact database, and recruiting, supporting, and educating customers and employees. Fortunately for small business owners with tight marketing budgets, seminars can be promoted effectively and with success for little cost, providing that you are prepared to roll up your sleeves to plan, promote, and host the seminar or workshop yourself. You can design and distribute fliers promoting the event, use direct mail to inform and invite prospects and customers, send out press releases about the event to the media, and use low-cost classified advertisements to promote the event.

You also have to decide on a location for your seminar or workshop. Depending on the types of services you sell, your current business location, and how many guests will be attending, you can hold the seminar at your office after hours or at your home. You can also rent boardroom space, restaurant or banquet hall space from a local business association or a supplier's business location. Regardless of the event venue, you want the seminar location to be central to the majority of the people attending. You also want on-site or nearby secure parking and access to public transit. And if guests will be attending from out of town, the location should also be central to hotels and the airport. You must also give thought to the timing of the event. If you want to reach businesspeople, a midweek daytime seminar works best. If you want to reach consumers, plan your event for when your target audience is not at work, generally weeknights and weekends.

If you are new to seminar and workshop hosting, you might want to pick up a copy of *Marketing and Promoting Your Own Seminars and Workshops* by Fred Gleeck (Fast Forward Press, 2001), which is full of helpful information. The

National Seminar Group also provides, via their web site, information, products, and services aimed at planning, promoting, and hosting seminars. The web site is located at www.natsem.com.

Contests

Contests have long been a great promotional tool for small business owners to generate sales leads and to help build awareness of their business, products, and services. But as with any promotional activity, you first need to identify your objectives. What do you want to achieve as a result of staging the contest? Do you want to capture and qualify sales leads from the entry ballots? Generate publicity and media coverage? Build or update your database for direct marketing purposes from the information you collect? Use the contest as a business grand opening, or to introduce a new service? Support a local charity or organization? Once you have determined your contest objectives, you will be in a better position to decide which type of contest is best suited to achieve your objectives. In addition to identifying your objective, you will also need to consider legal issues, contest budget, how you will promote the contest, what the grand and runner-up prizes will be, and how these prizes will be awarded for maximum promotional benefit.

A simple contest to organize is an entry-ballot contest format, which requires contestants to complete a ballot and deposit it into a box or mail it in for the drawing. Other contests include scratch cards that reveal prizes, counting games, and customer interactive contests such as celebrity look-alike or essay contests. If you decide that you want to stage a high-stakes contest, such as million-dollar hole-in-one, or a million-dollar basketball free-throw competition, you can purchase insurance to cover the cash prize value should a participant win. National Indemnity, www.nationalindemnity.com, offers insurance packages to cover up to one million dollars in prize money for hole-in-one contests, football field-goal contests, and half-court basketball shots, as well as insurance programs to cover other types of unique contests and promotional risks.

The next step is to seek legal advice to make sure that you will not be placing yourself, business, family, or contestants in a position of liability as a direct result of the contest or prize. In most cases, the lawyer who you deal with for your general business matters is qualified to advise you on the contest and potential liability issues. If the contest is just a small one-time or ongoing weekly draw, or a similar small promotional event with low-value prizes, legal advice is probably not warranted. In addition to seeking legal advice on larger contests, be sure to call your insurance broker and inquire about liability insurance to cover the event and matters relating to the contest. It should also be noted that not all states and provinces have the same rules and regulations governing promotional contests. You will need to check with local government agencies before conducting any contests to make sure you comply with the rules. Arent Fox Attorneys, www.arentfox.com, offers information and articles about the legalities of staging promotional contests.

Networking

It's a proven fact that people like to do business with people they know and like. They also like to refer others to businesses run by people they know and like. Personal-contact networking is still one of the best and easiest ways to form long-term and profitable business relationships. Networking gives you the power of one-on-one relationship-building that few other methods of marketing or advertising can match. Through proper networking activities, you are able to build your own powerful sales force of alliances that work tirelessly at selling your services by way of referral and word-of-mouth advertising. Like any business or marketing activity that you implement, you will get the most out of networking if you know why you are doing it and what you want to accomplish. Set networking goals and objectives so that you know what you want to accomplish, and have a yardstick to measure your performance. Your networking objectives will vary depending on your goals—generate sales leads, sell services, form business partnerships, research the market, find new employees, or become known as an expert in your industry.

If you are going to actively network with others, I strongly suggest that you create a high-impact mini sales pitch. Keep it short, simple, and directly to the point—the biggest benefit your customers will receive from doing business with you. Keep practicing this mini sales pitch until you have it down pat. Of course, all this information is great, but you still have to know where to network. You can network in any number of places and situations—business association events, social functions, organization and club events, community events, online discussion groups, chat rooms, and business networking e-communities such as Networking for Professionals, www.networkingforprofessionals.com, and Knowmentum, www.itsnotwhatyouknow.com.

Mastering Personal-Contact Selling

In this section you will discover many highly effective selling techniques and tips that top business owners and sales professionals use daily to find more prospects, sell more services, and keep every customer they get for life. Personal-contact selling is an important skill for service providers to learn. After all, in almost all instances you will need to persuade people in person, or on the telephone, that the services you sell are the best to meet their needs. The selling skills discussed here include setting the stage to sell, prospecting for new customers, qualifying buyers, getting past objections, mastering negotiations, closing every sale, and getting more referrals. Don't feel intimidated if you feel that "selling" is not your strongest skill. Remember that there is no such thing as *a natural-born salesperson*. The majority of people who start a business are not professional salespeople, nor do they have to be to succeed in business. Mastering personal-contact selling is a combination of education, practice, persistence, and building on your strengths.

Setting the Stage to Sell

Preparation is the starting point for mastering personal-contact selling. In other words, to pull off a flawless performance and leave your audience applauding for more you must first set the stage to ensure you cover the basics, which are your service, your target audience, the competition, and your sales tools. You have to know what you are selling inside out and upside down, and how customers will benefit by purchasing and using your service. Knowledge of the services you sell can be acquired from research, specialized training, your suppliers, information in books and other published formats, and two of the most important methods—feedback from customers and hands-on experience.

You must also know your target audience inside out and upside down. You know the people who need and want the services you are selling. Where do these people live? How can you access them? How often do they buy? And what do they base their buying decisions on? It is also handy to have additional customer information, such as what hobbies and recreational activities they enjoy and what newspapers they read, so you can effectively target your promotional activities. Perhaps more important, you must know the answers to the questions your prospects and customers have, in advance of their asking.

Being prepared to sell means you also must know your competition thoroughly—what people like and dislike about their businesses, services, prices, and guarantees; how they promote their business; and how they secure and keep paying customers. Basically, you need to know how your business and the services you sell stack up against competitors. You find out by using your competitors' services, subscribing to their newsletters, visiting their web sites, clipping and reading their ads, and by talking to their suppliers and customers.

The final aspect of setting the stage to sell is to have a toolbox packed with great sales tools. Think of your sales tools as the instruments you use to grab your prospects' attention, create desire to buy what you are selling, and motivate them to take action and buy. Depending on the services you sell, sales tools can include promotional literature, product samples, attention-grabbing signage, customer testimonials, specialized training, convenient 24-hour service, ironclad guarantees, and numerous purchase payment options.

Prospecting for New Business

In addition to advertising your business and the services you sell in newspapers, on the radio, and through direct mail, you also must take a more proactive approach to finding customers, which is known as prospecting. For the majority of new business start-ups, prospecting for customers will probably dominate the initial marketing effort. There are two reasons for this: (1) you lack an existing customer base to expand upon; and (2) your advertising budget is probably tight. This makes telephone calls, e-mail, and personal visits very attractive options for drumming up new business because they are cheap, quick to implement, and effective. Yes, this does mean having to make cold calls in person and on the telephone, but if you develop a simple prospecting strategy these quickly become habitual. At the same time, you begin to build a valuable contact pipeline.

One simple prospecting strategy to develop and implement is the three-by-four technique. This means that each day you make three telephone calls, send three sales letters, make three personal visits, and send three e-mails. Using this prospecting method enables you to make 12 new contacts a day, 60 per week, 240 per month, and 2,880 per year, which in turns affords you literally thousands of selling opportunities. If you are going to integrate telemarketing into your prospecting plans, be sure to follow federal telemarketing guidelines, which can be found online at, www.donotcall.gov.

You can also become more creative in how you prospect for new business and generate sales leads. For instance, you could develop a customer list and lead-swap program with business owners and sales professionals in your area who sell noncompeting but compatible products or services. For example, if you sell window-washing services, swap your customer and prospect list with a house-painting service.

Holding a contest is another great way to prospect for business by generating sales leads from the information you capture on the entry ballots. If you are a dog groomer, make the prize free dog grooming for a year; if you are a small business coach, make the prize 20 hours of free consulting. Even though in both examples there is only one winner, you could potentially have hundreds of entry ballots filled out by people looking for dog grooming services or small business coaching services. So it is important that you collect as much contact information as possible on the ballots.

Prospecting can also mean developing strategies that will result in people seeking you out for your expertise, which is referred to as expert prospecting. Get started by writing a book, newspaper column, or magazine feature, or actively look for places where you can speak about your specialty. If you operate a self-defense training school, give demonstrations at women's groups. If you operate a career-coaching service, write a weekly tip column on the topic for your local newspaper. Becoming known as an expert not only distinguishes you from the competition, it also means that, in all likelihood, people will seek your advice when they are trying to solve a problem or need advice or help in a decision, all of which can be turned into selling opportunities.

Qualifying Buyers

Perhaps you are the type of person who feels uncomfortable asking prospects qualifying questions; maybe you think it's being pushy, nosy, or aggressive? Don't, because the only way you can do your job properly and help people make informed buying decisions is to ask questions. Qualifying the buyer is the process of asking questions and using the responses to determine if they need and can afford what you are selling. The importance of qualifying cannot be overstated. The better qualified a prospect is, the greater the chance they will benefit from buying and using your service, and the greater the chance that you will close the sale. You do not want to try to sell your service to people who do not need what you are selling, can't make the buying decision, or cannot afford what you are selling, and you will be able to avoid these situations by applying the information below and asking the right qualifying questions.

The first step is to determine right away if the person you are attempting to sell needs or wants what you have to sell. If not, you are wasting your time and theirs by continuing the conversation. If you have in-depth knowledge of what you sell and how people benefit from using it, qualifying a prospect with a few simple questions should be easy: What problems need solving? What are their requirements? What needs to be improved? What is wrong with what they are currently using, or alternately, what would make their job or life easier?

Likewise, you must always make sure you are dealing with the person who has the authority to make the buying decision. The best way to find out upfront is to simply ask any of the following questions: Who will be making the purchasing decision? Will you be making the decision on your own, or will there be other people involved in the purchasing decision? If you find my _____ suitable, are you authorized to make the purchase?

Finally, you also do not want to waste time trying to sell to people who cannot afford to buy. You have to be able to determine if the person you are talking to has the money or access to the money needed to make the purchase. Ask your prospect if she has the money put aside to pay for the purchase, if she can afford it, and if it is in her budget. Regardless of how you phrase the question, you have to know they can afford to buy what you are selling. If not, then stop wasting time and move on to someone who needs and can afford to buy what you are selling.

First make sure, of course, that you have exhausted all payment options such as credit cards, consumer financing, leasing, and installment plans.

Getting Past Objections

The first thing you need to understand about objections is that they are nothing more than prospects telling you they need more information to help them make the right buying decision, one that fulfills their needs in beneficial ways, or answers lingering concerns. Doubt and fear are the biggest sales killers, and to close you must be able to remove all your prospects' doubts about what you are selling and their fears about making the purchase. When prospects start giving reasons why they shouldn't buy, don't take these as a rejection. Instead, welcome and overcome these objections. Depending on the services you sell, you will meet with various objections specific to your services, but the three most common objections you are likely to encounter are: The price is too high. I don't have the money. Let me think about it.

It should come as no surprise that most people automatically respond, "The price is too high" when asked to buy. It is a natural response that most people give. When this objection is raised you should ask, "The price is too much in comparison to what?" The majority of people have not actually considered why they think the price is too high, or in comparison to what; once again, it is just a natural response when asked to buy. Therefore, by asking, you force your prospect to reveal their real reason for objecting, or perhaps they honestly do feel the price is too high. Either way, you open the lines of communication so you can speak to lingering concerns and find a mutually agreeable solution. Another strategy for overcoming price objections is to simply agree that your price is indeed more than competitors', but explain why—superior quality, longer warranty, skilled workers, or some other competitive or beneficial advantage that justifies a higher selling price. Also ask, "Is price the only objection you have to proceeding with the sale?" The answer will let you know if price is the only objection or if there are other obstacles. If price is the only objection, look for suitable solutions—reduction in the level of services provided or creative financing options, for example.

A second common objection to overcome is when prospects tell you they cannot afford to buy. When this happens you must ask why, for the simple reason that you cannot overcome the no-money objection unless you know all the details, so you can develop workable solutions that might otherwise go unnoticed—credit cards, consumer loan, and leasing, for example. When you can show people they can purchase by using financing means they had not thought of, often the no-money objection fades and they warm up to the idea of buying because now they can. You must clearly demonstrate to prospects that the benefits of buying are so important to their particular situation that a no-money objection would not be wise. In other words, the cost of not buying far outweighs the cost of buying.

Finally, when a prospect tells you that he or she wants to think about it, suggest you go over the details again. This tactic opens the door once more and enables you to flush out the real obstacles to the sale. One way to cover the details again is to use the Benjamin Franklin technique by listing the advantages of a buy decision in one column, and listing the disadvantages of not buying in a second column. Often when people see in black and white that the advantages of buying far outweigh the disadvantages, it is all the persuasion they need to go ahead.

Mastering Negotiations

People who are new to business quickly discover that negotiation is a necessary skill that they will use daily. You negotiate with customers to buy more and at higher prices. You negotiate with suppliers for lower prices and better terms. You negotiate with your bank for lower merchant account fees. Consequently, taking the time and effort to master the art of negotiating is well worth the effort: usually you will sell your services at a higher price, while paying less for the products and services you need to operate your business.

Information is the cornerstone of mastering negotiations, and the more of it you have, the stronger your position becomes for getting what you want on your terms and conditions. Obtaining information means you have to find out as much as you can about what the person you are negotiating with wants and needs, and how these are prioritized—by benefits, budget, or by schedule. Having this information lets you know what the other person wants to achieve through negotiations—lower price, longer warranty, or faster installation, for example. And once you know what they want to achieve, your position in the negotiations is strengthened, while theirs is weakened. Information is the proverbial ace up your sleeve.

Also remember that if someone really needs the service you are selling, price often becomes secondary to user benefits—improving their lives, saving them money, making them money, solving a problem, or whatever the benefit may be. So before negotiations start, you must first position the value of your service in relation to the benefits the person will receive by buying and using your service. This is a critical step in the negotiation process. If what you have to sell is properly positioned in terms of value, it gives you increased leverage and power to get what you want out of the negotiations process, without having to accept less money or unfavorable conditions. And on that note, don't be afraid to walk away from negotiations if you are positive you have nothing to gain by continuing.

When the result of the negotiations is no longer beneficial to you, walk away. If not, be prepared to sacrifice profits or waste time.

Closing Every Sale

The golden rule of closing is simple: *Always ask for the sale*. You might have blown them away with your presentation, answered all of their questions, and fulfilled all their buying requirements, but remember: few people will take it upon themselves to offer you the sale unless they are asked to do so. Therefore, when you are selling services you have to get in the habit of asking for the sale every time you talk to a potential customer. If not, all you will have accomplished is to educate your prospect, which makes them a very easy closing target for your competitors. Closing is an essential selling skill, but at the same time it is nothing more than the natural progression in the sales cycle. You prospect, qualify, present, overcome objections, and you close. Therefore, asking for the sale should be nothing more than a formality.

One of the easiest closing techniques to master is the assumption close because it requires doing nothing more than assuming every person you talk to about your services will buy. You assumption-close by making statements like, "We can install this for you next week." "I just need your signature on this agreement so we can get started." Or, "How would you like to pay for this?" If your prospect is agreeable, you complete the sale, thank them, and move on to the next meeting.

Likewise, the alternate-choice close is also an easy one to master. As the name suggests, this closing technique means giving your prospect more than one service option, and asking a question such as, "So which choice would you prefer, the basic dog grooming package, or our premium dog grooming service?" The alternate-choice close pulls your prospect into making a buying decision and selecting one of the options. Not buying is no longer an available option, based on the alternate-choice closing question.

At the end of the day, volumes can and have been written about closing sales. The most successful salespeople are the ones who take the time to understand their prospects' needs, go out of their way to meet these needs so that both sides win, and simply ask for the sale, and close more times than not because of it. Remember, closing a sale is the easy part; it is bringing your customer to this point that involves 99 percent of the work required to sell.

Getting More Referrals

Hands down, for entrepreneurs selling services, the fastest way to increase sales and profits, while reducing sales cycle time and the costs associated with finding new prospects and developing profitable business and selling relationships, is to get more referrals. In fact, referrals can make all the difference between business success or business failure. How do you get more referrals? Getting more referrals requires you to develop and implement a referral strategy consisting of three important elements: asking for referrals, building a referral team, and rewarding people who refer your business to others.

Implementing the first part of your referral strategy is easy because it requires nothing more than getting in the habit of asking for referrals. Much as you ask for the sale to close, you have to ask every customer, and even prospects who did not buy, for a referral. Wording the question is simple. "Mrs. Jones, do you know anyone else who would benefit from the services we provide?" Or, "We take pride in providing the best services at fair prices. Do you know anyone else, like you, who needs our services and who wants to be treated fairly?"

The second part of the strategy is also straightforward. Enlist your family members, friends, suppliers, and business associates to refer your business to their friends, family, co-workers, and customers. The idea is to build an army of people who know and trust your business, as well as to have an in-depth knowledge of the services you provide so they can refer your business to others. You accomplish this by being the best businessperson that you can, offering great service, and by treating others the way that you like to be treated. You will quickly discover that when people believe in you, your business, and the services that you sell, they will be more than happy to tell others.

The final part of the strategy is also an easy one to master: never let a good deed go unnoticed, and do this by always rewarding people who refer your business to others. People do not expect to be rewarded, and are greatly appreciative when they are, so much so that they will work even harder to refer your business to others. Depending on the services you sell, rewards could be just about anything such as a nice thank-you note, a card, calendar, cash, service discounts, concert tickets, or a gift certificate for a great meal at a fine restaurant.

Options for Growing Your Business

At some point, most small business owners must make the decision whether to grow their business. Like any decision, you have to weigh the advantages and disadvantages. There are obvious benefits to business growth, including potentially higher profits, greater equity, and personal satisfaction. There are also disadvantages, such as increased operating costs, loss of control if partners are brought in, extra administration and paperwork, and just more stuff to do. If you decide that growing your business is the best option to achieve personal and business goals, you have five main growth options: geographic growth, people growth, offering more services, franchising, and mergers and acquisitions.

Grow Geographically

Geographic growth can be physical, electronic, or a combination of both. Physical growth means adding satellite locations in the same city, county, state, country, or even internationally. To grow your business geographically in the real world there are many choices, including agents, licensees, new offices with managers, new business partners, franchising, or mergers and acquisitions. Electronic growth means harnessing the power of the internet to make your services available electronically to a global audience of consumers. Growing your business via the internet is somewhat easier and definitely less expensive because there is no need to rent costly office space and pay employee and management wages. Once the decision has been made to expand via the internet, you can move into foreign markets relatively quickly, efficiently, and with virtually no red tape to worry about. Although not every service business is amenable to electronic expansion, attention should be paid to planning and executing growth strategies utilizing the internet if your business is suitable and this is the route you choose. Savvy business owners with an eye to substantial growth will usually elect to combine physical and electronic expansion methods to grow their small businesses.

Grow by People Power

You can also substantially grow your business by hiring more employees, installers, sales agents, or subcontractors to sell your services to a broader customer base to increase sales, revenues, and profits. If you choose to grow your business by bringing in new people, you must be prepared to invest the time necessary to find people who share your enthusiasm for the business and its long-term growth prospects. You must also be prepared to invest the money required to train, equip, and support employees until they can become productive team players. Before bringing in new people there are issues to consider such as: What type of training is required? What type of new equipment must you acquire for your expanded work force? How much do you have to pay your expanded work force, and how will they be compensated—salary, commission, or a combination? And, do you have to supply employee insurance and benefits? There are also other considerations such as labor laws, health and safety regulations, and management issues, especially in more specialized fields. At the end of the day, growing your small business into a larger business takes people; it simply cannot be accomplished without help. Consequently, you need to develop a strategy for bringing in new people so that you can maximize your potential for success.

Grow by Offering More Services

Another way to grow your business is to offer your existing customers new services and/or products in addition to the services that you currently provide. Growing by expanding the number of products and services you sell is highly advisable. You already have valuable customer relationships in place, which usually can be tapped for new sales quickly, with little resistance, and at minimal cost. Keep in mind, however, that your current customers must want and need your new products or services. Before expanding your line, talk to customers and ask: What additional products or services do you want or need? Would you be willing to purchase these from me? How much are you prepared to spend? It is a safe bet that your customers are purchasing products and services elsewhere that you could easily supply to them, probably at the same or a competitive cost.

Grow by Franchising and Licensing

Many small businesses have also expanded to become national and international corporations by successfully franchising their business model or by licensing their intellectual and proprietary properties. The potential for growth through franchising and licensing is nearly limitless, but these are very tricky waters to navigate. Small business owners who choose this route are advised to seek the services of a lawyer and accountant who are experienced in franchising laws and financial issues. You will also want to talk with a franchise consultant who, through analysis, can advise you on the viability of franchising your business. The most successful franchises are ones that keep things simple. The franchise is easy to operate, sells services that consumers want, and has the potential to cover expenses and the operator's income. The best franchises do not try to reinvent the wheel, but rather improve upon a current product or service and its distribution through their own unique selling proposition. Information about franchising can be obtained from the International Franchise Association, ☎ (202) 628-8000, www.franchise.org; members include franchisors, franchisees, and product and service providers to the franchise industry.

Grow by Mergers or Acquisitions

Mergers and acquisitions are also growth options, although certainly not as popular as the other options already discussed. It is, however, possible to merge your business with a competing or noncompeting business. If you do, your options include retaining a portion of ownership of the new operation or selling out completely and not retaining any ownership but remaining involved as an employee or consultant. Growing a business by merging it with another business can be a wise growth strategy. When the two businesses become one, they benefit by being able to take advantage of each other's resources and strengths while offsetting weaknesses through specialization. It may also afford you the opportunity to own a piece of a larger pie with further growth potential, instead of a larger piece of a small pie with little, if any, opportunity for growth. Business growth through acquisition can also prove a wise move because buying a business that sells complementary goods and services enables you to expand your current line quickly with a customer base in place. At the end of the day, both options warrant careful consideration, research, and planning.

CHAPTER

6

THE BEST 202 SERVICES YOU CAN SELL FOR BIG PROFITS

So far, you have learned about business structure and registration, legal and financial issues, how to set up an office, advertise and sell your service. Now the real fun begins! In this chapter you will discover the best 202 services you can sell for big profits, just like thousands of other entrepreneurs are doing right now with great success.

The criteria used to select the best services to sell were based on a number of factors, including:

- In-demand services in growth industries.

- Minimal to moderate investment levels.
- Excellent profit potential.
- A broad range appealing to different personalities, experiences, and skill levels.
- Service businesses with proven track records.

Keep in mind that not every person has the resources, knowledge, or finances needed to start each service business listed here. Some people will be better equipped than others to provide certain services. But don't worry, there is a service for everyone to provide and sell for big profits, as you will soon discover. Ultimately, once you have considered all the important issues such as your special skills and experiences, investment criteria, health, and level of commitment and interest, you will be the best judge of what service(s) you are best suited to provide.

The information presented in this chapter is in brief synopsis format. The service is explained, along with marketing information, and often equipment and training requirements. I have also endeavored to list franchise and business opportunity resources, which are flagged with a star ★ icon for many of the services featured. This is for people who would prefer to own and operate a franchise rather than starting their own business from scratch

At a Glance

At the end of each service listing is a section called At a Glance, where you will find capsulated information covering the amount of investment needed to start the business, current rate information, skill level requirements, and helpful resources. This information has been included to provide a helpful overview of the service featured so that, at a glance, you will have general information that answers the most frequently asked questions: How much money is needed to get started? How much money can I make? What skills are needed to run the business? And, what do I do next?

Investment

The business start-up investment information should only be used as a general guideline, as actual start-up costs may be higher or lower than indicated. Additionally, the investment figures shown are for new businesses started from scratch, and not reflective of the costs associated with purchasing and starting a franchise or business. Investment figures also do not take into account the need to purchase transportation, specialized tools and equipment, working capital reserve, or to buy or rent and substantially renovate or improve a business location. They do cover the basics such as business registration, basic tools and equipment, a computer, business cards, fliers, and a small initial advertising and marketing budget.

Business start-up investments are broken into four categories—under $2,000, under $10,000, under $25,000, and over $25,000. In Chapter 3, Business and Marketing Planning, you will find a business start-up costs worksheet that can help you calculate the total amount of money needed to start your business.

BUSINESS START-UP INVESTMENT CATEGORIES

Investment: Under $2K = Start-up investment less than $2,000
Investment: Under $10K = Start-up investment $2,001 to $10,000
Investment: Under $25K = Start-up investment $10,001 to $25,000
Investment: Over $25K = Start-up investment greater than $25,000

Rate

You will also find rate information that is based on industry averages. This should only be used as a guideline, as actual earnings per hour may be higher or lower than indicated. Likewise, rates vary between the United States and Canada, can vary between states and/or provinces, and can even vary from city to city within specific states and/or provinces. Specialized services, requiring a higher skill level, generally command the highest hourly rates.

RATE CATEGORIES

Rate: $15+ = $15 to $25 per hour
Rate: $25+ = $25 to $50 per hour
Rate: $50+ = $50 per hour and greater

Skill Level

Information is also provided about the skills needed, or in many instances not needed, to provide the service. This information is based on a scale, with level 1 representing the lowest skill requirement, which means there are no qualifications, previous experience, training, or certifications needed to provide the service. Skill level 2 means previous experience is recommended. Skill level 3 means previous experience and training are recommended. Skill level 4 is the highest, and training is required along with certification to provide the service.

Like rates, skill level requirements can vary from country to country, state to state, and province to province. Therefore, this information should only be used for general purposes and it is the responsibility of all entrepreneurs to check into legal, training, and licensing requirements prior to starting any business or selling and providing any service.

SKILL LEVEL CATEGORIES

Skill Level: 1 = No qualifications
Skill Level: 2 = Experience recommended
Skill Level: 3 = Training required or recommended
Skill Level: 4 = Certification or license required

Resources

Each service featured includes helpful resources such as associations, equipment suppliers, products, publications, franchise or business opportunities, and pertinent government agency information. None of the resources presented in this chapter is meant to promote or endorse any company, association, product, or service. All resources are included simply as helpful tools to get you to the next level should you decide to pursue any of these business ideas. You may elect to contact and even do business with sources listed, or you may choose not to. The decision is entirely up to you. However, I did endeavor to select only reputable companies, associations, products, and services to list as resources.

At the end of the day, you must be comfortable in the knowledge that you are doing business with reliable and honest sources. The only way this can be accomplished is through research. Learn everything you can about any company or organization you intend to do business with. All should be happy to answer questions and supply references. If not, look for companies that will. It is your time, money, and energy—all very valuable assets. Do your homework to protect these assets!

RESOURCE ICONS

☎ Contact telephone number
✐ Web address
📖 Book, magazine, or publication
★ Franchise or business opportunity

202 Services You Can Sell

Desktop Publishing

The desktop publishing industry is experiencing double-digit growth and will continue to flourish and keep pace with software and technological innovations for years to come, making this a great business start-up with incredible upside growth potential. In fact, the Bureau of Labor Statistics estimates that more than 50,000 people are currently employed in the desktop publishing industry.

Combining your design and computer skills, you can provide clients with a wide range of desktop publishing services. With the aid of desktop publishing software programs from Adobe, www.adobe.com, and Corel, www.corel.com, you can create and produce print and electronic promotional fliers, brochures, product catalogs, business reports, posters, presentations, coupons, and advertisements of all sorts. Create samples of your work and set up appointments with business owners and professionals to present your talents and explain the benefits provided by your service. Also attend business association meetings to network and spread the word about your desktop publishing services. You will need to invest in computer equipment, specialized software, scanner, digital camera, and high-quality printer, but with desktop publishing rates in the area of $40 per hour, you can be assured of a quick return on investment.

 INVESTMENT: Under $10K

 RATE: $25+

 SKILL LEVEL: 2–3

 RESOURCES

—Desktop Publishing Online, information and resources, www.desktoppublishing.com

—Elance Online, outsourcing and services marketplace, www.elanceonline.com

—*Layout Index: Brochure, Web Design, Poster, Flyer, Advertising, Page Layout, Newsletter, Stationery Index*, Jim Krause (North Light Books, 2001)

Newsletter Publishing

Making use of your research, writing, and design skills you can create informative print and/or electronic promotional newsletters to meet your clients' specific wants and needs. These potential clients may include stockbrokers, realtors, small business owners, service providers, sports clubs, nonprofit organizations, and corporations. Even though most organizations and businesses realize the benefits of newsletters, such as keeping clients and members informed about the latest news and promoting products and services, many do not have the skills, time, or people-power to get the job done on a regular basis. Writing, designing, printing, and distributing print and electronic newsletters will require an investment in computer hardware, software, and related equipment such as a scanner, laser printer, and digital camera. But at $25 to $40 per hour, the return on investment is quick. Create and print electronic newsletter samples to use as your main marketing tools. Print samples can be mailed and hand-delivered to potential clients, while e-newsletters can be delivered by e-mail. Networking at business functions and talking to small business owners will also go a long way in spreading the word about the services you offer.

 **INVESTMENT:** Under $10K

 **RATE:** $15+

 **SKILL LEVEL:** 2

 **RESOURCES**

—*Design It Yourself Newsletters: A Step-by-Step Guide*, Chuck Green (Rockport Publishers, 2002)

—E-Newsletter Pro, newsletter management software, www.enewsletterpro.com

—How to Write a Newsletter, newsletter tool kit software, www.howtowriteanewsletter.com

Electronic Magazine Publishing

Have you ever wanted to publish your own magazine, but the lack of the millions of dollars that are required to start a large-scale print magazine has always stood in the way? Well, now you can publish your own magazine on a shoestring start-up investment of only a few thousand dollars—but in electronic format rather than print. In spite of the estimated 100,000 electronic publications being distributed to millions of readers monthly, there is room for lots of newcomers in the ezine publishing world. Develop your ezine based on what you know and like—antiques, sports, entertainment, investment, family issues, or just about anything else that tickles your fancy. Ezines are generally free to subscribers and supported by advertising revenues, which means businesses pay for space in your electronic magazine to advertise their products and services. For instance, if you publish and distribute a monthly football ezine, logical advertisers would include sports retailers and sports gaming businesses. Due to the amount of competition in the marketplace, aim to serve a well-defined niche market, provide interesting and informative content that readers cannot get anywhere else, and build a large subscription base that will appeal to advertisers and marketers who want to reach your audience.

AT A GLANCE

 INVESTMENT: Under $25K

 RATE: $25+

 SKILL LEVEL: 1–2

 RESOURCES

—Ezine Director, ezine delivery and management software, www.ezinedirector.com

—Ezine Directory, lists over 2,400 electronic publications, www.ezine-dir.com

— *The Columbia Guide to Digital Publishing,* William E. Kasdorf (Columbia University Press, 2003)

Community Newsletter

Writing, publishing, and distributing your own community newsletter is a great way to earn extra money and have some fun at the same time. To keep your start-up, equipment, and printing costs to a minimum use 11-by-17-inch paper folded in half, as is your newspaper. This will give you four pages on which to feature content and advertisements. Featured content can be whatever you think will be beneficial to the community—entertainment, sports, real estate, the arts, senior issues, business news, or just games and trivia. The paper is supported financially by local business advertisers and, based on the 11-by-17-inch format, you can fit up to 24 business-card-sized ads in each issue, while still leaving lots of room for content. Charging $150 per month for each ad space will generate revenues of $3,600, of which approximately 20 percent will be needed to cover paper, printing, and distribution. The weekly newspapers can be delivered free of charge to community gathering places such as restaurants, community centers, coffee shops, fitness clubs, and pubs, for clients to read on location and/or take home. To get up and running you will need a computer, software such as Adobe PageMaker, a printer capable of using 11-by-17-inch paper, and reliable transportation to deliver the papers. Once you have typeset in the content and ads, you can print one copy of the paper and use a local copy shop to complete the run for pennies apiece.

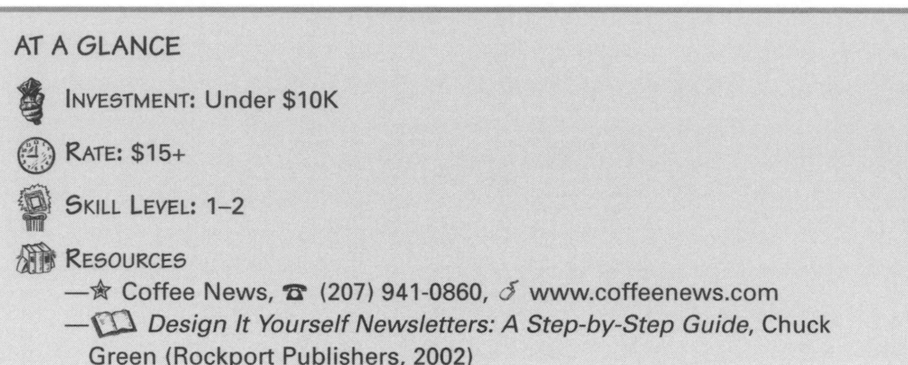

AT A GLANCE

INVESTMENT: Under $10K

RATE: $15+

SKILL LEVEL: 1–2

RESOURCES

—Coffee News, (207) 941-0860, www.coffeenews.com

—*Design It Yourself Newsletters: A Step-by-Step Guide*, Chuck Green (Rockport Publishers, 2002)

Logo Design

Great logos help to build and maintain instant brand recognition and consumer awareness by visually linking the logo to the business, product, or service it represents. If you have a creative flair and artistic abilities, you can put them to good use by starting a logo design service. You will need a computer, digital camera, printer, and design software to get started. But outside of these expenditures, start-up costs are minimal, as are the ongoing fixed overheads to operate the business because you can work from home and the majority of jobs can be serviced using e-mail and fax. Market your talents to business owners and professionals, product developers, profit and nonprofit organizations, government agencies, and basically anyone else in need of product, service, or personal branding through repetitive use of logo. Fees for designing logos vary greatly, from as low as $75 to literally thousands. The better known you become for your incredible design work and logos that perfectly describe what they represent, and the more well-known your customers are, the higher your fees will go.

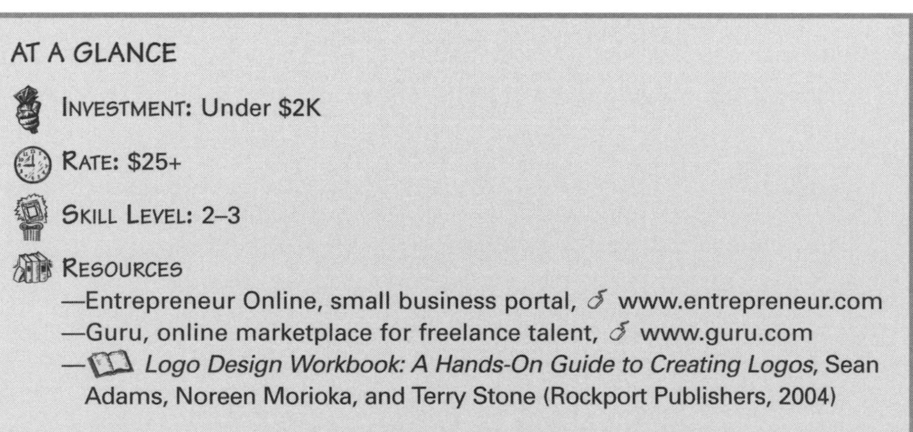

AT A GLANCE

INVESTMENT: Under $2K

RATE: $25+

SKILL LEVEL: 2–3

RESOURCES

—Entrepreneur Online, small business portal, www.entrepreneur.com

—Guru, online marketplace for freelance talent, www.guru.com

—*Logo Design Workbook: A Hands-On Guide to Creating Logos*, Sean Adams, Noreen Morioka, and Terry Stone (Rockport Publishers, 2004)

Self-Publishing Consultant

Here is your opportunity to help people fulfill their dreams of becoming a published writers by starting a self-publishing consulting business. Offer your clients numerous services in both print and electronic formats for nonfiction and fiction books, journals, and short stories, including proofreading, editing, printing, marketing, and distributing their projects. Potential clients are not limited to people who want to write the next Great American Novel, but also include trainers wanting to write and publish books to use as training aids; activists (political, environmental, or any other kind) wanting to write a book to help raise awareness of their causes; corporations wanting to produce a book for customers telling the history of their business, products, services, and employees; and people wanting to write books about their family histories or life experiences to give to friends and family members as gifts. Advertise your services in online writing portals and magazines, join writing associations and groups to network for business, and build alliances with copywriters, book printers, editors, and illustrators to capitalize on word-of-mouth referrals.

AT A GLANCE

 INVESTMENT: Under $10K

 RATE: $25+

 SKILL LEVEL: 2

 RESOURCES

—Self-Publishers Association of North America, ☎ (719) 395-5761, www.spannet.org

—Self-Pub Net, industry information portal, www.self-pub.net

Resume Service

Finding the perfect words to describe why people's experiences, special skills, and interests make them the right candidate for a job is difficult work. That's why resume services continue to flourish in spite of the fact that just about everyone has or has access to a computer and a word processing program. If you are a wordsmith with a human resources, management, or administration background, this may be the perfect opportunity for you. One of the best aspects about starting a resume service is that you can start small, part-time, and keep costs to a minimum by working at home and utilizing existing resources. All of which makes this the perfect opportunity for people looking to earn an extra few hundred dollars a month. In addition to resumes, you can also write cover, sales, and follow-up letters for clients, as well as offer duplication and binding services, all of which will help to boost revenues. As a way to separate your resume service from competitors,' consider creating a tips booklet to help clients land their dream jobs. This would include how to dress for interviews, how to handle themselves in a stressful interview situation, how to make follow-up telephone calls, how to prepare for interviews, and how to network for that dream job. Advertise locally, online, and through career expos. Once established, word-of-mouth advertising will go a long way to keeping you busy.

AT A GLANCE

 INVESTMENT: Under $2K

 RATE: $15+

 SKILL LEVEL: 1–2

 RESOURCES

—*The Resume Handbook: How to Write Outstanding Resumes & Cover Letters for Every Situation*, Arthur D. Rosenberg and David Heizer (Adams Media Corporation, 2003)

—WinWay, resume software, www.winway.com

Online Researcher

If you find yourself spending a lot of time surfing the web, and if you're looking to start your own business, consider an internet research service so you can get paid for the time you spend surfing. This business opportunity was once called information brokering, but, with the introduction of the internet, the name has changed. The business remains the same, however, as the information that was once researched and compiled from newspapers, trade magazines, and business and industry journals may now be found online. An internet research service operates in two ways. The first is to collect data and facts relevant to a specific topic or topics, and then sell the compiled data to individuals and businesses that require this information. Business owners also enlist the services of an internet researcher to source specific data and facts relevant to their particular business, industry, or market. In both cases, clients pay for information they are seeking.

Billing rates for the services vary, depending on how much research time is required to compile the data; however, many internet research services have base billing rates of $25 to $35 per hour.

AT A GLANCE

 INVESTMENT: Under $10K

 RATE: $25+

 SKILL LEVEL: 2

 RESOURCES

—Association of Internet Researchers, www.aoir.org

—*Building & Running a Successful Research Business: A Guide for the Independent Information Professional*, Mary Ellen Bates (Cyberage Books, 2003)

—Elance Online, outsourcing and services marketplace, www.elanceonline.com

Web Site Design

A huge opportunity exists to cash in on the boom in web site design because there are thousands of web sites and web pages being posted on the internet every day. Best of all, if you lack the skills needed to design highly effective web sites and pages, you can take a crash course in web site design at your local community college. Alternatively, you can capitalize on your sales and marketing skills and concentrate your efforts on finding new customers, and hire a high-tech wizard right out of school to take on design duties. Competition in web site design and service is steep, so you may want to take a more grassroots approach to marketing and start by servicing your local area. Get started by designing a few sample sites to showcase your talents, and be sure to mix up your sample work to include e-commerce, information portal, and so on. Next, initiate a letter, telephone, and e-mail direct marketing campaign, along with personal visits to introduce your design services to small business owners in your community who currently do not have a business web site or have a site in need of improvement. Armed with a notebook computer, you can meet with business owners, present your sample sites, and explain the benefits of your web site design services. Additional revenues can be generated by hosting sites, maintaining sites, providing content, and by creating online marketing programs to meet individual client needs.

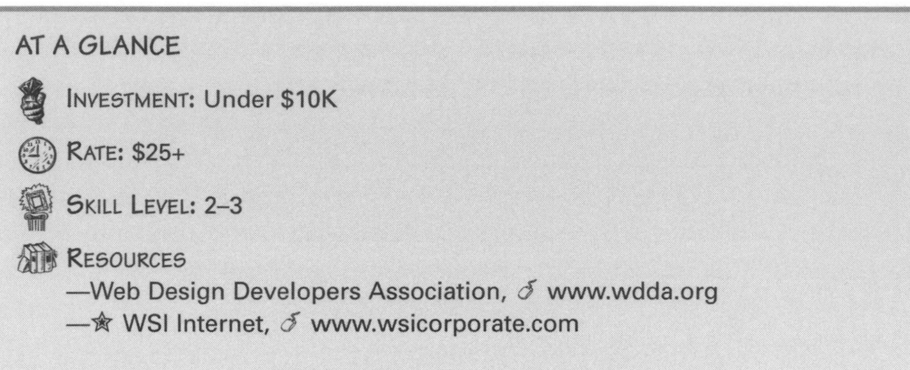

AT A GLANCE

INVESTMENT: Under $10K

RATE: $25+

SKILL LEVEL: 2–3

RESOURCES

—Web Design Developers Association, www.wdda.org

—★ WSI Internet, www.wsicorporate.com

Computer Repair

It's time for you to get in on the multibillion-dollar, ever-growing computer industry by starting your own computer repair service. Working from home, mobile, storefront, or office, you can offer computer and related technologies setup, repair, maintenance, and troubleshooting services. Market your services through traditional advertising formats such as the Yellow Pages and newspaper advertising, as well as through more direct methods such as networking at business functions and by creating and implementing a direct-mail campaign aimed mainly at commercial customers with multiple computer workstations. Don't worry if your computer troubleshooting skills are not up to par, because there are a plethora of training courses appropriate to every skill level and budget across the country. Some courses can have you up and running and repairing computers in a matter of months. Best of all, computer repair technicians earn up to $50 per hour.

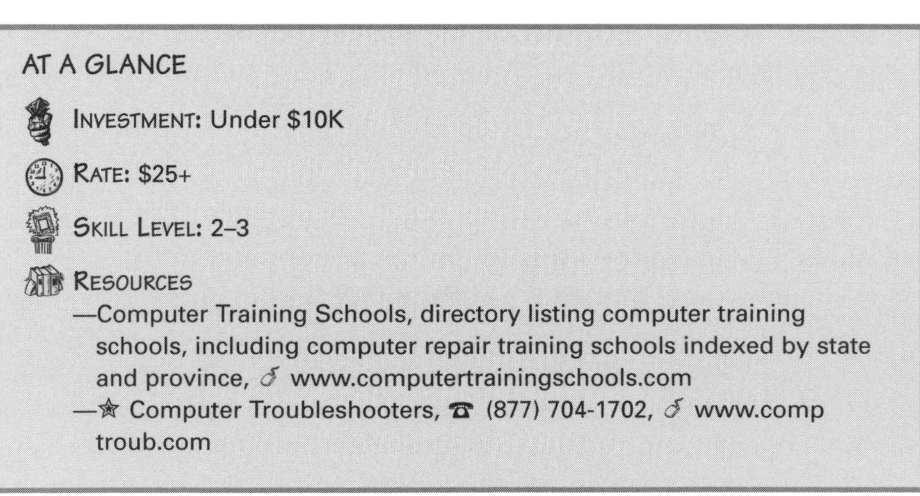

AT A GLANCE

INVESTMENT: Under $10K

RATE: $25+

SKILL LEVEL: 2–3

RESOURCES

—Computer Training Schools, directory listing computer training schools, including computer repair training schools indexed by state and province, www.computertrainingschools.com

—★ Computer Troubleshooters, ☎ (877) 704-1702, www.comptroub.com

Moblie Computer Trainer

Most computer training schools require students to come to their location for training classes. But for companies that have upgraded or purchased new computers and software, this is often not practical, especially if there are five to ten or more employees who are in need of training or retraining. Likewise, not everyone who purchases a new computer, software, or other hardware devices has time to attend classes to learn how to use the equipment. Herein lies the opportunity. Capitalizing on your computer, software, and marketing experience, you can start a mobile computer training service and train students one-on-one, or in a group format at their homes, businesses, or office. The proliferation of technological advances, and the constant new stream of software applications and hardware devices means that there will always be lots of people in need of training or skills-upgrading, so they can get the most benefit from their computer equipment and programs. Advertise your service with fliers, in newspaper classifieds, the Yellow Pages, and by networking at business and social functions.

 INVESTMENT: Under $10K

 RATE: $25+

 SKILL LEVEL: 2–3

 RESOURCES

—☆ Computer Moms International, ☎ (866) 447-3666, www.computermoms.com

—Computer Training Schools, directory listing computer training schools indexed by state and province, www.computertrainingschools.com

E-Commerce Specialist

While it may sound like doing business in cyberspace is a piece of cake, nothing could be farther from the truth. In fact, doing business online and achieving any kind of e-profitable success is probably more difficult than it is in the bricks-and-mortar world. For that reason many webpreneurs are turning to enlisting the services of an e-commerce specialist to help build, market, and maintain their e-commerce businesses. Right now, and for the foreseeable future, there is an incredible opportunity to build a super profitable e-commerce consulting business for entrepreneurs with web development, online marketing, e-commerce, and e-communications skills and experience. In short, if this describes you, the potential to earn $1,000 a day and more is presently available. E-commerce specialists do much more than just show businesspeople how to hawk their goods online. They also:

- Help businesses build or improve their web sites
- Develop productive database systems
- Create efficient e-showrooms and checkouts
- Create and manage electronic mailing lists
- Design e-mail communication systems and plans
- Increase search engine rankings
- Create effective advertising and pay-per-click promotions
- Develop and implement order processing and fulfillment systems
- And much more

Online sales are expected to top $1 trillion in 2005. Needless to say, the timing cannot get better than now for getting your piece of this very lucrative pie. The Institute of Certified E-Commerce Consultants provides training, and students graduate with the professional designation of Certified E-Commerce Consultant.

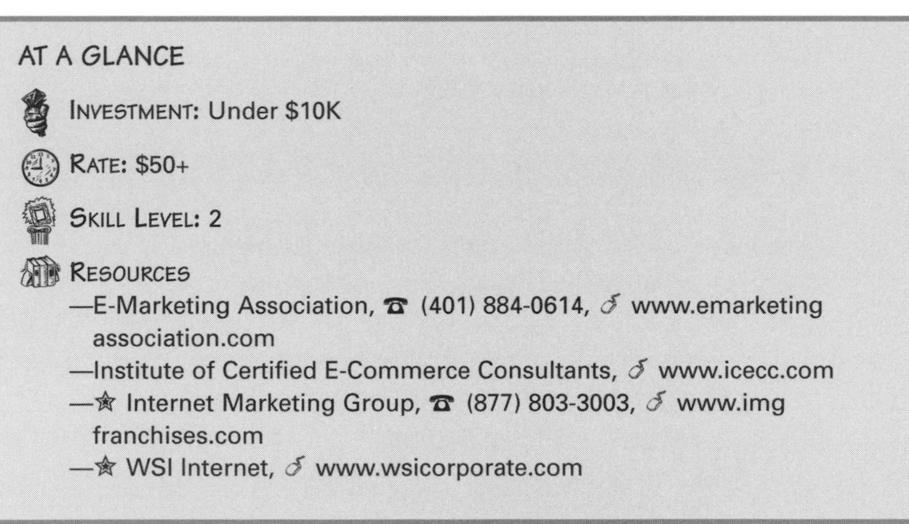

AT A GLANCE

INVESTMENT: Under $10K

RATE: $50+

SKILL LEVEL: 2

RESOURCES

—E-Marketing Association, ☎ (401) 884-0614, www.emarketingassociation.com

—Institute of Certified E-Commerce Consultants, www.icecc.com

—★ Internet Marketing Group, ☎ (877) 803-3003, www.imgfranchises.com

—★ WSI Internet, www.wsicorporate.com

e-Bay Consultant

With more than 100 million registered users, eBay generates billions in annual sales. This in turn has created a fantastic opportunity to start an eBay consulting business training small business owners to use the online marketplace giant to sell their goods and services and cash in big. Marketing your consulting services requires nothing more than setting appointments with businesses that are not currently using eBay, and explaining the incredible opportunity they are missing out on, along with the beneficial features of your service, and why they should hire you as their eBay consultant. Teach business owners how to list goods for sale using one or more of eBay's sellers' options, as well as how to increase interest in and promote their auctions, take online payments, and process and fulfill orders. Basically, your instruction covers everything that is required to list products on eBay, sell them, get paid, and have them delivered.

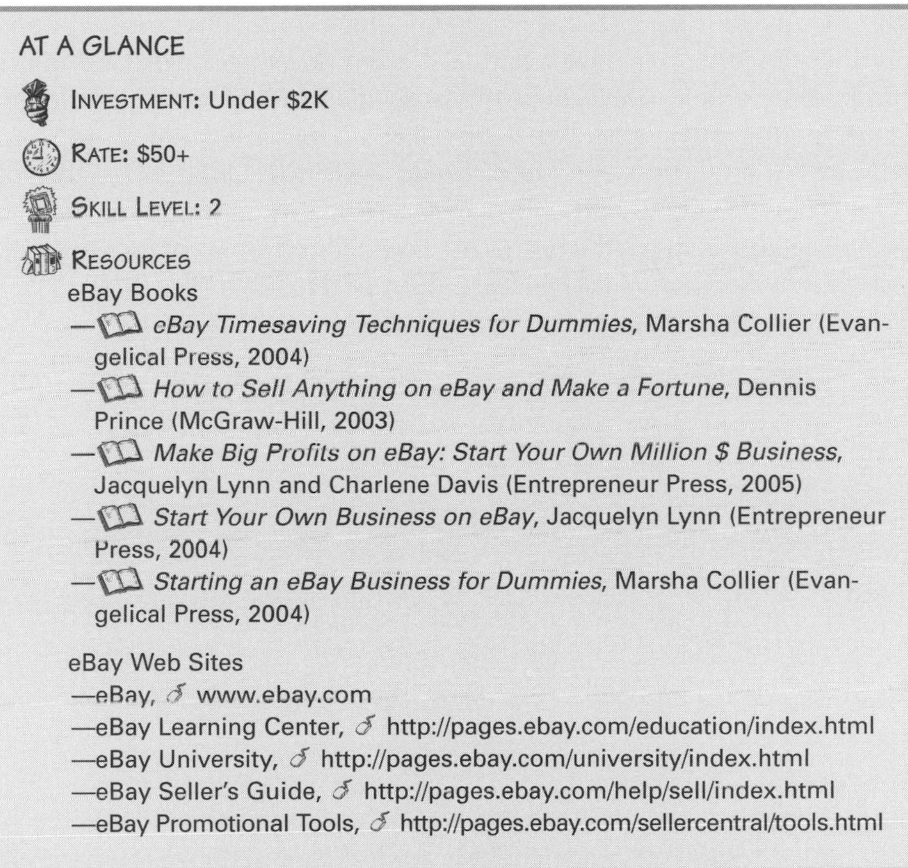

AT A GLANCE

INVESTMENT: Under $2K

RATE: $50+

SKILL LEVEL: 2

RESOURCES

eBay Books

—*eBay Timesaving Techniques for Dummies*, Marsha Collier (Evangelical Press, 2004)
—*How to Sell Anything on eBay and Make a Fortune*, Dennis Prince (McGraw-Hill, 2003)
—*Make Big Profits on eBay: Start Your Own Million $ Business*, Jacquelyn Lynn and Charlene Davis (Entrepreneur Press, 2005)
—*Start Your Own Business on eBay*, Jacquelyn Lynn (Entrepreneur Press, 2004)
—*Starting an eBay Business for Dummies*, Marsha Collier (Evangelical Press, 2004)

eBay Web Sites

—eBay, www.ebay.com
—eBay Learning Center, http://pages.ebay.com/education/index.html
—eBay University, http://pages.ebay.com/university/index.html
—eBay Seller's Guide, http://pages.ebay.com/help/sell/index.html
—eBay Promotional Tools, http://pages.ebay.com/sellercentral/tools.html

Community Web Site

Not all small business owners and professionals have the time, ability, or inclination to build, maintain, and regularly update a web site. But at the same time many would still like to have some sort of presence on the web. Therein lies the opportunity for internet-savvy entrepreneurs: Develop, maintain, and market a community-based web site, featuring local news and information, as well as participating businesses and professionals. Each business that joins would receive one or more web pages within the site to advertise, promote, and even sell their products and services, along with a web address extension, private e-mail, and a host of additional web and commerce features. Think of it as a bricks-and-mortar mall, but in virtual space. You can charge each participating business a monthly fee membership that includes fixed services, and additional fees for premium services such as content updating and web tools specific to that business. Promote the community web site locally with fliers, print advertisements in newspapers, and with the use of advertising specialties. Offer clients a noncompetition clause to entice them to join. This means one car dealer, one roofer, one clothing retailer, one chiropractor, and so on. Community web sites are truly a win-win-win situation. Participating businesses win by getting a fully functioning and regularly updated site for a fraction of what it would cost individually. Community residents win by getting news and information specific to their area, along with convenient online access to products and services offered by community businesses. And you win by building a successful and profitable business.

AT A GLANCE

INVESTMENT: Under $10K

RATE: $15+

SKILL LEVEL: 2

RESOURCES

—★ Rezcity.com, ☎ (201) 567-8500, www.rezcity.com

—★ WSI Internet, www.wsicorporate.com

Auctioneer

Have fun and make lots of money by starting and operating an auction service. The first thing you have to know about becoming an auctioneer is that training is required, and each state and province has its own criteria for auctioneer licensing. However, with that said, there are dozens of auctioneer schools across the United States and Canada. Contact the associations listed below to inquire about auctioneer training in your area. Auctioneers are more than just fast talkers; they are also expert marketers who have an excellent knowledge of the products they sell, the demand for these products, and the target audience of buyers. They must be knowledgeable about this audience, because without buyers in attendance it does not matter what's up for auction. That is why most auctioneers specialize in one or two types of goods, such as real estate, heavy equipment, antiques, automobiles, or general goods. Starting an auction service also requires relatively deep pockets unless you contract your auctioning services to other auctioneers. It is a costly business to establish because you have to pay for everything upfront to advertise, promote, set up, and run the auction before you receive your commissions which are based on the total value of the goods sold at auction.

AT A GLANCE

INVESTMENT: Over $25K

RATE: $50+

SKILL LEVEL: 4

RESOURCES
- —Auction Guide, industry information portal, www.auctionguide.com
- —Auctioneers Association of Canada, (866) 640-9915, www.auctioneerscanada.com
- —National Auctioneers Association, (800) 662-9438, www.auctioneer.org

Home Office Planner

First-time attempts to work or operate a business from home often meet with frustration and confusion about how to get started, because functional room design is more important than most people think. Being disorganized, too much noise, too small a work space, and the wrong office furniture and equipment are common problems for the new homebased worker. They're also the basis of starting a home office planning service with the focus on assisting employees and business owners to establish, or make the transition to, a homebased office. Working one-on-one with clients, you can develop successful work and organization plans that are tailored to their specific needs. Focus on topics such as office layout design, ergonomics, security systems and devices, storage solutions, recycling programs, work routine schedules, computer and technology integration, communications systems, and suitable equipment and supply requirements. Make sure you market your services to corporations, as many are now having key employees work from homebased offices as telecommuters.

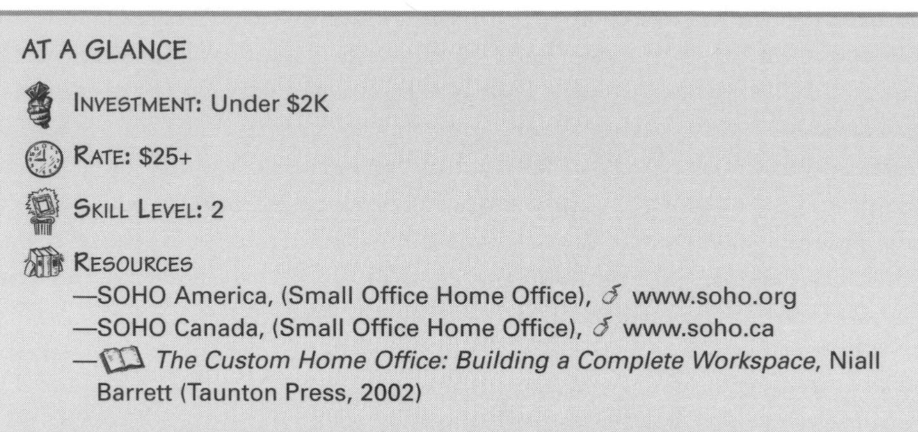

AT A GLANCE

INVESTMENT: Under $2K

RATE: $25+

SKILL LEVEL: 2

RESOURCES

—SOHO America, (Small Office Home Office), www.soho.org

—SOHO Canada, (Small Office Home Office), www.soho.ca

—*The Custom Home Office: Building a Complete Workspace*, Niall Barrett (Taunton Press, 2002)

Cartridge Refiller

One of the fastest-growing service businesses today is ink cartridge recycling. Ink and toner cartridges used in most photocopiers, fax machines, and laser and inkjet printers can be recycled by simply replenishing the ink or toner supply, thereby keeping them out of landfills and putting profits in your pockets. This creates a wonderful business opportunity for energetic entrepreneurs to start a toner cartridge recycling service operating from home, on a mobile basis, or from a retail location such as a mall kiosk or storefront. The requirements for operating the business are basic, and you will only need simple tools, which are very inexpensive, and the ability to refill cartridges with new ink, which is easily learned. Offer clients fast and free delivery of recycled cartridges right to their offices, stores, or homes, which can save them as much as 50 percent of the cost of new cartridges. This fact alone can become your most convincing marketing tool for landing new business, and don't be afraid to go after the large accounts with hundreds of machines that regularly must have ink and toner cartridges renewed.

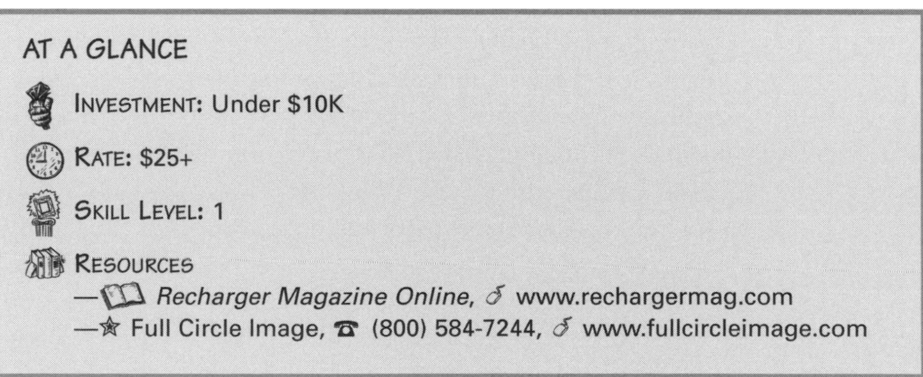

AT A GLANCE

INVESTMENT: Under $10K

RATE: $25+

SKILL LEVEL: 1

RESOURCES

—*Recharger Magazine Online*, www.rechargermag.com

—Full Circle Image, (800) 584-7244, www.fullcircleimage.com

Customer Service Training

At some point we've all received bad service from a store, restaurant, or office, both over the phone or in person. And it's probably happened a lot more than once. The end result of such an encounter is usually a vow never to return to the business, or refer others to the business. Rude or poorly trained employees cost companies millions of dollars each year in lost business and referral sales. But companies that take proactive steps to ensure that all employees receive professional customer service and appreciation training have a leg up on the competition. They wait in the wings with arms wide open to receive disgruntled customers when others screw up. You can earn incredible profits by starting a consulting service that offers customer service and appreciation training programs specifically designed to meet your clients' individual needs. The starting point is to choose a specialty, such as retail, food servers, receptionists, and so forth. Training can be based on your own expertise as well as on the input of other customer service professionals who help create the training curriculum and manuals.

AT A GLANCE

 INVESTMENT: Under $10K

 RATE: $50+

 SKILL LEVEL: 2–3

RESOURCES
- —International Customer Service Association, www.icsa.com
- —*Raving Fans: A Revolutionary Approach to Customer Service*, Ken Blanchard and Sheldon Bowles (William Morrow and Company, 1993)
- —The Training Registry, consultants and trainers marketplace, www.tregistry.com

Clutter Consultant

For the majority of us, frantic and busy lifestyles leave little time to get ourselves organized, let alone our family, homes, or businesses. Exploiting your own organizational and time management skills are the two main prerequisites for starting a clutter consulting business that helps clients get—and stay—organized. Aim your organizational efforts at two separate but equally important topics—physical organization of space (better known as de-cluttering), and time management.

On the physical side of the service, focus on issues such as clearing the clutter that is not needed, developing storage solutions, organizing office furniture and equipment for maximum attractiveness and productivity, rearranging closet space, and organizing items by use priority. On the time management side, assist clients in developing routines and schedules to eliminate overlap, streamline operations, and basically squeeze the most productivity out of each hour so they no longer have to work nights and weekends just to stay on top of their work at home and office. Without question, networking at business and social functions is the best way to get the word out about your service and to start building a valuable contact and referral base.

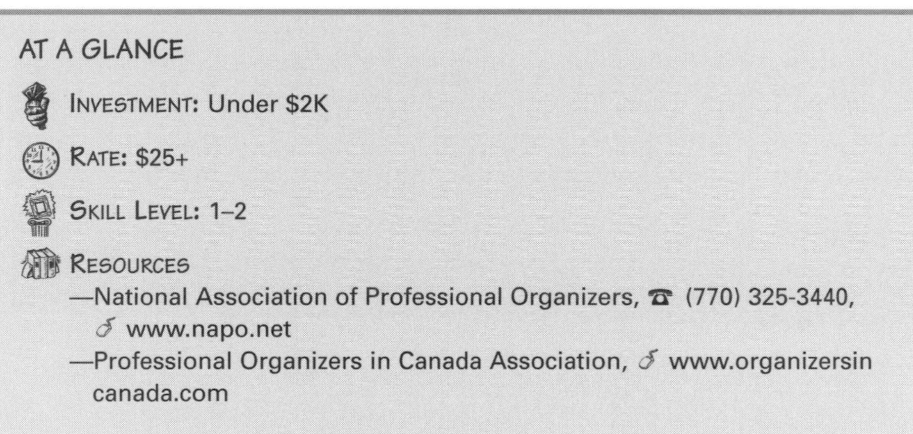

AT A GLANCE

INVESTMENT: Under $2K

RATE: $25+

SKILL LEVEL: 1–2

RESOURCES

—National Association of Professional Organizers, ☎ (770) 325-3440, www.napo.net

—Professional Organizers in Canada Association, www.organizersincanada.com

---

Import/Export Specialist

Considering the many red-tape barriers and all the issues surrounding importing products into this country, or exporting products out of this country, it's no wonder that so many businesses do not know how to get started, and just plain give up out of frustration. Of course, the smart business owners who do not want to miss a single opportunity to grow their businesses and revenues don't give up. Instead, they hire an import/export specialist to guide them through the complex issues of the import/export business—legal, transportation, warehousing, distribution, marketing, employment, environmental, political, and financial. Starting an import/export consulting business will require experience in the industry, or the willingness to learn about the industry. One simple way to market your services is to develop and host a free informational seminar on importing and exporting, and use the event to sign up businesses and individuals who want to get started in import and export.

AT A GLANCE

 INVESTMENT: Under $10K

 RATE: $50+

 SKILL LEVEL: 2

 RESOURCES

—American Importers Association, ☎ (727) 724-0900, www.americanimporters.org

—Canadian Association of Importers and Exporters, ☎ (416) 595-5333, www.importers.ca

—Import Export Coach, industry information portal, www.importexportcoach.com

—The Training Registry, consultants and trainers marketplace, www.tregistry.com

Residential Safety Consultant

Statistically speaking, the largest percentage of accidents causing injuries do not happen on the job, on the roads, or on playing fields, but right at home. Falls, accidental poisonings, burns, cuts, broken bones, and many other types of injuries take place in thousands of homes across the country every single day. The vast majority of these injuries are preventable through education, and by taking proactive steps to eliminate or reduce potential risks around the home. Working as a residential safety consultant, you can conduct inspections of your clients' homes, noting all the potential hazards inside and outside. The next step is to write a report outlining these hazards, along with your recommendations for removing, repairing, or reducing these hazards. At this point, at your client's request, you can carry out the recommended corrective measures, hire a handyperson to do the work, or refer your client to people who can do the work. So what are these potential hazards around the house that can cause harm to kids, pets, seniors, and, in fact, anyone? A few include trip hazards on exterior walkways, window-blind cords, the lack of grab bars and anti-slip surfaces in washrooms, the unsafe storage of cleaning solvents, and the lack of child-resistant latches on cabinets and cutlery drawers.

AT A GLANCE

 INVESTMENT: Under $10K

 RATE: $50+

 SKILL LEVEL: 2

 RESOURCES

—Safe Home Products, safety products for the home, www.safehomeproducts.com

—Safety Info, industry information portal, www.safetyinfo.com

Image Consultant

Image consulting is an exciting business in a booming industry, and you can get paid big bucks to help other people look and feel great. Working as an image consultant you can help people land a new job, spruce up for an important occasion, make a great impression on others, or just feel good about the way they look and the image they project. Image consultants help people on many fronts, including:

- Wardrobe consulting and updating
- Current image analysis, and the development of a new image program
- Etiquette training that can be used in business and social situations
- Assistance in developing better communication skills through vocabulary enhancement and voice projection
- Assistance in developing skills such as the perfect handshake and perfect posture

If you think only women enlist the services of a professional image consultant you would be wrong. In fact, the numbers are evenly split, 50 percent women and 50 percent men. Potential clients include corporate executives, people looking to land new jobs, politicians, people recovering from major illnesses and injuries, television and radio personalities, public speakers, sales professionals, and singles in or reentering the dating scene. Market your services by building a strong network of alliances that can refer their clients and contacts to your business. Be sure to include corporations, hair and makeup professionals, doctors, fitness trainers, and public relations consultants.

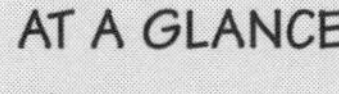

AT A GLANCE

 INVESTMENT: Under $10K

 RATE: $50+

 SKILL LEVEL: 2–3

 RESOURCES
—Association of Image Consultants International, ☎ (972) 755-1503, www.aici.org
—Gloria Starr Success Strategies, image and etiquette consultant training, ☎ (704) 922-6665, www.gloriastarr.com

Notary Public

Notaries public are legal officers with specific judicial authority to administer oaths, certify affidavits, and take depositions. Notaries prepare wills, mortgages, and other legal documents, which they certify with an official seal, as well as providing official witnessing of signatures. There is a growing need for notaries public to work in the areas of real estate, business, finance, insurance, and law. Imagine the flexibility that becoming a notary public affords. You can work from a homebased office, on a mobile basis going to your clients' locations, open an independent office, or work in conjunction with a compatible business such as a real estate office, insurance office, or law office. In a nutshell, if you are prepared to invest in the training required to become a notary public, you have lots of options for how you operate your business once you're certified. Notary Public Online, www.notarypublic.com, provides state-by-state notary public training and certification requirements. In addition to traditional advertising in the Yellow Pages and newspapers, the most successful notaries public are those who build a broad network of business alliances with professionals who require notary public services. Clients include realtors, health-care providers, insurance brokers, and professional service providers.

 INVESTMENT: Under $25K

 RATE: $50+

 SKILL LEVEL: 4

 RESOURCES
—National Notary Association, ☎ (800) 876-6827, www.nationalnotary.org
—The American Society of Notaries, www.notaries.org
—The Society of Notaries Public of BC, www.notaries.bc.ca

Corporate-Meeting Planner

Using your organization and event planning skills will enable you to start a corporate-meeting planner service. Long gone are the days of boring boardroom meetings for middle managers, executives, employees, investors, and business alliances. Today, corporations need and want to keep all executives, managers, employees, customers, investors, and alliances highly motivated, energized, productive, and happy. Consequently, they are more than happy to part with, in some cases, very big bucks to pay for innovative meeting locations, games, and preparations for same. The duties of the corporate-meeting planner are straightforward: They do what it takes to plan and execute a great meeting. You will make all arrangements including, if applicable, sending out invitations, making follow-up calls, catering, booking locations, booking speakers, making hotel arrangements for out-of-town guests, arranging suitable transportation, distributing meeting plans and documents, looking after equipment rentals, and everything else required to pull the event together without a hitch. The best way to market a corporate-event planning service is to simply get out and talk to business owners and managers, and pitch them on why your service is just the right service to meet and exceed their needs.

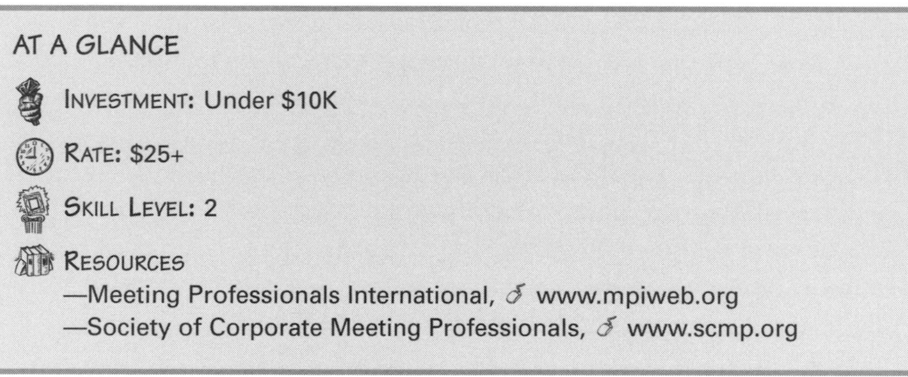

AT A GLANCE

INVESTMENT: Under $10K

RATE: $25+

SKILL LEVEL: 2

RESOURCES

—Meeting Professionals International, www.mpiweb.org

—Society of Corporate Meeting Professionals, www.scmp.org

Retail Loss Prevention Expert

Every year retailers lose billions of dollars in revenues and profits to acts of theft—shoplifters, delivery shorts, employee and subcontractor theft, and various acts of unaccountable "shrinkage." Ultimately, retail theft costs all consumers through higher prices needed to offset these losses. Here is your chance to save retailers and consumers big bucks, while also cashing in big time by providing clients with retail loss prevention training, products, and services. Ideal candidates to start a retail loss prevention service include private investigators, retail security specialists, security specialists, police personnel, or anyone with an interest in the industry who is prepared to obtain the proper training. Training business owners, managers, and employees to spot shoplifters; selling products such as security cameras and counterfeit money detectors; and providing undercover security personnel to retailers on a contract basis or for special events, are just a few ways to earn money operating a loss prevention service.

AT A GLANCE

 **Investment:** Under $10K

 **Rate:** $25+

 **Skill Level:** 2–3

 **Resources**

—Loss Prevention and Security Association, ☎ (888) 372-7214, www.lpsa.net

—The Training Registry, consultants and trainers marketplace, www.tregistry.com

---

Executive Recruiter

A star executive is as vital to a corporation's or an organization's success as a star pitcher is to a baseball team's chances of winning the World Series. If you want to win in today's super competitive global marketplace, you need the right executives who can lead the entire team to victory. This is why executive recruiting services are in big demand as corporations worldwide scramble to build the best executive team that will guide their ship in the new global economy. Executive recruiter is nothing more than a fancy term for a headhunter. The objective of the executive recruiter is to locate the best candidate to meet each client's needs and executive criteria. Many executive recruiters wisely choose to specialize in a specific field such as investment and finance, manufacturing, technology, food services, insurance, advertising and marketing, legal, health care, construction, engineering, or human resources. You would be well advised to do the same. So where do you find the right executives for your clients? The answer is simple—everywhere. You run advertisements on behalf of clients, you source out great talent at other corporations and lure them away with superior contracts and benefits, and you never stop networking and building your database of candidates.

 INVESTMENT: Under $25K

 RATE: $50+

 SKILL LEVEL: 2–3

 RESOURCES

—★ Global Recruiters Network, ☎ (866) 476-8200, www.grncorp.net
— *Start Your Own Executive Recruiting Service*, Mandy Erickson (Entrepreneur Press, 2003)
—Recruiter Connection, industry information portal, www.recruiterconnection.com
— *The Directory of Executive Recruiters*, (Kennedy Information, 2004)

Leasing Broker

Working as an independent or franchised leasing broker, you can help business owners lease the equipment they need to start, operate, and expand their businesses, including everything from computers to machinery to heavy equipment to specialized tools and lots more. The duty of a leasing broker is to bring together three parties—business owners and managers wanting to lease equipment for their businesses, equipment manufacturers and retailers wanting to sell equipment, and lending companies willing to purchase the equipment and lease it back to the business owner. Broker fees are generally paid by the lender or by the equipment manufacturer or retailer. Consequently, finding business owners to work with should not prove difficult because they have nothing to lose—if you cannot arrange suitable financing, they don't pay for the service. You can work from home and visit clients at their location, or rent suitable office space. You will need to establish working relationships with a number of lenders, and perhaps you will want to specialize in one particular type of equipment such as tools, computers, or vehicles so you can become known as an expert in that area. Once established, this is the type of business that thrives on repeat business and referrals.

 INVESTMENT: Under $10K

 RATE: $25+

 **SKILL LEVEL:** 2–3

 **RESOURCES**

—★ Lease One Corporation, ☎ (888) 852-3380, www.leaseoneri.com/join.htm

—United Association of Equipment Leasing, www.uael.org

Launch Service

Every new business, product, service, or event needs a great launch to propel it into the minds of consumers or the intended target audience. The time to start a grand opening service has never been better, especially when you consider that the United States Small Business Administration estimates that there are more than 700,000 new businesses formed each year. Launching provides a wide range of valuable services—everything from creating and sending out press releases, to hosting press conferences, creating photo opportunities, ribbon-cutting ceremonies, red-carpet events, hiring celebrities for appearances, sending out invitations, and arranging for catering services and entertainment. Basically, you do everything that is needed to launch the client's business, product, service, or event with a positive big bang. This opportunity suits a creative entrepreneur with excellent marketing, public relations, organizational, and communications skills.

 **INVESTMENT:** Under $10K

 **RATE:** $25+

 **SKILL LEVEL:** 2

 **RESOURCES**

—National Association of Manufacturers, ☎ (202) 637-3000, www.nam.org

—National Retail Federation, www.nrf.com

Expense Reduction Analyst

Calling all seasoned business managers, controllers, CFOs, operations managers, accountants, and administrators! You can greatly profit from your business experience and budgeting skills by starting an expense reduction consulting service aimed at all businesses, from small and local to multinational corporations. Expense reduction consultants provide clients with a multitude of services: developing short- and long-term budgets, analyzing fixed and variable overhead, increasing employee productivity, analyzing product and service costs, and developing expense reduction strategies to meet each client's specific needs. The objective of the expense reduction exercise is to uncover costs associated with doing business that can be reduced or eliminated entirely while maintaining or increasing the overall efficiency, productivity, and profitability of the business. Many expense reduction consultants specialize in their field of expertise—manufacturing, food services, retail, or small business, for example. The most powerful marketing asset that expense reduction specialists have at their disposal is the fact that through analysis of business operations, they generally save clients anywhere from 2 to 50 times their consulting fees in expense reduction savings.

AT A GLANCE

INVESTMENT: Under $10K

RATE: $50+

SKILL LEVEL: 3

RESOURCES

—★ ERA Canada, ☎ (416) 622-7720, www.eracanada.com

—Guru, online marketplace for freelance talent, www.guru.com

Expert Witness Referral Service

Starting an expert witness referral service is a unique opportunity for the innovative entrepreneur to tackle. Insurance companies, defense lawyers, activists, politicians, public prosecutors, health-care providers, unions, law enforcement agencies, government agencies, hospitals, and corporations often use expert witnesses to substantiate or refute claims and testimonies via their expertise on the topic or subject matter. The most common expert witnesses are forensic specialists, gun specialists, military experts, engineers, medical doctors, aviation experts, maritime experts, construction, investment analysts, computer scientists, security personnel, environmentalists, psychiatrists, transportation experts, and business experts. The service works very much like an employment agency; potential clients contact you with their expert witness needs and you refer them to a qualified expert who can fulfill those needs, but with a higher degree of security and anonymity to protect both clients and expert witnesses. You can charge expert witnesses a fee to be listed with your service, or retain a percentage of the fee they earn as an expert witness, which in some cases can range well into five figures.

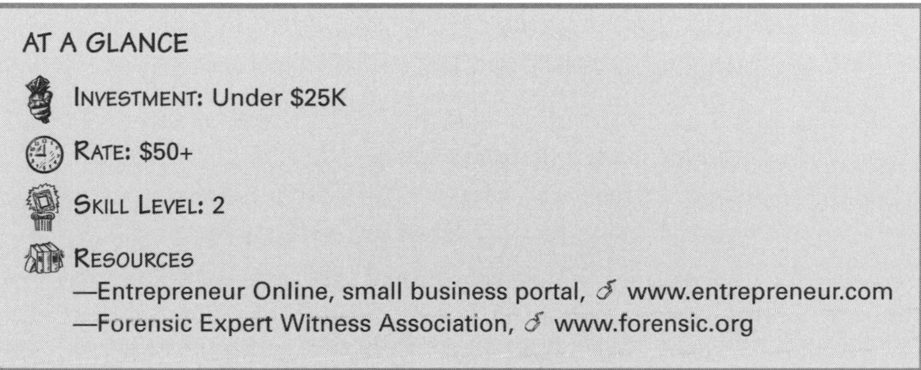

AT A GLANCE

INVESTMENT: Under $25K

RATE: $50+

SKILL LEVEL: 2

RESOURCES
—Entrepreneur Online, small business portal, www.entrepreneur.com
—Forensic Expert Witness Association, www.forensic.org

Bookkeeper

Bookkeeping is the process of recording every time money comes into or goes out of a business. Providing you have money management and bookkeeping experience, or are willing to take bookkeeping training, a very comfortable living can be earned by providing clients with bookkeeping services. Clients will largely be comprised of small business owners and professionals without the time, skills, or inclination to keep their own books and file and remit tax forms and the like. Accounting software such as QuickBooks, www.quickbooks.com, is, of course, a mandatory tool of the trade for every bookkeeper. Attracting clients requires a combination of traditional advertising in newspapers and getting out in the community and talking to business owners to tell them about the services you provide. Work can be completed at your client's location, or you can work from home offering free pickup and delivery of documents and forms. Rates are in the range of $25 to $40 per hour, depending on services provided and your qualifications.

AT A GLANCE

INVESTMENT: Under $2K

RATE: $25+

 SKILL LEVEL: 2–3

 RESOURCES

—American Institute of Professional Bookkeepers, ☎ (800) 622-0121, www.aipb.com

—Canadian Bookkeepers Association, ☎ (250) 860-4130, www.canadianbookkeepersassociation.com

—★ Ledger Plus, ☎ (888) 643-1348, www.ledgerplus.com

Business Broker

In Canada all business brokers are required to have a real estate license to list and sell businesses. In the United States, however, at the time of this writing only 17 states require people to obtain a real estate license to legally start and operate a business brokerage. These states include AK, AZ, CA, FL, GA, ID, IL, MI, MN, ME, NV, OR, SD, UT, WA, WI, and WY. This is exciting news because it is estimated that there are as many as 1,000,000 businesses for sale at any one time in the United States. Needless to say, the potential to earn enormous profits from listing, marketing, and selling businesses is very great. Even if you do invest the time and money to obtain a real estate license, the potential rewards easily justify the effort. So what do business brokers do? They source people wanting to sell their businesses, prepare a business valuation for fair market pricing, list the business for sale, market the business, qualify potential buyers, show the business, answer questions, work on behalf of their clients to negotiate an appropriate selling price, and help in all closing matters. In other words, a business broker looks after everything that is required to sell a business, taking all the stress and work off the seller's shoulders. You might also want to consider specializing in selling a specific type of business such as restaurants, hotels, retail establishments, or manufacturing companies. Specialization is the fastest way to become known as an industry expert and will increase repeat and referral business.

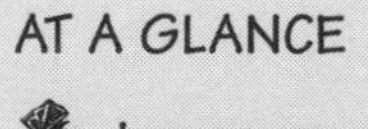

AT A GLANCE

 INVESTMENT: Under $25K

 RATE: $50+

 SKILL LEVEL: 4

 RESOURCES
—American Business Brokers Association, ☎ (239) 425-0677, www.americanbusinessbrokers.com
—International Business Brokers Association, ☎ (888) 686-4222, www.ibba.org
—★ Sunbelt Business Advisors, ☎ (800) 771-7866, www.sunbeltnetwork.com
—★ Xpert Business Brokers, ☎ (416) 367-4141, www.xpertbusinessbrokers.com

Management Trainer

Management consulting and training generates more than $100 billion in annual revenues worldwide, and according to the Association of Management Consulting Firms, management trainers earn an average of $150 per hour! Leadership management training is one of the fastest-growing segments of the corporate training industry, and for good reason. A corporation's or organization's management team needs to be able to lead, unite, and motivate everyone on the team, including executives, employees, suppliers, and vendors, if the business is to succeed in today's highly competitive marketplace. Most management trainers also coach clients in their field of expertise—marketing, logistics, technology, international business, manufacturing, human resources, finance, health care, etc.—and you would be advised to do the same. The objective of the management trainer is to assess the client's management team and operational systems, identifying weaknesses and strengths. Once the assessment is complete, a plan can be developed which includes recommendations to reorganize as required, retrain as required, refocus as required, and eliminate all weaknesses and build upon all strengths.

AT A GLANCE

INVESTMENT: Under $10K

RATE: $50+

SKILL LEVEL: 2–3

RESOURCES
—American Management Association, www.amanet.org
—Canadian Management Professionals Association, www.workplace.ca
—★ Leadership Management Inc., ☎ (800) 568-1241, www.lmi-bus.com

Sales Trainer

Are you recognized as a top-producing sales professional who knows how to prospect for new business, win negotiations, and close the sale every time? If so, why not share your sales knowledge and experience and make huge profits in the process by training employees, managers, small business owners, and executives to also become top-producing sales professionals? Even if you don't want to rock the boat and interrupt your current sales position, you do not have to. You can train students online, via correspondence, with personal conference calls, and by way of evening and weekend workshops and seminars. This way, you can make the transition to full-time sales training as your business and client list grows. Target customers will include small business owners, salespeople, retail clerks, corporate managers and executives, students enrolled in business and marketing courses, professional service providers, volunteer fundraisers, and real estate professionals.

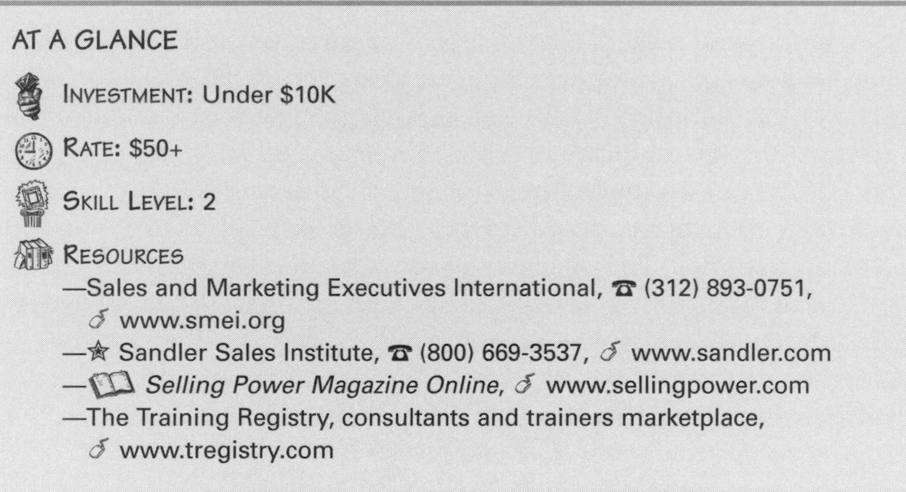

AT A GLANCE

INVESTMENT: Under $10K

RATE: $50+

SKILL LEVEL: 2

RESOURCES

—Sales and Marketing Executives International, ☎ (312) 893-0751, www.smei.org

—★ Sandler Sales Institute, ☎ (800) 669-3537, www.sandler.com

—*Selling Power Magazine Online*, www.sellingpower.com

—The Training Registry, consultants and trainers marketplace, www.tregistry.com

Small Business Coach

In the United States and Canada more than 800,000 businesses are started annually. Combine this with the millions of small to medium-sized businesses already operating, and I'm sure you would agree that the future looks very bright, not to mention potentially profitable, for a small business coaching service. This hot opportunity will appeal to entrepreneurs who are past or present small business owners, business managers, or corporate executives, especially those with strong marketing, administration, operations, and financial forecasting skills. Because there is a plethora of small business training schools and courses offered by non-profit government agencies and for-profit businesses in both countries, you will be well advised to specialize in a specific industry, such as retail or manufacturing, and to offer clients a more personalized one-on-one training service as opposed to a classroom setting. Small business coaches help new and existing business owners with any number of tasks, including business planning, marketing strategies, financial budgets, logistics issues, technology issues, and expansion challenges.

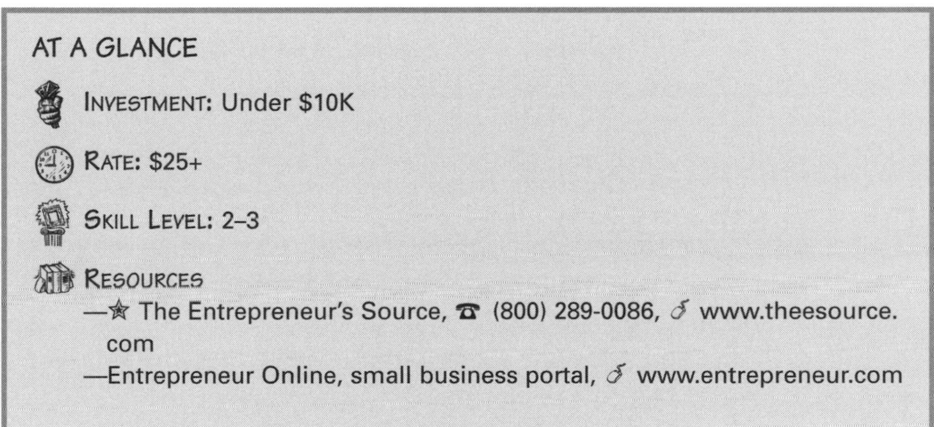

AT A GLANCE

INVESTMENT: Under $10K

RATE: $25+

SKILL LEVEL: 2–3

RESOURCES
—★ The Entrepreneur's Source, ☎ (800) 289-0086, www.theesource.com
—Entrepreneur Online, small business portal, www.entrepreneur.com

Marketing Consultant

Let's face it: Without marketing, businesses cannot survive. So it is no surprise that topnotch marketing consultants are in high demand across North America. Consequently, if you are an experienced marketer, the time has never been better to put that experience to work leading other businesspeople down the path to marketing success. Marketing consultants offer a wide range of services, including developing marketing plans, establishing marketing budgets, hiring and training salespeople, and developing advertising, telemarketing, and direct marketing programs to meet each client's needs and budget. Marketing consultants also help businesses expand into new markets, and even new countries, as well as build new distribution channels and profit centers. In short, marketing consultants are the Jacks-of-all-trades in terms of helping clients build their businesses, revenues, and profits. Market your services through networking activities, and by setting appointments with business owners and managers to explain how your services will benefit and ultimately profit their business.

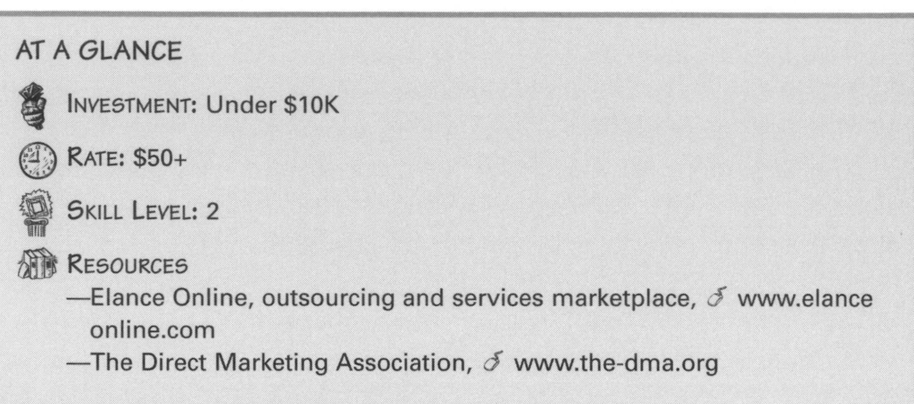

AT A GLANCE

INVESTMENT: Under $10K

RATE: $50+

SKILL LEVEL: 2

RESOURCES

—Elance Online, outsourcing and services marketplace, www.elanceonline.com

—The Direct Marketing Association, www.the-dma.org

Public Opinion Survey Service

From the smallest independent businesses to the largest international corporations, businesses often rely on public opinion surveys to learn more about their products, services, competition, and customers, and they react accordingly based on results. Politicians rely on opinion polls to gauge what voters feel are the most important issues, so they can champion these issues in hopes of getting elected. Just about every level of government agency relies on public opinion polls to find out and prioritize what services and programs taxpayers want and need. Public opinion polls and surveys can be conducted on the telephone, by mail, e-mail, web site polling, or by way of personal interview. Your communications, marketing, and organizational skills will be your main tools to make this business prosper. To get started, create and conduct a few of your own public opinion polls on topics that would be interesting to the public at large. Send local media the results in the form of a press release or media alert, and use the media coverage of your polls and surveys as a marketing tool to secure paying customers for the service.

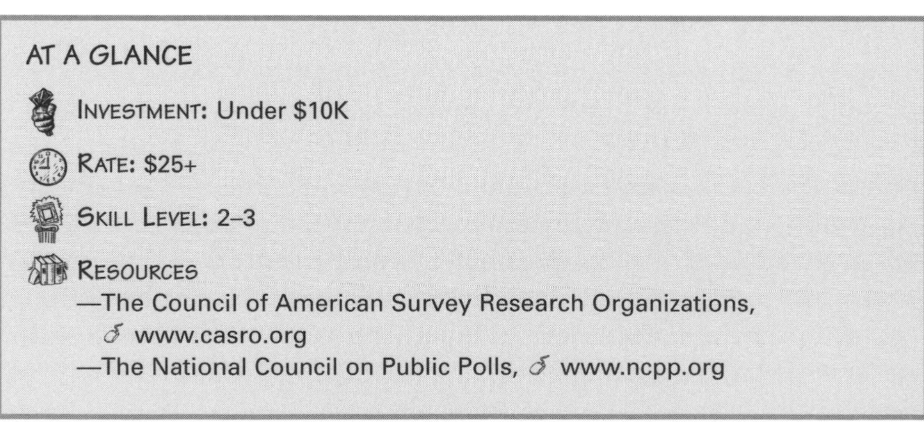

AT A GLANCE

INVESTMENT: Under $10K

RATE: $25+

SKILL LEVEL: 2–3

RESOURCES

—The Council of American Survey Research Organizations, www.casro.org

—The National Council on Public Polls, www.ncpp.org

Temporary Help Agency

Outsourcing, downsizing, and consolidation are buzzwords in today's business world, and all have helped to make the placement of temporary workers a thriving industry. In short, when businesses and organizations need temporary or seasonal help, many turn to the services of a temporary help agency to fulfill their manpower needs. It is often cheaper that way, and always more convenient than having to run help wanted ads and interview candidates. In starting your temp help agency, I suggest that you specialize in supplying qualified workers in one particular industry or area of expertise, such as the construction industry, retail sales, home care, domestic work, office work, or warehouse staffing. Recruiting workers prepared to work on a temporary basis should not prove difficult. Just target students, early retirees, homemakers, and even other home-based business owners seeking to earn extra income periodically. Marketing can be as easy as creating an information package describing the service and your available work force, and distributing it to businesses and companies that occasionally rely on temporary workers. You can network for clients at business and social functions, and use the Yellow Pages and newspaper classifieds for advertising.

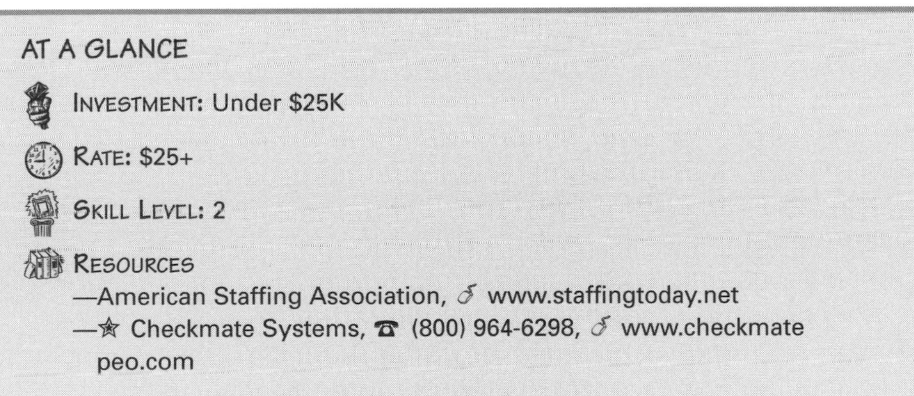

AT A GLANCE

INVESTMENT: Under $25K

RATE: $25+

SKILL LEVEL: 2

RESOURCES
—American Staffing Association, www.staffingtoday.net
—★ Checkmate Systems, ☎ (800) 964-6298, www.checkmatepeo.com

Business Plan Service

Did you know that a recent survey of new business owners revealed that fewer than 25 percent of the 250 owners surveyed had created a business plan for their new venture? Asked why they hadn't, the number-one reason was that they simply did not know how. According to the Small Business Administration, approximately 750,000 new businesses are started each year in the United States, which in turn creates an outstanding opportunity for entrepreneurs with business planning experience to offer research and business plan development services to those businesses. Market your service by attending business networking meetings; also attempt to obtain a list of all new and renewal business registration licenses through your local business service center. In addition to new businesses, you can also aim marketing efforts at existing businesses and professionals who are expanding or need to update or create a new business plan. This service costs little to start and can be operated part-time or full-time, depending on your needs. Billing rates vary depending on the size and scope of the business plan being developed.

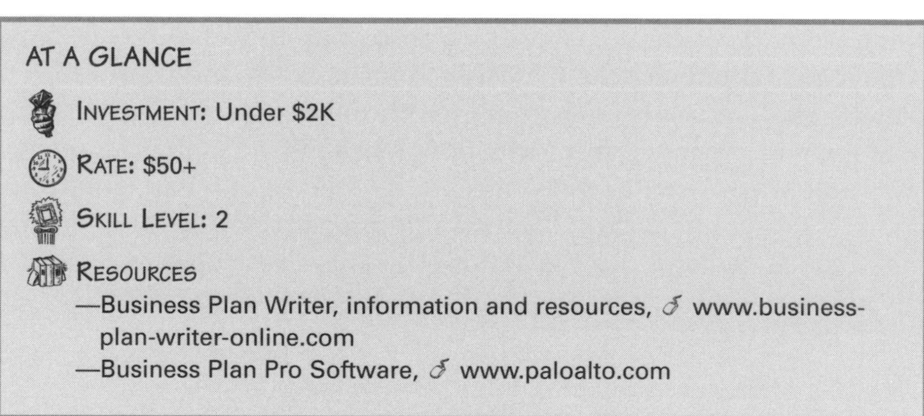

AT A GLANCE

INVESTMENT: Under $2K

RATE: $50+

SKILL LEVEL: 2

RESOURCES

—Business Plan Writer, information and resources, www.business-plan-writer-online.com

—Business Plan Pro Software, www.paloalto.com

Manufacturers' Representative

Manufacturers commonly contract with professional representatives to market their products within a specific country, state, or even city, and these reps are known as manufacturers' sales agents or manufacturers' representatives. The reason that manufacturers contract with professional reps is to help grow their businesses by having reps sell their product lines to wholesalers, distributors, corporations, small businesses, and institutions. For instance, a bicycle manufacturer in Australia might contract with a sales agent in the United States to represent and market his bicycle line here, calling on sporting goods distributors to set up supply accounts, or meeting directly with bike retailers to set up supply accounts. It is not uncommon for manufacturers' reps to earn well into the six-figure range annually after expenses. If you have sales and marketing experience, this may well be your opportunity to capitalize on it by starting a manufacturers' representative service. Get started by researching manufacturers' that are currently looking for reps. The web sites and associations listed below are good places to start your research. Next, decide on a manufacturer(s) and product(s) to represent. I strongly advise you to create a marketing plan to ensure that there is sufficient demand for the product first. Experience and knowledge of the product are also helpful, especially if you are going to capitalize on your current contact base to generate business.

AT A GLANCE

 INVESTMENT: Under $10K

 RATE: $50+

 SKILL LEVEL: 2–3

 RESOURCES
—Find A Sales Agent, directory service, www.findasalesagent.com
—Manufacturers' Agents National Association, (949) 859-4040, www.manaonline.org
—National Association of Manufacturers, (202) 637-3000, www.nam.org

---

For-Sale-by-Owner Specialist

Many people attempt to sell their own homes, properties, and cottages every year. And while some are successful, many are not. This creates a fantastic opportunity for the clever entrepreneur to start a for-sale-by-owner consulting business to assist these people in selling their homes and properties quickly, conveniently, and for top dollar. Duties include instructing clients in how to prepare their home for listing, helping them to establish a value, teaching them how to market their property, having signs made, instructing them on the finer points of hosting an open house, and providing them with template forms that can be used to write an offer and sale agreement. The for-sale-by-owner specialist is not working as a real estate agent or broker, but merely as a consultant to guide clients through the steps to help them sell their own homes. Securing clients is as easy as calling people who currently have their homes for sale by owner, and by advertising locally in the real estate section of the newspaper. Charge clients a flat fee for providing the service, and charge separately for extras like printing fliers, creating For Sale and Open House signs, and for listings on your Homes for Sale by Owner web site and in any for-sale-by-owner publications that you print and distribute.

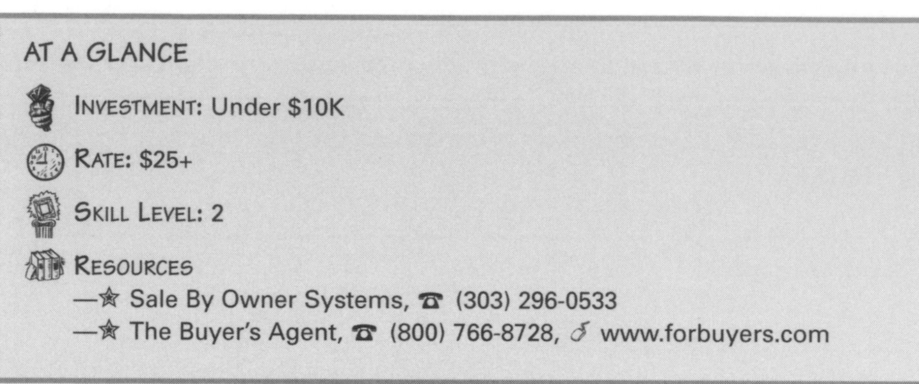
AT A GLANCE

INVESTMENT: Under $10K

RATE: $25+

SKILL LEVEL: 2

RESOURCES

—★ Sale By Owner Systems, ☎ (303) 296-0533

—★ The Buyer's Agent, ☎ (800) 766-8728, www.forbuyers.com

Energy Management Consultant

Corporations, organizations, and homeowners spend billions of dollars annually on energy costs to light, heat, and air-condition their homes and buildings. Just imagine how much healthier the environment would be, as well as how much money each of us could save every year, if we all could reduce our energy consumption by a mere 10 percent! Working as an energy management consultant, you can teach home and business owners practical and useful energy management strategies to reduce energy consumption and eliminate energy waste. Your tips can be put into practice easily, quickly, and inexpensively. Getting this enterprise off the ground will require a great deal of research, planning, and perhaps training, depending on your background and experience in this area. However, with energy costs continuing to soar, the need to take care of the environment and save money at the same time is becoming more of a concern for everyone. Given this, the future for energy management consulting looks very bright.

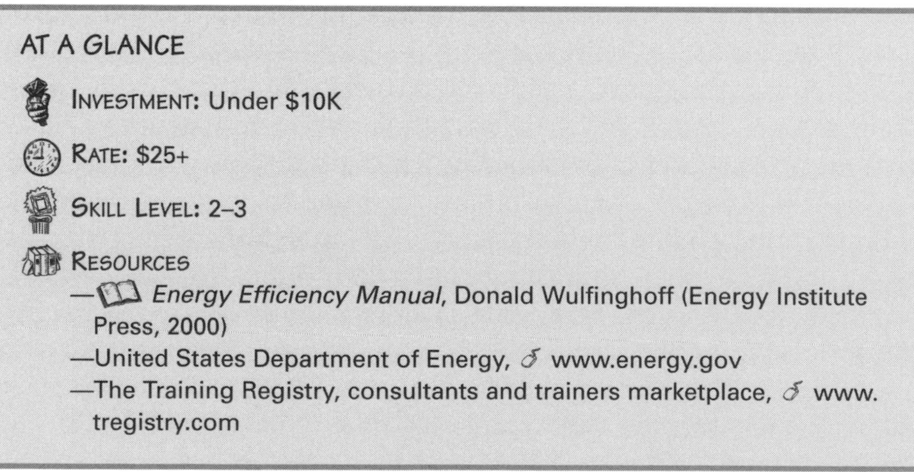
AT A GLANCE

INVESTMENT: Under $10K

RATE: $25+

SKILL LEVEL: 2–3

RESOURCES

—*Energy Efficiency Manual*, Donald Wulfinghoff (Energy Institute Press, 2000)

—United States Department of Energy, www.energy.gov

—The Training Registry, consultants and trainers marketplace, www.tregistry.com

Recycling Consultant

Taking the time to educate yourself on the subject of recycling industrial and household materials can really pay off, especially if you apply that knowledge and start a recycling consulting service. Across North America millions of homeowners, small businesses, corporations, and organizations now recycle waste materials. But millions more would be—if they knew what could be recycled, and where to start! This is where you put your recycling knowledge to work by teaching homeowners, business owners, and employees how to recycle, what to recycle, and where it can be recycled. Charge clients a fee to design a tailor-made recycling plan, specific to their particular needs. In addition to creating the recycling program, you can also provide a brief instructional course on the program you have created for them, as well as on the topic of recycling in general. The timing has never been better because the need for every person on the planet to practice recycling measures has never been more urgent. Potential income ranges from $25 to $40 per hour, plus markup on products sold.

AT A GLANCE

 INVESTMENT: Under $10K

 RATE: $25+

 SKILL LEVEL: 2–3

 RESOURCES

—Guru, online marketplace for freelance talent, www.guru.com
—*McGraw-Hill Recycling Handbook, 2nd Edition*, Herbert F. Lund (McGraw-Hill, 2000)
—Solid Waste Association of North America, www.swana.org

Retail Merchandiser Specialist

Retailers often must rely on elaborate window displays to grab the attention of passing consumers and draw them into their stores. Once people are inside, retailers must also rely on exciting in-store displays to create buying desire and urgency for their goods. Even though most retailers realize that creative merchandise displays can double or even triple sales, few have the ability or time to actually create attention-grabbing displays on a regular basis. Starting a business that specializes in creating effective window and in-store merchandise displays for retailers is the focus of this opportunity. People with a design and retail background will be well suited to take up the challenge, and have the potential to cash in for big profits. Marketing the service can be as easy as approaching local retailers and offering a free trial period so they can realize the benefits and increased sales that well-designed product displays inspire. Once this happens, most will sign up for the service on the spot. The free display you create can also be used as a powerful marketing tool by taking photographs and video and using them to present your work to other retailers. Also, be sure to build an inventory of interesting props, signage, and lighting so you can provide clients with an all-inclusive display service.

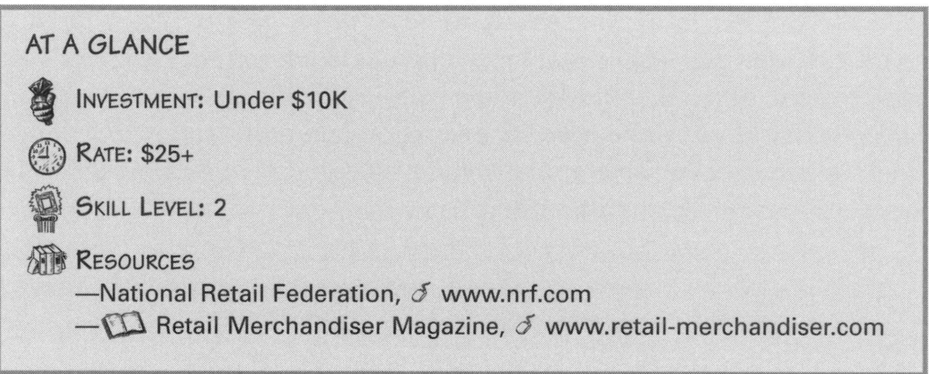

AT A GLANCE

INVESTMENT: Under $10K

RATE: $25+

SKILL LEVEL: 2

RESOURCES
—National Retail Federation, www.nrf.com
—Retail Merchandiser Magazine, www.retail-merchandiser.com

Association Manager

Many clubs, associations, and organizations simply do not have the time, money, or people-power to manage the day-to-day operations of their enterprise. Needless to say, a fantastic opportunity exists to provide these small organizations with management services that run the gamut from database management, to membership recruitment, bookkeeping, writing and publishing association newsletters, shipping and receiving, and providing meeting space. Associations can include nonprofit groups, sports clubs, entertainment clubs, charity groups, social clubs, union associations, and community associations. The best way to market association management services is to compile a list of all the clubs and associations in your community, regardless of size, create a complete package detailing all services you provide, set appointments, and present your services to each. Generally you will find that some of the associations and clubs you contact will want to try out one or more of the services you provide, while others will elect to jump at all the services you offer, especially membership recruitment. There are a few requirements to get started: you will need great organizational skills, strong marketing skills, administration and management skills, and a fully equipped office.

AT A GLANCE

 INVESTMENT: Under $10K

 RATE: $25+

 SKILL LEVEL: 2–3

 RESOURCES

—Marketing Source, directory listing over 5,000 associations, www.marketingsource.com

—Guru, online marketplace for freelance talent, www.guru.com

Proposal Writer

Government agencies on the federal, state, and local levels put thousands of RFPs (requests for proposals) out for bid annually. Proposals can range from construction of new buildings to supplying computer equipment for government offices, and just about anything in-between. Although these proposals can be very lucrative for the company or individual that successfully bids for the contract, many small-to-medium-sized contractors simply do not complete the proposal and bid forms. Because the process is extremely involved and usually requires technical drawings, action plans, and contingency plans, business owners and managers often have neither the time nor ability to complete these required documents. A proposal writer compiles and completes the proposal documents on behalf of the contractor. Proposal writers charge fees based on the amount of time it takes to complete the proposal, typically in the range of $30 to $40 per hour, but as high as $100 an hour for very specialized industries. Some will even charge a commission based on the value of the contract should their client win it. Most proposal writers specialize in specific areas, such as nonperishable goods, construction, services, or maintenance. A proposal writer must also have access to a wide range of research resources and in almost all cases a technical writing ability and knowledge.

AT A GLANCE

 INVESTMENT: Under $10K

 RATE: $25+

 SKILL LEVEL: 2

 RESOURCES

—Association of Proposal Management Professionals, www.apmp.org

—Elance Online, outsourcing and services marketplace, www.elanceonline.com

Freelance Sales Consultant

Freelance sales consultants who produce results—meaning lots of profitable sales—are in high demand and earn annual incomes that go well into the six-figure range. In a nutshell, freelance sales consultants represent companies selling products ranging from manufactured goods and equipment, to services (home improvements, internet technology etc.), to associations seeking to expand their membership base, and everything imaginable in-between. Freelance professional sales consultants find securing clients to represent very easy, because they generally supply all the tools of the trade needed to find new customers and close the sale—transportation, communications, and computer hardware. Not to mention that almost all also generate and qualify their own sales leads. What's more, clients have little to lose by bringing on freelance sales consultants to represent their business: not only will they supply the needed sales tools as well as, find, qualify, and close buyers, but they also sell for more, easily covering their commissions. Remuneration is always by way of commission, which ranges between 10 and 25 percent of the total sales value depending on what is being sold.

 INVESTMENT: Under $10K

 RATE: $50+

 SKILL LEVEL: 2

 RESOURCES

—Find A Sales Agent, directory service, www.findasalesagent.com

—The Training Registry, consultants and trainers marketplace, www.tregistry.com

Public Relations

An outstanding PR person representing an individual, business, politician, celebrity, product, or service can be the equivalent of having someone in your corner who can pick the winning lottery numbers long before the draw. The main duty of a public relations specialist is to promote in a positive and informative manner, regardless of what is being promoted. Promotion techniques and services include creating press releases and press kits, organizing media and special events, performing damage control services when things go awry, and networking around the clock on the client's behalf. Getting started in the business can be difficult, given that the public relations industry is fiercely competitive. As an entry strategy, consider starting small and representing one or two clients in your local area until you have mastered the art. It could be your current employer, a businessperson, someone running in an election, or a local celebrity. Remuneration is generally by way of a flat fee plus additional fees depending on the services rendered, frequency, and length of contract.

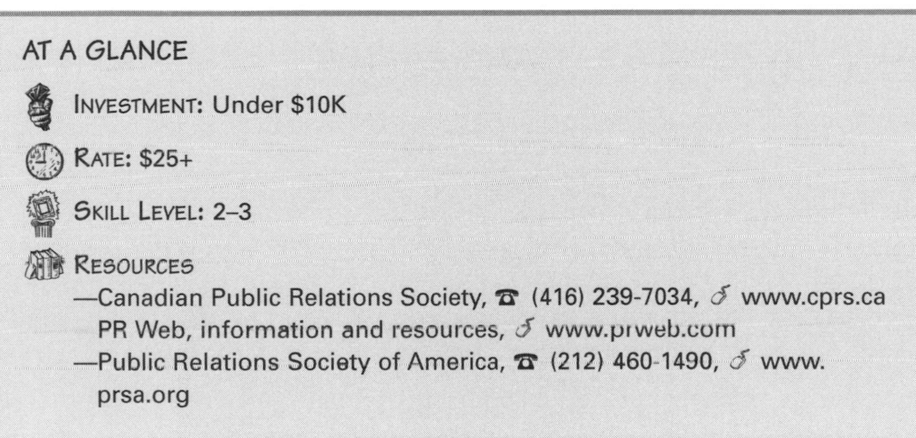

AT A GLANCE

INVESTMENT: Under $10K

RATE: $25+

SKILL LEVEL: 2–3

RESOURCES

—Canadian Public Relations Society, ☎ (416) 239-7034, www.cprs.ca

—PR Web, information and resources, www.prweb.com

—Public Relations Society of America, ☎ (212) 460-1490, www.prsa.org

Protocol Consultant

In this age of political correctness, disputes between employees or between employees and management based on allegations of sexual harassment, racism, or other forms of abusive behavior within the office environment can bankrupt a business, morally and financially. Needless to say, the time has never been better to start a business as an office protocol consultant. The concept is very straightforward. As an office protocol consultant, you can advise clients on issues pertaining to these subjects as well as create a training program for employees and management on how to avoid, or respond to any unfavorable situations that arise in the office environment. The demand for this type of consulting service is gigantic, as thousands of corporations rush to retain the services of protocol consultants as a proactive measure to ensure that they are not involved in politically or socially inappropriate situations. The protocol consultant may thus be viewed as a guardian of corporate image, morale, and financial stability. Scheduling meetings with human resources managers and networking at business and social functions is a good way to get started.

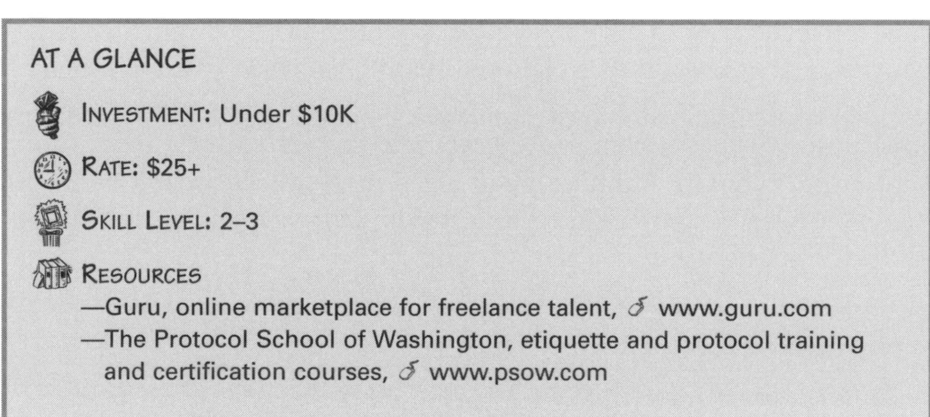

AT A GLANCE

INVESTMENT: Under $10K

RATE: $25+

SKILL LEVEL: 2–3

RESOURCES
—Guru, online marketplace for freelance talent, www.guru.com
—The Protocol School of Washington, etiquette and protocol training and certification courses, www.psow.com

---

Small-Business Advertising Agency

Put your advertising and marketing skills and experience to good use by starting an advertising agency focused on assisting small business owners to create knockout advertising campaigns that get the results they want and need from their tight advertising budgets. Many advertising agencies concentrate on big corporations with massive advertising budgets, leaving small business owners to figure out how to best advertise their products and services. Advertising is costly, and small business owners cannot waste money on advertising that does not hit the target and get results. Creating cost-effective advertising campaigns is one of the toughest challenges that most small business owners face. Advertising is an all-encompassing task that requires experience and creative skills to determine what type of advertising and message will work best for what is being sold. Confusing the matter even more is that small business owners are bombarded daily by advertising salespeople, each with the "greatest offer." Capitalizing on your advertising, marketing, or public relations experience, you can create specialized advertising campaigns for small business clients that will directly reach their target market, stay within their budget, and get the results they want.

AT A GLANCE

 INVESTMENT: Under $10K

 RATE: $25+

 SKILL LEVEL: 2

 RESOURCES
—American Association of Advertising Agencies, ☎ (212) 682-2500, www.aaaa.org
—American Home Business Association, ☎ (800) 664-2422, www.homebusiness.com
—Association of Canadian Advertisers, ☎ (416) 964-3805, www.aca-online.com
—Pub List, online directory listing 150,000 publications, www.publist.com

---

Flier Delivery

Small business owners, salespeople, and marketers of all sorts have utilized promotional fliers for decades as a fast and frugal, yet highly effective, method of advertising their products and services. After all, you can fit an enormous amount of promotional information, pictures, and contact details on one flier, especially if both sides are used. A flier delivery service is easy to start and operate and has the potential to generate a great full-time or part-time income. Best of all, it requires no more than a telephone and a good pair of walking shoes to get started. Flier delivery services are charging in the range of 5 to 10 cents for each flier individually hand-delivered. Of course, revenues increase exponentially if you are delivering more than one flier to each home. Imagine: delivering five fliers for five separate clients but all in the same area, you could be raking in up to 50 cents per home, and spending less than half a minute to get the job done. To increase revenues, hire students, retirees, and homemakers to deliver fliers during busy times, and concentrate your efforts on marketing and managing the business. Creating your own flier detailing the service and rates you offer, and delivering it to businesses and professionals in your community is the easiest way to get the telephone ringing and clients lining up to get their promotional fliers delivered.

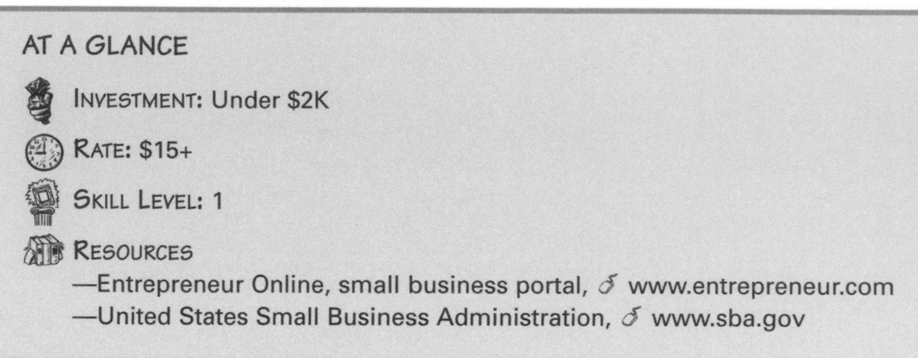

AT A GLANCE

INVESTMENT: Under $2K

RATE: $15+

SKILL LEVEL: 1

RESOURCES

—Entrepreneur Online, small business portal, www.entrepreneur.com

—United States Small Business Administration, www.sba.gov

Bulletin Board Service

Take flier delivery to the next level by starting a community bulletin board service. The concept is very straightforward. In exchange for a flat monthly fee, you post promotional fliers for retailers, professionals, and service providers on bulletin boards throughout the local trading area. Community bulletin boards are typically found in supermarkets, schools, laundries, libraries, gas stations, community centers, and fitness clubs. Most, however, have a policy of removing fliers after a week so that boards do not get overcrowded, and to allow space for new fliers to be posted. Even though most small business owners realize that posting fliers on community bulletin boards is a fast, frugal, and effective way to advertise their products and services, most miss out on the opportunity because they do not have the time to drive around town posting them. Like hand-delivering fliers to homes and businesses, this service can also be very profitable because you have the potential to post fliers for more than one client at a time. Charging clients $20 (not including the cost of the fliers) per week to post fliers on 50 bulletin boards may not be worthwhile, but a mere 50 clients will earn you $52,000 a year. And, at 40 cents per flier posted, with the potential for thousands of people stopping to read it, you will find little resistance in selling this service to small business owners.

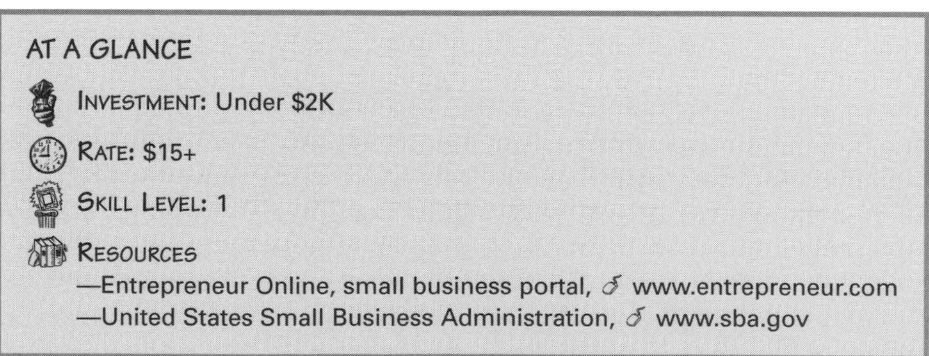

AT A GLANCE

INVESTMENT: Under $2K

RATE: $15+

SKILL LEVEL: 1

RESOURCES

—Entrepreneur Online, small business portal, www.entrepreneur.com

—United States Small Business Administration, www.sba.gov

Human Billboards

We have all seen them—people in wacky costumes holding signs or banners emblazoned with promotional messages in high-traffic areas of the community. They're usually standing outside, in front of or in close proximity to the business they're promoting. These people are called human billboards, and they advertise everything from retail store sales, to car dealerships, to restaurants, to homes for sale. Human billboards are really catching on as a highly effective, cost-efficient method of promoting services and products. The objective of a human billboard is to grab the attention of passing motorists and pedestrians and get them to visit the business or event being promoted. Don't worry if you don't think you're cut out to be a human billboard yourself, because you can hire homemakers, students, actors, musicians, and retirees—basically anyone who is available to work on a part-time, as-needed basis. Doing so enables you to focus on marketing the service and managing the business. Set appointments with local business owners to explain the benefits of your service. Joining business networking clubs is also a good way to get the word out. Rates for human billboards vary based on considerations such as the number of people (billboards), the length of the promotion, and other factors like signage and special costumes.

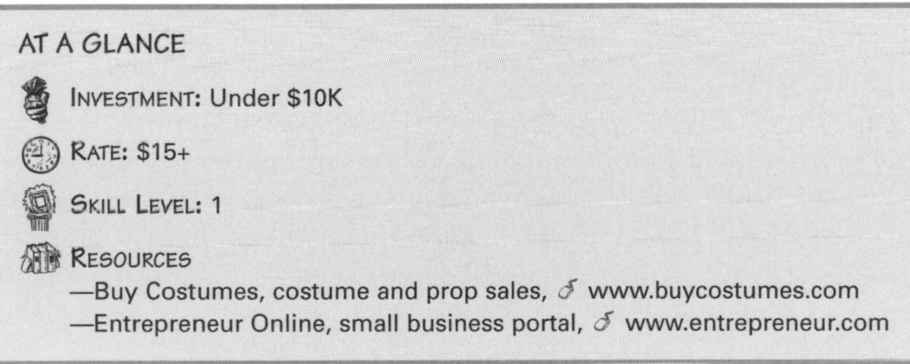

AT A GLANCE

INVESTMENT: Under $10K

RATE: $15+

SKILL LEVEL: 1

RESOURCES
—Buy Costumes, costume and prop sales, www.buycostumes.com
—Entrepreneur Online, small business portal, www.entrepreneur.com

Inflatable Advertising Rentals

Twenty-foot-high inflatable gorillas, holiday Santa Clauses, and cartoon characters get noticed by traffic, especially when these large inflatables are sitting on a retailer's rooftop or in a parking lot with a "sale in progress" sign brightly emblazoned across them. Renting inflatable advertising objects is a fantastic new business venture to get up and going. You can operate the business on a full- or part-time basis right from home, and potential clients can include retailers, sports teams, realtors, property developers, car dealers, community organizers, event planners, or just about anyone who wants to draw attention to a sale or special event. New cold-air advertising inflatables are retailing in the range of $5,000. But to reduce start-up investment, you can purchase secondhand inflatables in good condition for half the cost of new. Short-term rental rates start at $150 per day, including delivery, setup, and removal. Long-term rental rates are in the range of $500 per week, depending on the inflatable rented. Outside of suitable transportation for delivery and pickup, requirements are few, making this an excellent new business enterprise for just about anyone.

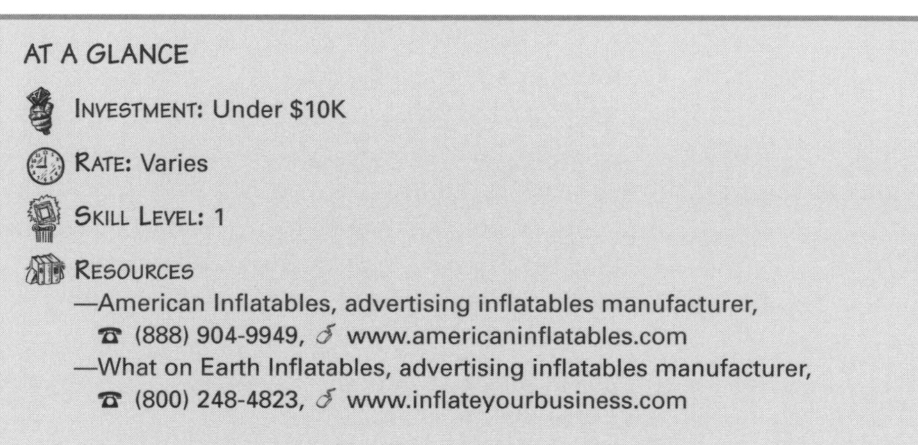

AT A GLANCE

INVESTMENT: Under $10K

RATE: Varies

SKILL LEVEL: 1

RESOURCES

—American Inflatables, advertising inflatables manufacturer, ☎ (888) 904-9949, www.americaninflatables.com

—What on Earth Inflatables, advertising inflatables manufacturer, ☎ (800) 248-4823, www.inflateyourbusiness.com

---

Announcement Service

Help your clients tell the world about their special occasion or milestone by starting your own yard announcement service. If you are handy with tools and have a creative flair, you can design and build your own special occasion yard announcement cutouts from wood or plastic, designed and painted to resemble a stork for birth announcements, a mortarboard for graduation, or a happy-birthday character, for example. Or for the nonhandyperson, you can purchase predesigned and constructed special occasion cutouts. Customers include any person or business that wants to surprise people by having an announcement placed in their front yard to let everyone in the neighborhood know about the special occasion—birthday, newborn, anniversary, graduation, etc. Or for businesses it could mean a sale or a special milestone such as 25 years in business. Depending on the size of the announcement, rental rates are in the range of $30 to $60 per day, including delivery and pickup.

AT A GLANCE

INVESTMENT: Under $10K

 RATE: $15+

 SKILL LEVEL: 1

 RESOURCES
—★ Special Delivery, ☎ (630) 871-2680, www.special-delivery.com
—★ Stork News of America, ☎ (800) 633-6395, www.storknews.com

On-Hold Promotional Messages

Right now hundreds of thousands of retailers, service providers, professionals, and business owners of all sorts are missing out on a fantastic opportunity to market their goods or services to a captive audience for next to no cost. How are they missing out? By not having prerecorded promotional messages advertising their products or services playing while telephone customers wait on hold. To create an on-hold advertising message for your clients, simply write the ad based on their input and needs, and hire a professional voice person to record it in a studio. Clients pay for this service on a one-time fee basis or on a monthly contract basis that includes a fixed number of changes to their on-hold promotional message. Opting for the second method means you will build a steady revenue stream. The best way to market the service is to produce sample recordings and hit the streets, setting appointments to meet with business owners to pitch the benefits of your service.

AT A GLANCE

 INVESTMENT: Under $10K

 RATE: $25+

 SKILL LEVEL: 1

 RESOURCES
—Elance Online, outsourcing and services marketplace, www.elanceonline.com
—★ Impressions On Hold, ☎ (800) 580-4653, www.iohi.com

Business Support Service

Homebased and small businesses are opening at a record pace, which means the time has never been better than right now to start a business support service. Most new businesses are small operations with few employees and more often than not are lacking a support team to properly handle all the work involved in running a business on a day-to-day basis. Business support services offer clients a wide range of services, including bookkeeping, inventory management, on-call support staff, training, secretarial services, database management, desktop publishing services, editing, inventory fulfillment services, and internet technology services. One of the best ways to find clients is to join small and homebased business associations, such as the chamber of commerce, www.uschamber.com, and SOHO (Small Office Home Office), www.soho.org, to network with other small and homebased business owners and inform them about the wide range of business support services you offer.

AT A GLANCE

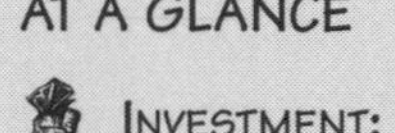

INVESTMENT: Under $10K

RATE: $25+

SKILL LEVEL: 2

RESOURCES

—International Virtual Assistants Association, www.ivaa.org

—International Association of Virtual Office Assistants, www.iavoa.org

—*Start Your Own Business Support Service* (Entrepreneur Press, 2003)

—American Home Business Association, (800) 664-2422, www.homebusiness.com

Freelance Writer

It has often been said that everyone has a book in them, and perhaps this is true. If you enjoy writing, but are not quite ready to pen the next Great American Novel, you might want to give freelance writing a try to sharpen your skills and earn some extra money. Freelance writing is competitive; some writing sources peg the number of freelancers in the United States at more than 100,000. There is lots of competition, but for those who make it, freelance writing can offer a fulfilling career. As the majority of successful freelance writers will tell you, if you want to make it, you must specialize. Pick a topic that you know, practice, practice some more, and keep practicing and submitting your work until you find your voice and a market. You could specialize in business, sports, entertainment, real estate, finance, health, retirement, travel, or venture into more specialized niche markets.

Writing fees are paid in two ways, per word or a fixed amount for each story or article, and sometimes with further royalties, depending on republishing rights. Expect to write a few freebies to get your name out there and have publishing credits. The best-paying markets tend to be major monthly magazines. The least attractive pay is usually for web content.

AT A GLANCE

 INVESTMENT: Under $2K

 RATE: $15+

 SKILL LEVEL: 2

 RESOURCES

—*2004 Writer's Market*, Kathryn S. Brogan and Robert Lee Brewer (Writer's Digest Books, 2003)

—Freelance Online, information and resources, www.freelanceonline.com

---

Copywriter

Copywriters prepare copy or text for advertising, marketing materials, press releases, TV and radio commercials, catalogs, web sites, and packaging labels, just to mention a few. This business depends on you having a talent for writing in a clear and concise manner that can get the message across, building excitement and interest, and motivating readers, listeners, and viewers to take the desired action. The demand for copywriting services is high, as most business owners, managers, and marketers do not have the time, skills, or inclination to prepare effective copy. More so, most are aware that paying a professional copywriter is not an expense, but the best way to ensure a high return on investments made in advertising and marketing materials. Establishing alliances with graphic designers, publishers, editors, advertising agencies, and public relations firms is a good way to get your foot in the door and get your name out there. Copywriting fees vary greatly depending on what is being prepared and the size of the assignment, but generally average in the range of $50 per hour.

AT A GLANCE

 INVESTMENT: Under $10K

 **RATE:** $25+

 **SKILL LEVEL:** 2

 **RESOURCES**

—Elance Online, outsourcing and services marketplace, www.elanceonline.com
—Freelance Online, information and resources, www.freelanceonline.com

Calligraphy

Turn your talent for exquisite handwriting into a profitable business by providing customers with calligraphy services. Even people with minimal artistic ability can easily learn calligraphy. There are numerous books and kits available that can help you master the craft, as well as training classes offered through the resources listed below. Calligraphy can be used to create one-of-a-kind handwritten wedding and event invitations, restaurant menus, gift basket cards, high-end product labels, business cards, award certificates, greeting cards, thank-you cards, stationery, and logo designs. Likewise, print shops and stationers are often asked for special designs requiring calligraphy and because the majority only offer machine-printed calligraphy, there is a great opportunity to subcontract your services to them to fill this void in the marketplace. Also be sure to create a portfolio of work that can be distributed to wedding consultants, restaurants, banquet facilities, associations, and clubs throughout your community, as well as print and stationery shops. This is a low-cost business to get started, and rates are in the range of $25 to $50 per hour.

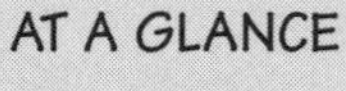

AT A GLANCE

 **INVESTMENT:** Under $2K

 **RATE:** $25+

 **SKILL LEVEL:** 2

 **RESOURCES**

—Association for the Calligraphic Arts, www.calligraphicarts.org
—Calligraphy Centre, industry information portal, www.calligraphycentre.com
—Society for Calligraphy, www.societyforcalligraphy.com
—*The Calligrapher's Bible: 100 Complete Alphabets and How to Draw Them*, David Harris (Barron's, 2003)

Greeting Card Service

The majority of business owners, salespeople, and service professionals know that one of the keys to successful customer retention is regular contact. At the same time, many are so busy working 60 hours a week running their business, that little time is left to even send a simple thank-you, thinking of you, or congratulatory greeting card. By starting a greeting card service, you will be able to help all your clients stay in regular contact with all of their clients, and in all probability they will retain a higher percentage of customers for the effort. You will need to build a database and create files for all clients. Each client file should include full contact information for their customers including telephone, e-mail, and mailing address, as well as more specific information such as birthdays and anniversaries. Having this information will enable you to automatically send your clients' customers greeting cards regularly—Christmas, birthdays, Fourth of July—and to announce special sales or other information that your clients want to periodically include. Additionally, you should work with a graphic designer and print shop so that each greeting card can be specific to each of your clients' businesses. Ideal candidates for a greeting card service include car dealers, realtors, corporations, associations and clubs that will send cards to members, lawyers, accountants, and doctors. Rates will vary depending on the quantity of cards sent for each client, frequency of the cards, and each client's greeting card design and selection.

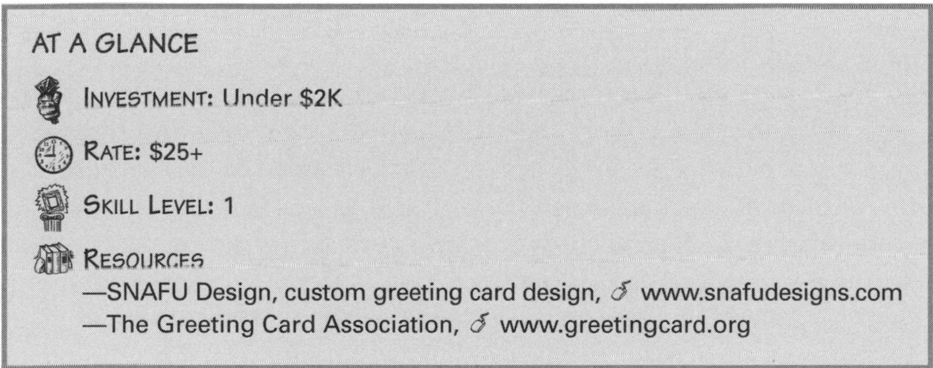
AT A GLANCE

INVESTMENT: Under $2K

RATE: $25+

SKILL LEVEL: 1

RESOURCES

—SNAFU Design, custom greeting card design, www.snafudesigns.com

—The Greeting Card Association, www.greetingcard.org

Catering

Turn your love of food and your incredible cooking skills into a gold mine by starting your own full-service catering business. Weddings, Christmas parties, corporate meetings, anniversaries, graduations, grand openings, product launches, tours and trips, and just about any other type of social function or business event can be catered for big profits. You will need to set up a fully equipped and permitted commercial kitchen in your own home, or if space or zoning do not allow, rent commercial space or strike a deal with a restaurant to share kitchen space in exchange for rent or a cut of the profits. Likewise, you will also need to invest in cooking equipment, dishes, utensils, uniforms for staff, and a number of other items required to offer full-service catering. Cooking, serving, and bar staff may be hired on an as-needed basis, and additional revenues can also be earned by providing valet parking services, coat-check services, and by renting party items such as tents, tables, chairs, and PA systems to your clients to create a more all-inclusive service.

 INVESTMENT: Under $10K–over $25

 RATE: $25+

 SKILL LEVEL: 2–3

 RESOURCES

—Food Service, industry information portal, www.foodservice.com

—National Association of Catering Executives, www.nace.net

—*Successful Catering: Managing the Catering Operation for Maximum Profit*, Soni Bode (Atlantic Publishing Group, 2002)

Exhaust Hood Cleaning

In many regions of the United States and Canada, restaurants are required by health board regulations to have their kitchen exhaust hoods and filters cleaned on a regularly scheduled basis to prevent bacteria growth and to eliminate the potential for grease fires. Needless to say, given the vast number of restaurants in North America, an incredible opportunity exists to start a restaurant exhaust hood-cleaning service and cash in big-time. Don't worry if you are scratching your head because you don't know how to clean exhaust hoods, because there are numerous schools such as the ones listed below that offer classes to become a certified hood and duct cleaner. This can be accomplished in only a few weeks in the classroom. Cleaning rates vary by size, access, and frequency, but average between $30 and $50 per working hour.

 INVESTMENT: Under $10K

RATE: $25+

SKILL LEVEL: 2–3

 RESOURCES

—★ Advanced Cleaning Systems, ☎ (888) 848-6636, www.hoodcleaningschool.com

—Phil Ackland's Exhaust Hood Cleaner Training, ☎ (403) 720-4055, www.philackland.com

Personal Chef

Take your pots and pans, cooking skills, and love of food mobile, and hit the road as a personal chef for hire. Prepare gourmet meals for people hosting house parties, special-occasion events such as birthdays or anniversaries, and for corporate luncheons—basically anywhere there is a kitchen on-site that you can use. Personal chef services are quickly becoming a very popular alternative for people who do not have the budget for a full-scale catered event, and for others hosting small gatherings not requiring complete catering services. The advantages for start-up are apparent: low overhead and initial investment, full-time or part-time operating hours, and easy management from home. Promote the service by joining business associations and community social clubs to network and spread the news. The service can be easily supported by word-of-mouth advertising and repeat business once established, providing the food is great and the service is second to none. Rates vary according to factors such as the supply of food and the type of menu requested. However, on average earnings are in the range of $35 to $50 per hour.

AT A GLANCE

 INVESTMENT: Under $2K

 RATE: $25+

 SKILL LEVEL: 2–3

 RESOURCES

—American Personal Chef Association, ☎ (800) 644-8389, www.personalchef.com

—*Become a Personal Chef: An Introduction to the Industry*, Brian T. Koning (AuthorHouse, 2004)

—United States Personal Chef Association, www.uspca.com

Freelance Bartender

Hiring your bartending skills out on weekends, evenings, and even on a full-time basis is a great way to earn a terrific living, or just some spare cash to help cover living expenses, depending on your needs. You can market your services as a freelance bartender to catering companies, event and wedding planners, banquet halls, hotels, and pubs for relief duties, earning up to $300 per day when you tally up your wages and tips. Even if you are not 100 percent up-to-speed on the latest drink recipes or the finer aspects of working behind a bar, fret not, because all across the country there are a multitude of schools providing bartending training. A definite prerequisite, however, is an outgoing and sociable personality. Employing other bartenders on an as-needed, on-call basis can generate additional revenue for your bartender-for-hire business by paying them $10 per hour while perhaps renting them out at $15 per hour.

AT A GLANCE

 INVESTMENT: Under $2K

 RATE: $15+

 SKILL LEVEL: 2–3

 RESOURCES

—American Bartenders Association, www.americanbartenders.org

—*The Bartender's Best Friend: A Complete Guide to Cocktails, Martinis, and Mixed Drinks*, Mardee Regan (Wiley, 2002)

—World Bartenders Training Organization, www.wbto.net

Romantic Catering

Who needs Cupid when your client can hire your romantic catering service and surprise that someone special with a unique and unforgettable romantic dinner for two? Romantic catering is just that. You plan and play host to a memorable dining experience for clients. The evening could start with a ride in a horse-drawn carriage through a park, complete with wine, roses, and mood-setting music. The ride could end on a secluded beach under the stars where your clients would dine on lobster and caviar, picnic-style. Of course, your service would provide the gourmet meal, make all the arrangements, supply the transportation, and even serve the meal on the finest china while dressed in exquisite formal wear. Best of all, you do not need to be a chef, have the horse-drawn carriage, or even the ability to serve the meal. All these can be contracted to qualified people who do possess these abilities and the needed equipment. What is required, however, is the ability to market the service and have the creative imagination to plan the best romantic dinner adventure possible.

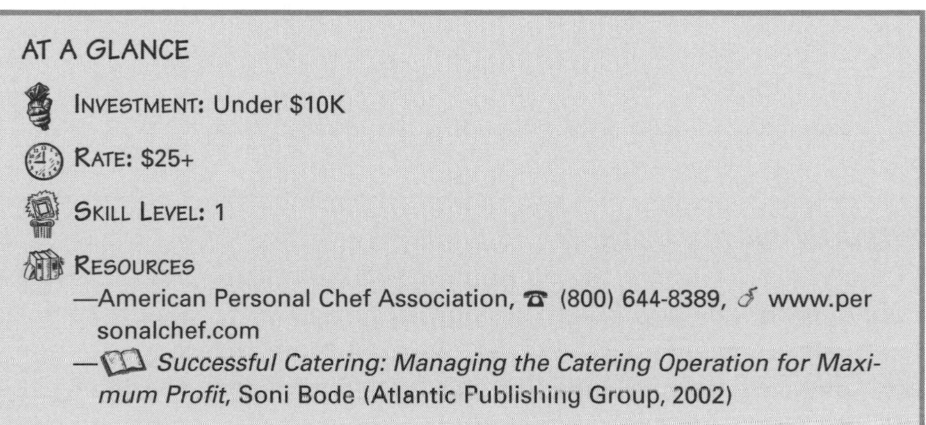

AT A GLANCE

INVESTMENT: Under $10K

RATE: $25+

SKILL LEVEL: 1

RESOURCES

—American Personal Chef Association, (800) 644-8389, www.personalchef.com

—*Successful Catering: Managing the Catering Operation for Maximum Profit*, Soni Bode (Atlantic Publishing Group, 2002)

Washroom Sanitizing

Next to bad food, the number-one reason people will not return to certain restaurants is dirty washrooms. This fact alone can be used as your greatest sales and marketing tool for convincing restaurant owners and managers that they need your washroom sanitizing services. Concentrate your marketing efforts on busy fast-food restaurants, family restaurants, coffee shops, and donut shops with a high turnover of customers—businesses that would stand to benefit the most from a daily washroom sanitizing service. Outside of reliable transportation, basic cleaning equipment and supplies, and a strong work ethic, other requirements to start this service are no more than a business license, a cell phone, and business cards. Call directly on restaurant owners and managers to pitch the benefits of your service, staying close to the core sales argument—that people do not return to restaurants with dirty washrooms. Charging $6 to $12 per washroom may not seem like a lot of money, but considering the average washroom will only take 10 to 20 minutes to fully clean and sanitize, you stand to earn upwards of $50 an hour, even allowing for travel time between jobs.

AT A GLANCE

INVESTMENT: Under $2K

 **RATE:** $15+

 **SKILL LEVEL:** 1–2

 **RESOURCES**

—★ Aire-Master, ☎ (800) 525-0957, www.airemaster.com

—Parish Maintenance Supplies, cleaning equipment and supplies, ☎ (800) 836-0862, www.parish-supply.com

---

Nonmedical Home Care

One of the reasons that nonmedical home care is an exploding industry is our aging population. The over-50 group is the fastest-growing demographic, and as a general rule, as people age they tend to need more personal attention. Nonmedical home-care services provide clients with a wide range of services specific to each individual's needs. These services can include companionship, meal preparation, medication reminders, light housekeeping duties, laundry, running errands, trips to appointments, and shopping for groceries and other personal needs. In addition to seniors, nonmedical home-care workers also provide similar services for new moms, people with disabilities, and people recovering from injury or illness. People who are reliable, compassionate, and who care about the welfare of others thrive in this field. This is an easy service to start, with minimal skill and experience requirements, although all nonmedical home-care service workers are required to carry insurance and be bonded.

 **INVESTMENT:** Under $10K

 **RATE:** $25+

 **SKILL LEVEL:** 2

 **RESOURCES**

—★ Homewatch Caregivers, ☎ (800) 777-9770, www.homewatch-intl.com

—National Private Duty Association, ☎ (317) 844-7105, www.privatedutyhomecare.org

Day Spa

The day spa industry is booming, as both women and men look for ways to pamper themselves and their loved ones. Forget about boring mudpacks—today's day spas offer clients a wide range of services, including aromatherapy, reflexology, facials, manicures, pedicures, herbal wraps, microdermabrasion, acrylic nails, airbrush bronzing, massage, wedding makeup, waxing, and a whole assortment of take-home skin, makeup, and relaxation products. The cost to open a day spa offering a full-service menu is not cheap; be prepared to shell out high five and even into six-figure sums to get started. Even so, the profit potential is excellent and the return on investment can be swift for ambitious entrepreneurs. Day spas can be opened and operated from home, but if you want to offer lots of services, you will need to rent a large commercial space, in the range of 2,000 to 3,000 square feet. Make sure to contact corporations, wedding planners, and hotels in your area to inform them about your spa and services, and also be sure to have elegant gift certificates printed so you will be ready for the rush of men lining up on Mother's Day, Valentine's Day, and at Christmas to purchase them.

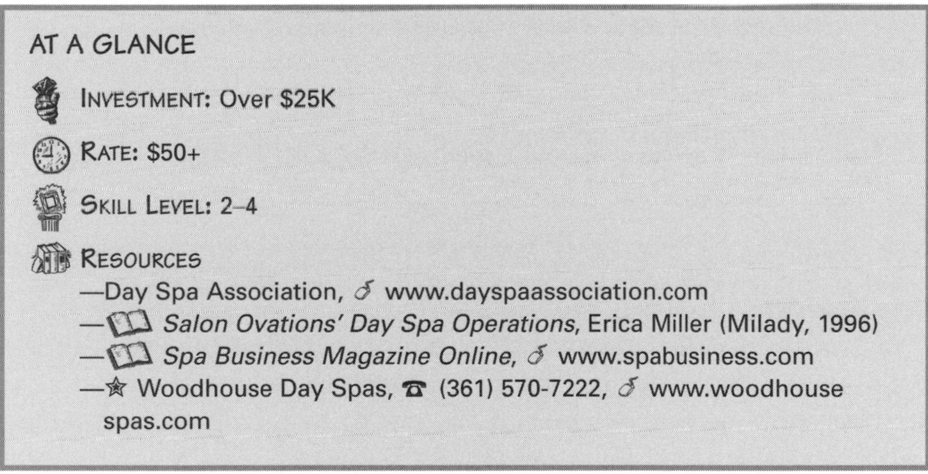

AT A GLANCE

INVESTMENT: Over $25K

RATE: $50+

SKILL LEVEL: 2–4

RESOURCES

—Day Spa Association, www.dayspaassociation.com
—*Salon Ovations' Day Spa Operations*, Erica Miller (Milady, 1996)
—*Spa Business Magazine Online*, www.spabusiness.com
—★ Woodhouse Day Spas, ☎ (361) 570-7222, www.woodhousespas.com

Hair Salon

For entrepreneurs with hair styling experience, or for those willing to learn the trade, there are three excellent options for starting your own family hair care service. First, if space and zoning permit, you can establish a hair styling salon in your home—a converted garage, basement, or family room are all excellent choices. Second, you can rent commercial storefront space in a mall, strip plaza, or town center location. Third, you can operate the business on a mobile basis, styling hair right at your customer's location. A mobile operation is perfect for seniors who find it difficult to get out, busy executives, brides at home before the big day, and anyone else who finds it more convenient to have his or her hair cut and styled at home. The third option is also the least costly to get started, but at the same time, commuting time could lessen profit potential. If you are going to rent space, location is the primary concern, and if you are going to work from home, zoning and related issues are the primary concern. Additional revenues and profits may be earned by selling complementary services like pedicures, manicures, facials, waxing, and makeup artistry, as well as hair and skin-care product sales.

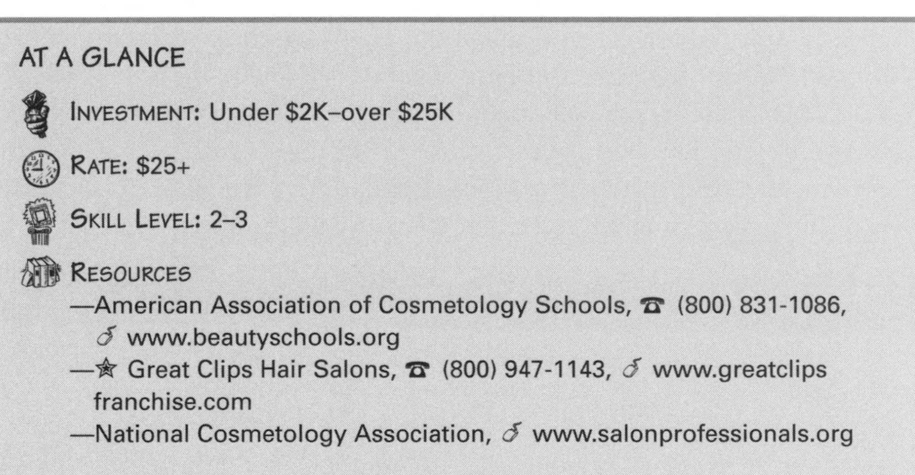

AT A GLANCE

INVESTMENT: Under $2K–over $25K

RATE: $25+

SKILL LEVEL: 2–3

RESOURCES

—American Association of Cosmetology Schools, ☎ (800) 831-1086, www.beautyschools.org

—★ Great Clips Hair Salons, ☎ (800) 947-1143, www.greatclipsfranchise.com

—National Cosmetology Association, www.salonprofessionals.org

---

Tanning Salon

Every day more and more people are giving up natural suntanning in favor of artificial salon tanning because of the convenience and ability to tan before taking a tropical vacation. So here is your opportunity to open your own tanning salon and cash in on the craze. Salon location will be one of the more important issues to address when getting started. You can operate from home, but doing so will mean that you will miss out on pedestrian and motorist traffic. I would suggest renting a storefront in a busy strip plaza with lots of parking and great street visibility as the best option. You will also need to purchase tanning beds and related equipment, which are not cheap but can be rented or leased if your investment budget is tight. This is a competitive industry, so careful research and planning will be needed. Suntanning.com provides business planning assistance to entrepreneurs wanting to open their own salon, and they may be contacted at, www.suntanning.com. The majority of tanning equipment manufacturers and distributors also provide training and other support to new salon owners, so you will not be totally on your own. To help boost revenues and profits, also consider selling sun protection, bathing suits, and sportswear.

AT A GLANCE

INVESTMENT: Over $25K

RATE: $25+

SKILL LEVEL: 1

RESOURCES

—★ Planet Beach, ☎ (888) 290-8266, www.planetbeach.com

—Tanning Online, commercial suntanning equipment and products wholesaler, ☎ (888) 777-7577, www.tanningonline.com

Massage Therapist

Massage therapy is one of the fastest-growing segments of the health-care industry, and massage therapists can earn upwards of $75 per hour. Massage therapy has been clinically proven to help reduce stress, help people recover more quickly from sports and other physical injuries, help people gain relief from pain, and help them achieve an overall deeper feeling of relaxation. In fact, many corporations believe so strongly that regular massage therapy helps to increase employee productivity, while decreasing absenteeism, that they now offer the service as an employee benefit. There are numerous opportunities that certified massage therapists can pursue. They can open their own massage therapy clinic, work as freelancers at day spas, work on a mobile basis visiting corporations and clients' homes, work with health clinics, work with fitness clubs and sports rehabilitation clinics, and even work with pet groomers and vets giving dog massages. Don't laugh; massage therapy for dogs is also one of the fastest-growing segments of the pet health-care industry. To become a massage therapist, you will need to obtain training, which in turn will qualify you for the professional designation of Certified Massage Therapist. You can contact the associations and resources listed below to inquire about massage therapy training available in your area.

AT A GLANCE

INVESTMENT: Under $10K

 RATE: $50+

 SKILL LEVEL: 3

 RESOURCES

—American Massage Therapy Association, www.amtamassage.org

—Canadian Massage Therapist Alliance, www.cmta.ca

—Natural Healers, directory of massage therapy schools, www.naturalhealers.com

Medical Claims Billing

The medical billing industry is extremely competitive, but for the determined entrepreneur, there is a good opportunity to earn $40,000 or more per year operating either a franchise or independent medical claims billing service. All medical claims billing is processed electronically and sent directly to Medicare clearinghouses, so the ability to use computer hardware and medical billing software programs is required. You will also need to familiarize yourself with the diagnostic and procedure coding system used by doctors and health-care professionals on medical claim forms to indicate the type of service being billed. Currently, medical billing services charge clients in the range of $2 to $3 per claim processed, and the overall profit potential for the service is good, providing you can process medical claims on a volume basis. There is a fairly steep learning curve for operating this service, and careful research and planning will be needed to ensure initial and continued success.

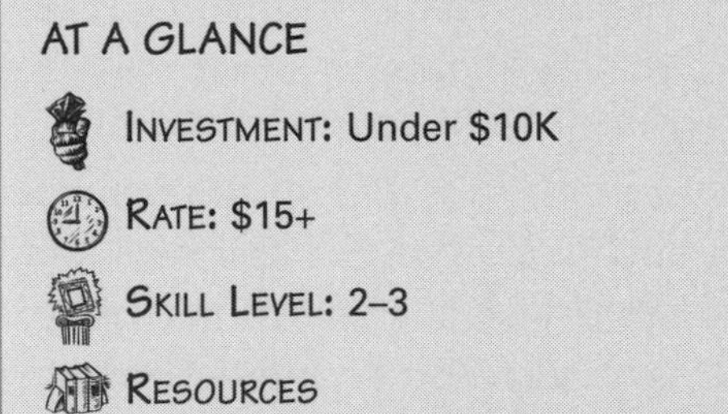

AT A GLANCE

INVESTMENT: Under $10K

RATE: $15+

SKILL LEVEL: 2–3

RESOURCES

—American Association of Medical Billers, www.billers.com

—★ American Billing Systems, www.americanbilling.com

Renovation Service

Capitalize on your carpentry and construction skills and cash in on the ever-growing multibillion-dollar home improvement industry by starting your own renovation service. Small additions, basement remodels, carport conversions, painting and drywall, fencing, siding, and general cosmetic changes all fall under the umbrella of home renovations. You can keep your start-up costs to a minimum by renting more expensive tools and equipment on an as-needed basis, and buy these items from the profits you earn. You will need to brush up on your estimating skills, so calling other renovation contractors in your area and asking about costs for the various improvement services they offer is a good way to get a handle on the competition's pricing. Skills that you may lack can be contracted out to qualified tradespeople, especially the more specialized work like tile flooring, electrical and plumbing, and insulating. Quality workmanship and reliability are essential to prosper in this industry, as it is not uncommon for top renovation companies to do strictly repeat and referral business, without the aid of any advertising.

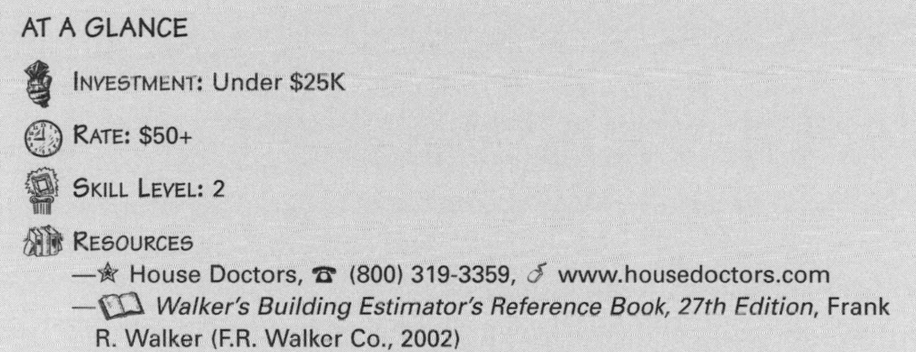

AT A GLANCE

INVESTMENT: Under $25K

RATE: $50+

SKILL LEVEL: 2

RESOURCES

—House Doctors, (800) 319-3359, www.housedoctors.com

—*Walker's Building Estimator's Reference Book, 27th Edition*, Frank R. Walker (F.R. Walker Co., 2002)

Parking Lot Power Sweeping

Look around at many parking lots and what you'll see are leaves, paper, cups, food wrappers, cigarette butts, and broken glass. All leave a negative impression about the business. Here is your opportunity to clean up your community and help business and property owners project the right image, by starting a parking lot power sweeping service. There are basically two styles of power sweeping equipment—truck chassis mounted sweepers and vacuums, and portable sweepers. The first are classified as heavy equipment, the type cities use to power-sweep streets. These models are very expensive, which will put them out of the financial reach of many entrepreneurs. The second style, portable power sweepers, are inexpensive and can be mounted on the back of any pickup truck. The second biggest advantage of portable power sweeping equipment, next to the cost savings, is that your truck can be a duel-use vehicle—power sweeper in place for business, and power sweeper removed for personal use. The equipment is also small enough to allow for sweeping of underground parking lots where the larger power sweepers cannot get in. This also creates a great opportunity to operate the business part-time on nights and weekends. Potential customers will include property managers, shopping centers, schools, strip plazas, hospitals, car dealerships, grocery stores, and every other business, agency, or organization with parking lots that need to be kept clean.

AT A GLANCE

 INVESTMENT: Over $25K

 RATE: $50+

 SKILL LEVEL: 1

 RESOURCES

—Schwarze Industries, mobile parking lot sweeping equipment manufacturer, ☎ (800) 879-7933, www.schwarze.com

—Sweeprite, parking lot sweeping equipment manufacturer, ☎ (888) 446-4494, www.sweeprite.com

Remodeling Project Management

Turn your knowledge of construction and home renovation into big bucks by starting a remodeling project-management service focused on helping clients to manage their home, office, or store renovations, but especially in the red-hot residential home improvement industry. Regardless of whether a homeowner tackles his own renovation job, or if a renovation company is hired to perform the work, a nonbiased remodeling project-management service can save thousands of dollars, while ensuring that all work conforms to code and that the highest-quality products and installations are used. This is especially true for homeowners doing their own work: What permits do they need and where do they get them? In what order is the job completed? And the granddaddy of them all: How much will the entire project cost, including possible extra charges to deal with unforeseen circumstances? These are common questions that project managers answer, along with attending to other duties such as contacting and screening potential trades, establishing budgets, signing off on materials and labor, and keeping the project on-time and on-budget. Remuneration is by way of a flat pre-quoted fee to oversee the entire project or portions of the project, or by using a percentage, such as 12 percent of the total project value.

AT A GLANCE

 INVESTMENT: Under $10K

 RATE: $25+

 SKILL LEVEL: 2

 RESOURCES

—📖 *2004 National Repair and Remodeling Estimator*, Albert S. Paxton (Craftsman Book Company, 2003)

—★ U-Build-It, ☎ (425) 821-6200, www.ubuildit.com

Concrete Cutting

Interior and exterior concrete often needs to be cut, ground, or drilled for plumbing repairs, sidewalk removal, trip-hazard removal, leveling for handicap accessibility, tree root damage, section replacement, installation of anchors and lags, and many other reasons. This need provides great opportunities to capitalize on your construction knowledge and to start a concrete-cutting and drilling service. The American Concrete Sawing and Drilling Association provides classroom training workshops on numerous services related to concrete cutting, and you can contact them at the phone number and web site below. Customers include plumbers, homeowners, property managers, and general contractors. In addition to concrete-cutting and drilling equipment, you will also need suitable transportation to carry it from job site to job site. This service is easily managed from home, and you can operate on a full- or part-time basis, depending on demand and your own business goals. Concrete-cutting rates vary depending on the scope of the job, but on average expect to earn between $50 and $80 per hour providing this specialized service.

AT A GLANCE

 INVESTMENT: Under $10K–over $25K

 RATE: $50+

 SKILL LEVEL: 2–3

 RESOURCES

—American Concrete Sawing and Drilling Association, ☎ (727) 577-5004, www.csda.org

—★ Precision Concrete Cutting, ☎ (800) 833-7770, www.pccccon crete.com

Demolition Service

Forget about starting a traditional demolition service, the kind that requires heavy equipment to knock down office buildings and houses, and instead specialize in small residential and commercial demolition jobs overlooked by the big guys. These small demolition jobs include knocking down walls for homeowners and contractors, removing decaying fences and small outbuildings like garages, and removing kitchen cabinets, carpets, and plumbing fixtures to make way for new renovations. I operated a renovation service for many years and can tell you first-hand that demolition services specializing in small jobs that remove debris from job sites are in big demand. What makes this a great opportunity is simple: Contractors and renovation companies typically carry out demolition work needed to clean an area so they can get started on the rebuilding process involved with renovations. The problem is that in most situations, the contractor ends up using carpenters to do the job, carpenters who are overqualified and overpaid to much to do work that could be done for much less. This means less profit for the contractor, and a sore back for the carpenter. So by forming a crew of qualified laborers capable of demolition work, you can subcontract your small-job demolition crew to contractors, renovators, and homeowners. You will need to invest in trucks and equipment, but the return on investment is quick.

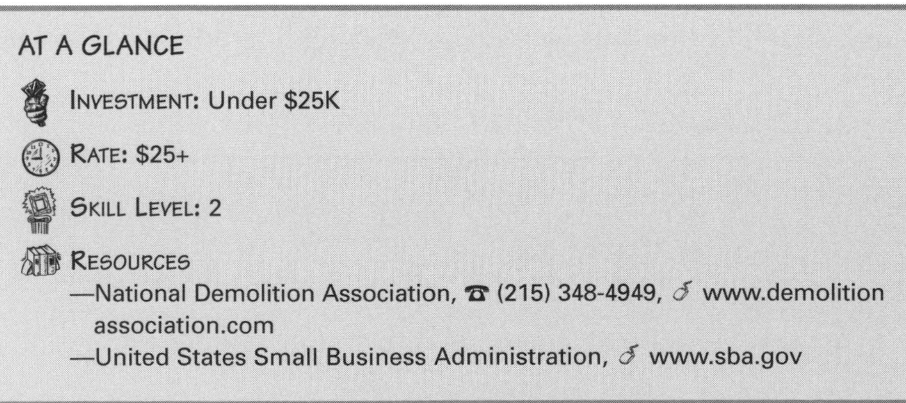
AT A GLANCE

INVESTMENT: Under $25K

RATE: $25+

SKILL LEVEL: 2

RESOURCES

—National Demolition Association, ☎ (215) 348-4949, www.demolition association.com

—United States Small Business Administration, www.sba.gov

House Painting

There are two main reasons why even the most hardcore do-it-yourself homeowners call in the pros when it comes time to paint the interior or exterior of their homes—heights and tedious labor-intensive work. As with most labor-intensive services, you can pretty much be guaranteed work, regardless of economic conditions. House painters who are not afraid to roll up their sleeves and get to work can earn a substantial living—six-figure annual incomes are not unheard of. Of course, those who do prosper provide clients with uncompromising quality and service, which in turn secures more repeat and referral business than most can handle. You will need some prior painting experience to get started, but with that said, much about the painting trade can be learned as you go, especially if you paint your own home, and friends and family members' homes for practice before you start charging. Tools and equipment requirements are no more than ladders, brushes, roller trays, sanding blocks, and reliable transportation. Providing free value-added services such as cleaning the rain gutters or windows while on the job site is a great way to separate your company from the competition, especially when you're just starting out.

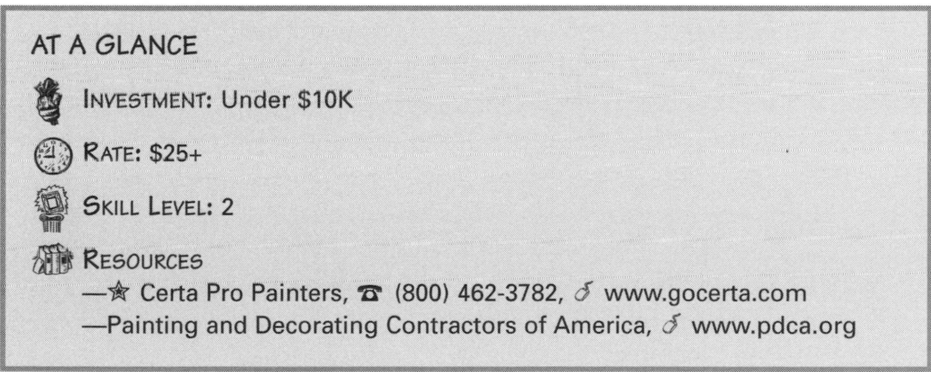

AT A GLANCE

INVESTMENT: Under $10K

RATE: $25+

SKILL LEVEL: 2

RESOURCES

—★ Certa Pro Painters, ☎ (800) 462-3782, www.gocerta.com

—Painting and Decorating Contractors of America, www.pdca.org

Hardwood Floor Refinishing

All across North America, homeowners are tearing out old carpet to expose real maple, oak, cypress, or walnut hardwood floors, which in many cases have been hidden away for decades. The majority of these hardwood floors have a few things in common—they need slight repairs, they need to be sanded, and they need to be refinished to bring them back to their former glory. When you consider that the cost to install new real hardwood floors is in the range of $10 to $25 per square foot, depending on the wood selected, most homeowners find refinishing their current floors a bargain at $1 to $3 per square foot. Needless to say, it does not require a lot of persuasion to talk homeowners into refinishing. You will need to purchase floor-sanding equipment and supplies, as well as identify sources for used hardwood flooring so that you can match to the old in section-replacement situations. Used building materials and antique architectural-building supply yards are good sources. If your start-up investment is tight, you can rent floor-sanding equipment on an as-needed basis, and purchase it from profits earned as your business grows. Hardwood floor sanding and refinishing is generally quoted on a per-square-foot basis before starting, so you will want to call around your area to find out the rate your competitors are charging.

 INVESTMENT: Under $10K

 RATE: $25+

 SKILL LEVEL: 2

 RESOURCES

—Floor Sanding Online, industry information and resources, www.floorsanding.com

—IVIE Enterprise, flooring sanding equipment and supplies, ☎ (918) 254-5161, www.hardwood-floor-sanders.com

—The Wood Flooring Manufacturers Association, www.nofma.org

Deck Builder

One of the fastest-growing segments of the home improvement industry is designing and building custom sundecks that can easily reach $25,000 and beyond, and include features such as built-in planters, hot tub gazebos, glass or cast-iron handrails, atmosphere lighting, and custom-manufactured wood patio furniture to match the deck's design. There are a number of ways that you can get started marketing deck design and building services. One is to sell directly to homeowners using advertising and home-and-garden-show displays to collect and qualify leads. If you choose this route of establishing alliances with landscape designers, real estate agents, and architects, their referral of your services to their clients will prove invaluable. A second way is to subcontract your services to established building and renovation companies, and design and build sundecks for their clients. This option will likely mean less overall profit, but it is generally faster to get up and running. Do keep in mind that in most areas of the country, installing sundecks requires a building permit. There are also building codes in place for the construction specifications of sundecks that must be met. Equipment such as table saws, compound power miter saws, drills, and a host of hand tools will also be required, but many of these can be rented at first to keep start-up costs to a minimum. Starting this business requires construction experience and skills, as well as creative design abilities.

AT A GLANCE

 INVESTMENT: Under $10K

 RATE: $25+

 SKILL LEVEL: 2

 RESOURCES

—☆ Archadeck, ☎ (800) 722-4668, www.archadeck.com
—Deck Industry Association, www.deckindustry.org
— *The Complete Guide to Building Decks* (Creative Publishing International, 2001)

Carpet and Upholstery Cleaning

What makes starting and operating a carpet and upholstery service such a terrific new business venture? A great number of reasons—low investment, minimal skill requirements, suited to full- or part-time hours, enormous consumer demand for the service, proven marketplace, easy to market, and great growth potential. If these are not enough reasons to tempt you to start a carpet-cleaning service, consider that on average, independent carpet and upholstery cleaners earn in the vicinity of $35 per hour. A fast-start method for securing work is to print and distribute two-for-one coupons. "Have one room's carpet cleaned and get a second room's carpet cleaned for free." Or, "Let us clean your sofa and we'll steam-clean your loveseat for free." You will also want to focus many of your marketing efforts on securing customers who will become regular users, or refer their clients and friends to your business. These people include property managers, real estate agents, landlords, retailers, car dealers, used furniture store proprietors, and RV dealers.

AT A GLANCE

 INVESTMENT: Under $10K

 RATE: $25+

 SKILL LEVEL: 1–2

 RESOURCES

—Advantage Cleaning Systems, carpet-cleaning equipment and supplies, ☎ (847) 838-3246, www.startcleaning.com

—★ Chem-Dry Carpet and Upholstery Cleaning, ☎ (800) 243-6379, www.chemdry.com

—Rotovac, carpet-cleaning equipment, www.carpet-cleaning-equipment.com

Furniture Repairs and Refinishing

Big bucks can be earned repairing office and residential furniture, as well as refinishing antique furniture. The furniture-repair side of the business can be operated on a mobile basis working right from a fully equipped van repairing furniture at your customer's location. Potential customers that commonly require furniture repair services include home and office movers, business owners, property managers, restaurants, hotels, schools, hospitals, institutions, government offices, and retailers of new and used furniture. The furniture-refinishing side of the business, namely antiques refinishing, can be conveniently operated from a well-equipped home workshop. Advertise this feature of the business by building alliances with antique dealers and interior designers who can refer their clients to your service. Additional money may be earned by attending auction sales and buying furniture and antiques in need of repair and refinishing. Once they have been repaired and refinished, they can be sold for a profit via classified ads in your local newspaper, on eBay, and at collector's shows.

AT A GLANCE

 INVESTMENT: Under $10K

 RATE: $25+

 SKILL LEVEL: 2

 RESOURCES

—★ Furniture Medic, ☎ (901) 820-8600, www.furnituremedicfranchise.com

—📖 *Furniture Repair and Refinishing*, Brian Hingley (Creative Homeowner Press, 1998)
—The Furniture Wizard, industry information portal, www.furniturewizard.com

---

Carpentry Shop

A terrific opportunity exists for carpenters of every skill level to earn a substantial full- or part-time income by setting up a fully equipped carpentry shop at home if space and zoning allows, or in a rental shop space. Offer customers various woodworking and carpentry services, including lumber milling, planing, joining, sawing, and gluing, as well as custom work such as shaping and sash construction. Commercial-grade carpentry equipment such as a table saw, joiner, planner, radial arm saw, compound miter saw, shaper, bandsaw, and dust-collection system will be required. Most if not all of these items can be purchased in good secondhand condition from auction sales, newspaper classified ads, and shop closeouts for about half the cost of new. Potential customers include homeowners in need of custom-milling and woodworking, as well as commercial clients such as contractors and renovators also in need of custom-milling and woodwork. Selling exotic woods, related tools, and supplies to hobbyist woodworkers and craftspeople can also help to boost revenues and profits.

AT A GLANCE

INVESTMENT: Under $25K

RATE: $50+

SKILL LEVEL: 2

RESOURCES
—Mammoth Tools, ☎ (516) 942-0905, www.mammothtools.com
—My Crazy Tools, ☎ (416) 944-8605, www.mycrazytools.com
—Quality Tools 4 Less, ☎ (808) 779-1311, www.qualitytools4less.com

---

Trim Carpenter

The home improvement industry is red-hot in North America and shows no signs of cooling off anytime soon, which is great news for entrepreneurs with basic carpentry skills, especially if those skills are utilized in starting a trim service. Trim carpenters install interior windowsills and doorsills, jambs, and casings, as well as baseboard trim and ceiling crown molding. They trim out built-ins like fireplaces, bookcases, and wall niches. For home exteriors, trim carpenters trim out windows, doors, fascia and bargeboards, as well as add decorative trim and gingerbread molding. Fortunately, equipment requirements are minimal to get started—a compound miter saw, air compressor, nail gun, ladders, suitable transportation, and basic hand tools. In addition to installing trim directly for homeowners, you can also subcontract your services to general contractors, new-home builders, renovation contractors, kitchen and bath installers, flooring installers, and painters. Rates vary depending on the type of trim being installed, stain or paint requirements, and the total footage installed. Call around to other trim services in your area to find out about current rates.

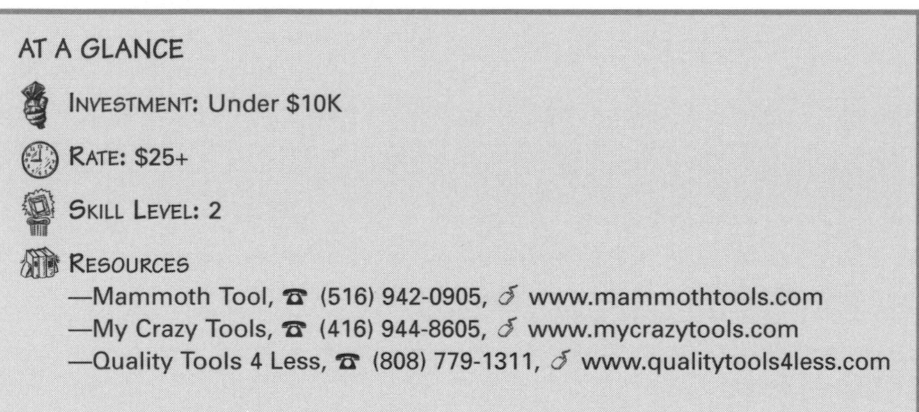
AT A GLANCE

INVESTMENT: Under $10K

RATE: $25+

SKILL LEVEL: 2

RESOURCES
—Mammoth Tool, ☎ (516) 942-0905, www.mammothtools.com
—My Crazy Tools, ☎ (416) 944-8605, www.mycrazytools.com
—Quality Tools 4 Less, ☎ (808) 779-1311, www.qualitytools4less.com

Decorating Service

A myriad of popular television programs aimed at home decorating such as "Trading Spaces," "The Designer Guys," and "While You Were Out" have fired up people's imaginations about how they can dramatically change the look of their homes on a relatively small budget. But there is a hook; anyone involved with the decorating makeover must have a creative flair for decorating and design, and the skills and tools necessary to pull it all together. Not all homeowners have these skills and talents, but if you do, operating a decorating service might be right up your alley. For budget-minded clients, you can spend time at garage and estate sales, scrounge through flea markets, and scan local classified ads for wacky decorative items, recycled building materials, and unique home furnishings. All can be purchased and resold to clients at a profit as you redecorate rooms or their entire house. For your well-heeled clients, stick with designer and brand-name products to transform their homes and offices into designer masterpieces. Market your service through home-and-garden shows and by creating colorful before-and-after brochures that showcase your decorating talents.

 **INVESTMENT:** Under $10K

 **RATE:** $25+

 **SKILL LEVEL:** 2–3

 **RESOURCES**

—International Interior Design Association, www.iida.org

—★ Interiors by Decorating Den, ☎ (800) 686-6393, www.decoratingden.com

---

Kitchen Facelift Service

If you launch a kitchen facelift service, your most powerful sales argument could easily become, "Why spend $20,000 to replace your kitchen, when we can give you an entirely new look for a fraction of the cost?" The average cost of a complete kitchen replacement now tops $20,000, making it out of the reach of many homeowners. Yet many of these same homeowners have the financial resources to part with a few thousand dollars to get the next best thing—a professional kitchen facelift. Leaving the wall and floor cabinets in place, install new doors, countertops, hardware, tile backsplash, accent lighting, and trim to make even the dullest kitchen look new and exciting for a fraction of the cost of a total kitchen replacement. You will need carpentry skills and woodworking tools and equipment to successfully start and operate this service. Exhibiting at home-and-garden shows with the aid of a before-and-after kitchen facelift display will enable you to generate sales leads from people interested in having their kitchens updated. Traditional forms of advertising in newspapers, on the radio, site signs, and via direct mail will also get the telephone ringing.

AT A GLANCE

 **INVESTMENT:** Under $10K

 RATE: $25+

 SKILL LEVEL: 2

 RESOURCES
—★ Kitchen Tune-Up, ☎ (800) 333-6385, www.kitchentuneup.com
—★ Surface Specialists Systems, ☎ (866) 239-8707, www.surfacespecialists.com

---

Driveway Sealing

Sealing or coating asphalt driveways is very easy: edge the driveway, removing grass and weeds, fill cracks with asphalt crack compound, power sweep, blow or wash the surface clean, and finally apply the asphalt sealer. There is self-propelled and tank-fed spraying equipment available, or for entrepreneurs on a tight business start-up budget you can use the good old Armstrong method and roll on the sealer straight from a five-gallon bucket using a coarse roller or squeegee. And forget about just plain old black asphalt sealer, because new age acrylic driveway coatings are now available in a wide range of colors so you can match your clients' driveway colors to their trim, siding, or even hair color if they want. Therefore, you are not limited to sealing only older driveways in need of a spruce-up. Any driveway is a candidate if the homeowner would like to change its color. You will find all the necessary supplies and equipment available at most major building centers or online. On average, you can earn between $25 to $40 per hour sealing driveways on a full- or part-time basis, which makes this the perfect service for students, retirees, and weekend entrepreneurs to sell.

AT A GLANCE

 INVESTMENT: Under $10K

 RATE: $25+

 SKILL LEVEL: 1–2

 RESOURCES

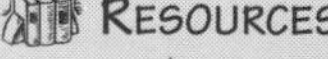

—★ Jet-Black, ☎ (888) 538-2525, www.jet-black.com
—Seal Master, asphalt sealing equipment and products, www.sealmaster.net

Roof Repair

The prerequisite for selling roof-repair services is obvious; you need to know how to repair all or most types of roofing—asphalt, cedar, tile, steel, torch-on, and tar and gravel. Although this may sound like a major requirement, in fact it is not. Just about anyone with basic carpentry and construction skills can quickly learn how to repair roofs. You will, however, need proper equipment to ensure quality and effective repairs as well as safety. Tools and equipment include basic hand tools, an assortment of extension ladders, roof jacks, safety harnesses, and reliable transportation. Potential customers can be divided into two camps—residential homeowners, and commercial property owners, managers, and renters. The best way to spread the word to residential homeowners about your roof-repair services is through print advertisements, both in the classified section of your local newspaper under Trades, and by placing ads in your local Yellow Pages directory. You can also join home-repair referral services if they are available in your community. The best way to reach commercial customers is to contact them directly by telephone, letter, personal visit, or all three. These include landlords, property managers, roofing companies that only provide reroofing services and not repair services, and other renovation companies that do not repair roofs. It is also a good idea to establish alliances with businesses and individuals who can refer your service to their clients, including realtors, property inspectors, and painters.

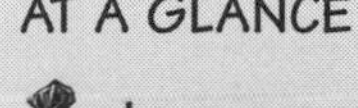
AT A GLANCE

 INVESTMENT: Under $10K

 RATE: $25+

 SKILL LEVEL: 2

 RESOURCES
—Entrepreneur Online, small business portal, www.entrepreneur.com
—United States Small Business Administration, www.sba.gov

Gutter Cleaning

Armed with nothing more than a ladder, garden hose, and basic transportation that will take you from one job to the next, it is possible to earn $200 to $300 per day cleaning leaves and other debris from rain gutters. You will also need to obtain liability insurance coverage as well as workers' compensation coverage, especially if you employ people, but these are great sales tools because they give customers the peace of mind in knowing that they will be protected in the event of an accident or damage to their homes; they also project a professional image for your business. Market your gutter-cleaning services by designing a flier outlining the details of your service, along with contact information. Hand-deliver the fliers to homes in residential neighborhoods, and be sure to advertise a special promotion on the flier, such as a 20 percent discount to help secure work quickly. In addition to single-family homes, you can also contact condominiums and property managers and pitch the benefits of your service.

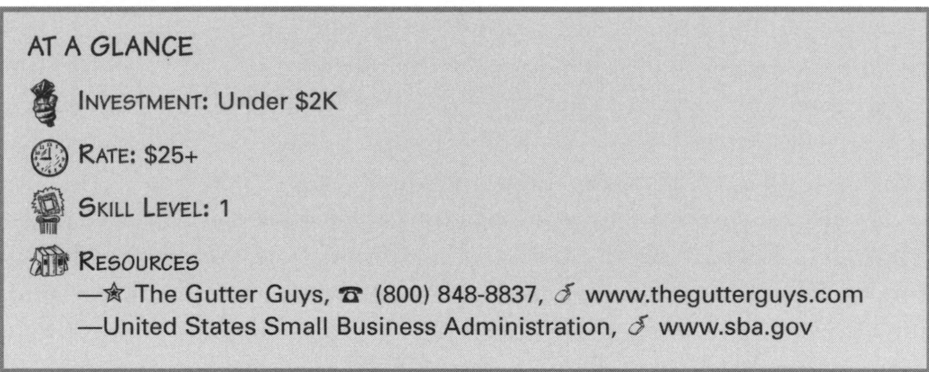

AT A GLANCE

INVESTMENT: Under $2K

RATE: $25+

SKILL LEVEL: 1

RESOURCES
—★ The Gutter Guys, ☎ (800) 848-8837, www.thegutterguys.com
—United States Small Business Administration, www.sba.gov

Construction Cleanup Service

Operating a construction cleanup service is a bit different than a residential or commercial cleaning service mainly because the work is much more labor-intensive. There is often heavy lifting, ladder work, and some debris removal required. Construction cleanup crews are the people who make sure newly built or renovated homes are spic-and-span before the owners move in and take possession. Duties can include cleaning windows inside and out, dusting and washing all surfaces, removing stickers on windows and appliances, hauling away the last of the construction debris, polishing all the interior glass, marble, and tile surfaces, dusting and washing walls and ceilings, and vacuuming the floors. Rates are generally based on an estimate prior to doing the work and vary greatly depending on the size of the job and scope of the work, but expect to earn in the $30-an-hour range. Renovation companies, contractors, and property developers are all potential customers. Therefore, creating a detailed brochure or promotional package that can be delivered to them is your best marketing tool, along with calling and visiting them in person to pitch your services.

AT A GLANCE

 INVESTMENT: Under $2K

 RATE: $25+

 SKILL LEVEL: 1

 RESOURCES

—Advantage Cleaning Systems, cleaning equipment and supplies, ☎ (847) 838-3246, www.startcleaning.com

— *Construction Cleanup: A Guide to an Exciting & Profitable Cleaning Specialty*, Don Aslett (Marsh Creek Press, 1997)

Home and Property Inspector

People with some construction background who are prepared to invest some money and time in a training course that will qualify them as a Certified Home and Property Inspector, can earn a very good living from owning and operating a home and property inspection service. How much money can be made? Many home and property inspectors routinely earn six-figure incomes after business expenses. Millions of homes and properties are bought and sold each year in North America. As a condition of sale, most buyers, and often mortgage lenders, insist that the property be professionally inspected to make sure the building does not have major structural or mechanical problems, so the investment is sound. Home and property inspection rates range from $150 for a small and basic residential home to more than $1,000 for larger commercial buildings and complexes. Be sure to build alliances with realtors, mortgage brokers, property appraisers, lawyers, notaries public, and insurance agents, all of whom can refer their clients to your property inspection service.

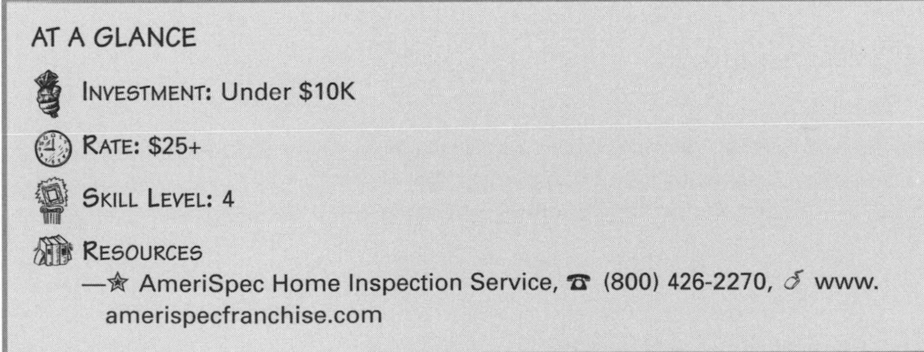

AT A GLANCE

INVESTMENT: Under $10K

RATE: $25+

SKILL LEVEL: 4

RESOURCES

—★ AmeriSpec Home Inspection Service, ☎ (800) 426-2270, www.amerispecfranchise.com

—Canadian Association of Home and Property Inspectors, www.cahi.ca
—National Association of Home Inspectors, www.nahi.org
—*Start Your Own Home Inspection Service*, Claire Ginther (Entrepreneur Press, 2003)

Draft Proofing

Starting a draft-proofing service allows you to save homeowners money, help the environment by reducing energy consumption, create a more comfortable living environment for homeowners, and build a successful and profitable business. Your service should focus around a report that you present to homeowners that explains the recommended draft-proofing measures, which could save them money on heating and cooling energy costs. These measures could include increased insulation and ventilation, caulking, installation of door and window weather stripping, replacement of electrical wall receptacles to draft-proof versions, and even replacement of old doors and windows with new high-efficiency models. Providing you have the experience and tools required, you can carry out the repairs needed to draft-proof the home or improve its energy efficiency. If not, the repairs could be contracted to a qualified local handyperson or to renovation contractors. Ideally, draft-proofing services are best marketed by establishing working relationships with utility companies, real estate brokers, home inspectors, renovation contractors, and property management firms, all of which can recommend your service to their clients.

AT A GLANCE

 INVESTMENT: Under $10K–over $25K

 RATE: $25+

 SKILL LEVEL: 2–3

 RESOURCES

—*2004 National Repair and Remodeling Estimator*, Albert S. Paxton (Craftsman Book Company, 2003)
—Building Performance Contractors Association, www.home-performance.org

Reglazing Service

Whether it's bathtubs, sinks, showers, tub surrounds, clawfoot tubs, or tile, most bathroom fixtures and surfaces can easily be reglazed, and these services are in high demand throughout the country. Why? Lots of reasons, including:

- Reglazing costs up to 75 percent less than replacement.
- There's zero mess and no need to renovate or call in a plumber, because fixtures are not removed, but reglazed in place.
- It's fast and convenient. Tubs and sinks can be used the same day of application.
- There's a wide range of available colors, including faux marble and granite finishes.
- Slip-proof safety coatings are available for seniors, kids, and people with disabilities.

Equipment and training is readily available, especially if you opt to purchase a franchise as a complete package, or purchase equipment and products from suppliers like Midwest Chemicals that also provide reglazing training and ongoing workshops. The business can be managed from home and operated from a van with no more than a cell phone. In addition to homeowners, potential customers include contractors, property managers, and landlords. Spreading the word through realtors is a great way to get referral work.

 **INVESTMENT:** Under $10K

 **RATE:** $25+

 **SKILL LEVEL:** 2–3

 **RESOURCES**

—★ Perma-Glaze, www.permaglaze.com
—Midwest Chemicals, bathtub and fixtures reglazing training, products, and equipment, ☎ (800) 270-0777, www.midwestchemicals.com

Fabric Restoration

Fabric restoration is big business for both residential and commercial applications, mainly because, if you stop to think about it, fabric covers just about everything in the home and office. Working from a well-equipped van on a mobile basis, you can repair and restore torn, cracked, faded, stained, and burned fabrics like leather, suede, vinyl, cloth, plastic, carpet, and velour. Market your fabric restoration services through traditional advertising mediums like the Yellow Pages and classified ads, and build working relationships with other businesses that have the potential to utilize your services on a regular basis. These businesses include hotels, motels, movie theaters, hospitals, carpet cleaners, furniture stores, boat dealerships, car and recreational vehicle dealerships, bus and limousine companies, and restaurants. There is quite a bit of learning to be done, which makes starting a franchise operation a good choice because training is provided. At the same time, entrepreneurs with handyperson skills can master the trade on their own through trial and error, and practice, practice, and more practice.

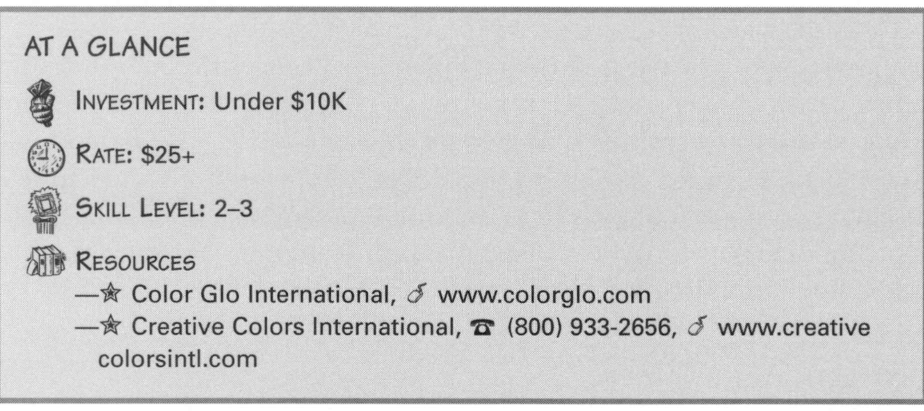

AT A GLANCE

INVESTMENT: Under $10K

RATE: $25+

SKILL LEVEL: 2–3

RESOURCES
—★ Color Glo International, www.colorglo.com
—★ Creative Colors International, ☎ (800) 933-2656, www.creativecolorsintl.com

Chimney Sweep

Some experience is needed to clean chimneys, which makes a franchise chimney-cleaning business a good choice for entrepreneurs without experience because training is provided when you purchase the franchise, as well as the necessary tools and equipment. The Chimney Safety Institute of America and the National Chimney Sweep Guild provide chimney sweep training. If you do elect to work independently you will need to purchase cleaning equipment such as ladders, roof jacks, and flue brushes, but these items are readily available at large centers and online, and are relatively inexpensive. In addition to experience and tools, another prerequisite is that you have no fear of heights, as much of your time working will be spent on rooftops and ladders. The average chimney will take one to two hours to clean and rates are in the $75 to $150 range per chimney cleaned, with discounts for houses with multiple chimneys. If you also have experience in masonry repairs, you can offer services such as repointing, brick sealing, installation of new liners, chimney rebuilding, and new pots and crowns to boost revenues and profits.

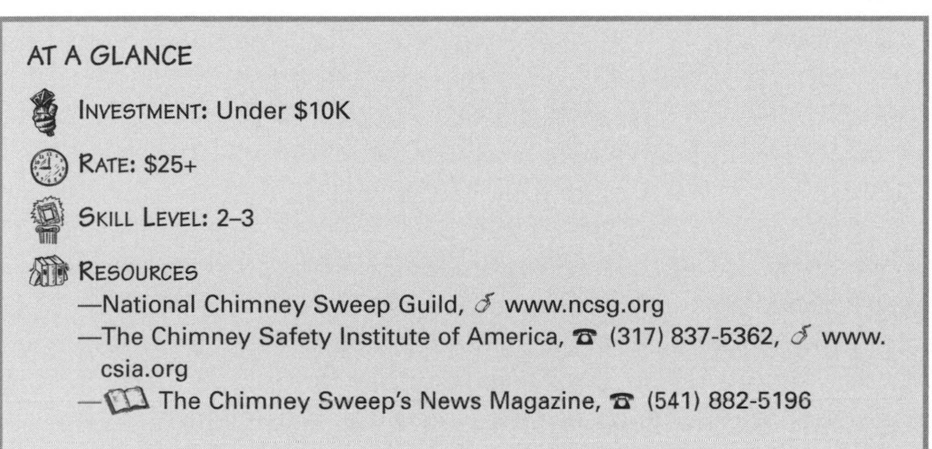
AT A GLANCE

INVESTMENT: Under $10K

RATE: $25+

SKILL LEVEL: 2–3

RESOURCES
—National Chimney Sweep Guild, www.ncsg.org
—The Chimney Safety Institute of America, (317) 837-5362, www.csia.org
—The Chimney Sweep's News Magazine, (541) 882-5196

Bug Screen Repair

Starting a screen repair and replacement business could put you on the road to riches, especially in light of the recent mosquito-borne West Nile virus and ever-present threat of killer bees. You will need basic tools and materials to get started—a miter saw, screen rollers, various screen replacement parts, and a selection of fiberglass and aluminum screen rolls in various widths. The business can be operated from an enclosed trailer or van to provide protection from inclement weather for onsite screen repairs and installations. Or, you can operate from a homebased workshop and pick up the screens, repair them at the workshop, and return to install them. To market your service, contact companies and individuals who require screen repairs and replacements on a regular basis. These include residential and commercial property management firms, condominium strata corporations, apartment complexes, government institutions, and renovation contractors. The profit potential is excellent, as there is limited competition and consumer demand for screen repairs and replacements is high.

AT A GLANCE

INVESTMENT: Under $10K

RATE: $25+

SKILL LEVEL: 1–2

RESOURCES

—★ The Screen Machine, ☎ (877) 505-1985, www.screenmachine.com

—★ The Screenmobile, ☎ (866) 540-5800, www.screenmobile.com

Handyperson

Cash in on the multibillion-dollar home repair industry by starting your own handyperson service. Handyperson services require little explanation about the business opportunity. The main requirement for starting such a service is, of course, that you are handy with tools, have the required tools and equipment, and have a good understanding and working knowledge of many trades—painting, carpentry, flooring, plumbing—basically, that you are a jack-of-all-trades. Currently, handyperson billing rates are in the range of $25 to $40 per hour, plus materials and a markup to cover the costs associated with handling and delivery. The service can be promoted and marketed to both residential and commercial clients through traditional advertising and marketing means such as the Yellow Pages, newspaper advertisements, fliers and door hangers, site and vehicle signage, door knocking, and home-and-garden shows. Repeat business and word-of-mouth referrals will become your main source of new business once you are established, providing you offer clients good value and excellent service.

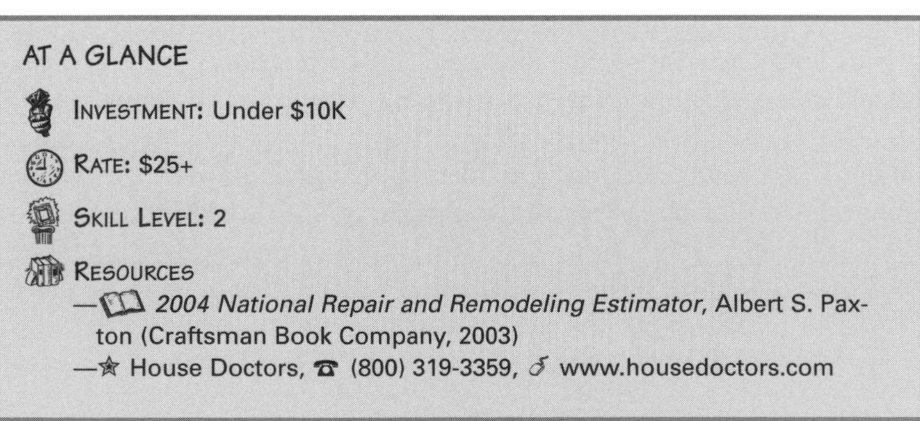
AT A GLANCE

INVESTMENT: Under $10K

RATE: $25+

SKILL LEVEL: 2

RESOURCES

—*2004 National Repair and Remodeling Estimator*, Albert S. Paxton (Craftsman Book Company, 2003)

—★ House Doctors, ☎ (800) 319-3359, www.housedoctors.com

Graffiti Removal

Look anywhere and you're sure to find graffiti—walls, sidewalks, signs, and fences—making a graffiti removal service a very timely and in-demand start-up. Removing graffiti does not require a great deal of work experience. In fact, it can be learned on the job through trial and error. The market is unlimited, largely untapped, and is constantly being renewed so there is lots of upside growth potential. The only equipment required is a portable pressure washer (water) and perhaps a portable sandblaster, but in recent years most graffiti removal services have been getting away from sandblasting because of the potential to damage surfaces. Regardless, both machines can be conveniently mounted on a trailer for easy transportation to and from job sites. Likewise, both can also be rented as needed to help keep initial start-up costs to a minimum, and then purchased from the profits the business earns. One marketing option is to visit businesses that are often the victims of graffiti vandalism and offer them a low-cost graffiti-removal solution. Provide clients with a monthly graffiti-removal option in which, for a fixed monthly fee, you will check in once a week to see if there is any new graffiti to be removed. If new graffiti is present, you simply remove it. If no graffiti is present, you move on to your next client's location. In addition to business owners, graffiti removal services can also be marketed to schools, libraries, homeowners, and just about any other location with graffiti problems.

AT A GLANCE

INVESTMENT: Under $10K

RATE: $25+

SKILL LEVEL: 1–2

RESOURCES

Graffiti Genies, graffiti-removal products and training, ☎ (604) 516-6136, www.graffitigenies.com

—★ Off The Wall Graffiti, ☎ (512) 328-7776, www.graffiti-removal.com

Duct Cleaning

Furnace and air-conditioning duct cleaning have become routine maintenance practices for many homeowners, small businesses, and building owners. Duct cleaning is relatively inexpensive and the health benefits are numerous, as anyone suffering from allergies or other breathing-related health ailments will attest to. You will need to purchase the required equipment, as well as training if you have no previous duct-cleaning experience. Contact the National Air Duct Cleaners Association at the web site listed below to inquire about training courses in your area. In addition to utilizing classified advertising and Yellow Pages advertising, also market your services by building relationships with businesses and individuals who can use your service or can refer their clients to your service. These include property managers, building contractors, realtors, commercial cleaners, and residential cleaners. Duct-cleaning rates vary, depending on the job and access, but average in the range of $50 to $80 per hour.

AT A GLANCE

INVESTMENT: Over $25K

RATE: $50+

SKILL LEVEL: 2–3

RESOURCES
—★ Ductbusters, ☎ (800) 786-3828, www.ductbusters.com
—Goodway, duct-cleaning equipment, ☎ (800) 333-7467, www.goodway.com
—National Air Duct Cleaners Association, www.nadca.com

Blind Cleaning

Whether wood, plastic, or fabric, window blinds now rank as the most popular window-covering choice for home and office owners across North America. So with millions of window blinds hanging out there, all needing to be cleaned regularly, it makes a lot of sense to cash in by starting a blind-cleaning service. The most efficient way to clean window blinds is by using ultrasonic cleaning equipment, which is basically a tank filled with cleaning solution that gently cleans blinds ultrasonically with no risk of damaging the blinds' materials or operational parts. This equipment can be mounted on a van or trailer so you can offer blind-cleaning services on site, or you can set up the cleaning equipment at home or in a warehouse space and offer clients free pickup, delivery, and reinstallation after the blinds have been cleaned. In addition to homeowners, be sure to aim your marketing efforts at winning blind-cleaning contracts from schools, hospitals, hotels, institutions, corporations, and others with large numbers of window blinds.

AT A GLANCE

 **INVESTMENT:** Under $10K

 **RATE:** $25+

 **SKILL LEVEL:** 1

 **RESOURCES**

—★ Hang & Shine Ultrasonics Inc., ☎ (800) 976-6427, www.dirtyblinds.com

—S. Morantz Inc., manufacturer of ultrasonic blind-cleaning equipment, ☎ (800) 695-4522, www.morantz.com

---

Pest and Critter Control

You can cash in on the booming pest management and critter control industry by starting your own pest-control service. You'll be in good company, considering that there are an estimated 65,000 people working in the pest-control industry in the United States. Specialize in ridding homes, offices, and commercial buildings of pesky insects such as termites, roaches, spiders, ants, and bees. Or concentrate on ridding your clients' properties of larger critters such as squirrels, snakes, rats, mice, and raccoons. For the more ecologically-minded client, some services even provide live catch-and-release services for the removal of raccoons, snakes, skunks, and squirrels. In short, pest-control services locate, identify, destroy, catch, control, or repel pests by applying chemicals, setting traps, installing physical barriers, or by manual removal techniques. Keep in mind that laws in both Canada and the United States require training and licensing before you can offer customers pest-control services, especially those involving the application of pesticides. You can contact the associations listed below for information regarding training and licensing in your area.

AT A GLANCE

INVESTMENT: Under $25K

RATE: $25+

SKILL LEVEL: 4

 RESOURCES

—Canadian Pest Management Association, ☎ (877) 595-0504, www.pestcontrolcanada.com
—★ Critter Control, ☎ (231) 947-2400, www.crittercontrol.com
—National Pest Management Association, ☎ (703) 573-8330, www.pestworld.org
—Pest Control Portal, industry information portal, www.pestcontrolportal.com

Residential Cleaning

Residential cleaning is a multibillion-dollar industry, and getting your piece of this very lucrative pie is very easy. Cleaning requires no special skills, start-up investment and equipment costs are minimal, and there is no shortage of work. Residential cleaners perform duties such as dusting, vacuuming, washing surfaces, mopping floors, polishing mirrors and fixtures, and some also offer interior window washing. For the most part, residential cleaners supply all cleaning products and equipment needed to perform these services. So you will need to invest in things like a vacuum cleaner, buckets, dusters, mops, rags, cleaning solvents, a stepladder, and reliable transportation. Ideally, you want to land customers who will be using the service on a regular basis—daily, weekly, monthly, instead of only occasionally. Market your services with flier and coupon drops, as well as by running classified advertisements in your local newspaper. Referrals will also make up a large percentage of new business, so quality and excellent customer service are musts. Expanding the business requires no more than subcontracting cleaners with their own transportation to work on an hourly rate or an income-splitting basis. On average, most cleaners charge in the vicinity of \$15 to \$25 per hour.

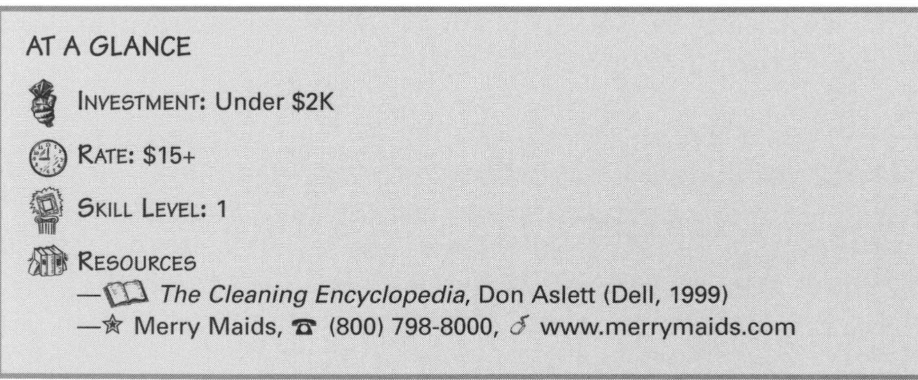
AT A GLANCE

INVESTMENT: Under \$2K

RATE: \$15+

SKILL LEVEL: 1

RESOURCES

—*The Cleaning Encyclopedia*, Don Aslett (Dell, 1999)
—★ Merry Maids, ☎ (800) 798-8000, www.merrymaids.com

Commercial Cleaning

Like residential cleaning, commercial cleaning is a booming industry, generating billions in sales annually. Commercial cleaners basically perform the same services as residential cleaners—dusting, vacuuming, and polishing, but on a larger scale and with the addition of services like replenishing paper products and soaps, washing windows, stripping floors, and emptying trash and recycling receptacles. The only real downside to commercial cleaning is that in most cases the cleaning must be performed nights and/or on weekends after the business or office closes, which is actually a positive for people who want to keep their day jobs but still be able to earn extra money working nights and weekends. Rates generally tend to be higher for commercial cleaning than residential cleaning, in the range of $20 to $30 per hour, plus paper and other special supplies. Rates are typically higher because equipment costs are more, work such as floor stripping and waxing is more specialized, and once again, the nighttime aspect of the work enables you to charge a premium. Landing contracts will require you to get out and knock on doors. Visit businesses in your community to learn if they need cleaning services, or when their cleaning services contracts come up for renewal. You can also buy commercial cleaning contracts, which is a common practice in this industry but expect to pay about three to five times the monthly value. For instance, if you want to earn $1,500 per month, this will cost you in the range of $4,500 to $7,500.

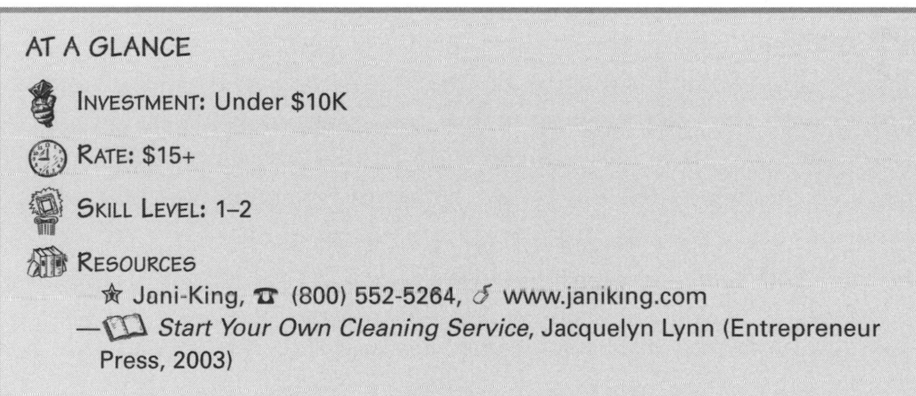

AT A GLANCE

INVESTMENT: Under $10K

RATE: $15+

SKILL LEVEL: 1–2

RESOURCES

★ Jani-King, ☎ (800) 552-5264, www.janiking.com

— *Start Your Own Cleaning Service*, Jacquelyn Lynn (Entrepreneur Press, 2003)

Rubbish Removal

It isn't pretty, but trash could put you on the road to riches. A secondhand truck or trailer, shovels, rakes, and a few garbage cans are all you need to start a rubbish removal service. Rubbish removal is charged by the hour, truckload, or by a quote before removing the junk. If you can offer home and business owners fast and convenient rubbish removal services at competitive prices, I guarantee that word-of-mouth advertising will generate more work than you can handle. Be sure to build alliances with people who can refer your business to their customers and clients; these referral brokers include real estate agents, residential and commercial cleaners, and home service companies such as carpet cleaners, contractors, and property managers. If you're looking for a low-cost business start-up that requires little in the way of skills or experience, a rubbish removal service is one of the better choices. After expenses and dumping fees, you should have no problem earning in the range of $25 to $40 per hour.

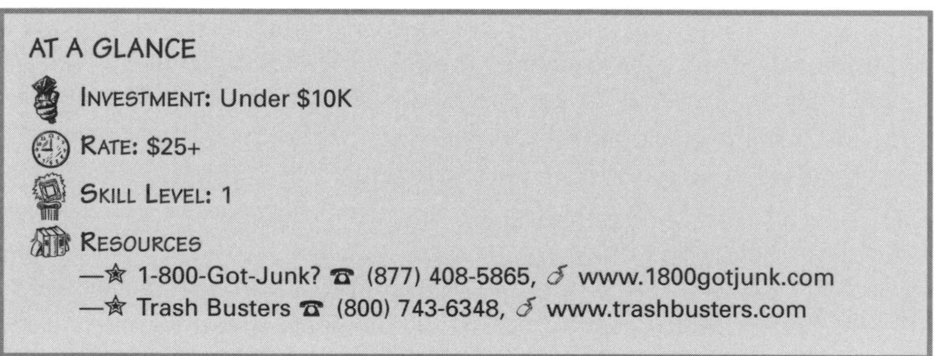

AT A GLANCE

INVESTMENT: Under $10K

RATE: $25+

SKILL LEVEL: 1

RESOURCES

—★ 1-800-Got-Junk? ☎ (877) 408-5865, www.1800gotjunk.com

—★ Trash Busters ☎ (800) 743-6348, www.trashbusters.com

Power Washing

There are hundreds of items that can be cleaned using power-washing equipment, including driveways, patios, parking lots, recreational vehicles, mobile homes, cars, boats, store signs, awnings, metal roofs, trailers, and construction and farm equipment. Not only is there a nearly unlimited number of items to pressure wash, rates are also excellent and it is not uncommon to earn as much as $400 per day pressure washing. The only fixed costs to operate the service are for a telephone, liability insurance, transportation, the occasional equipment repair, and a bit of initial advertising until repeat business and referrals kick in and make up the bulk of your work. A helpful hint to keep in mind as you start marketing is to aim your efforts at clients who will become repeat clients. These include companies with fleet vehicles and retailers who want to keep their storefronts spic-and-span. It costs much more to find 100 clients and service each client one time than to find one client and service that client 100 times. You can also visit marinas, trailer parks, and RV campgrounds on weekends and offer your power-washing services to owners at reduced rates because you can make up the difference (and more) through volume power washing.

> **AT A GLANCE**
>
> **Investment:** Under $10K
>
> **Rate:** $25+
>
> **Skill Level:** 1
>
> **Resources**
>
> —E-Power Wash, industry information portal, www.epowerwash.com
>
> —★ Sparkle Wash International, ☎ (800) 321-0770, www.sparklewash.com

Window Washing

Window washing is perhaps the granddaddy of all service businesses, especially when you consider all the advantages such as steady demand, low start-up investment and operating overhead, no special skills or business experience required, flexible operating hours, fantastic profit potential, and unlimited growth opportunities. Promoting a window-washing service is just as easy as starting one. Print and distribute fliers that describe your service, run low-cost classified ads under Home Services in your community newspaper, network with potential customers at business association functions and social events, and piggyback your service with existing service providers such as house painters, window installers, property managers, real estate agents, and renovation contractors. You will need to purchase equipment such as ladders, buckets, and squeegees, as well as suitable transportation, but these can be bought inexpensively. Most window washers specialize in residential and/or low-rise commercial establishments fewer than three stories. High-rise window cleaning is much more lucrative, but specialized training is required to do this work, and it is best left to professionals with the training and experience. Offering clients complementary services such as rain gutter cleaning and pressure washing is a great way to increase profits.

 RESOURCES

—ABC Window Cleaning Supply, window-cleaning products and equipment, ☎ (800) 989-4003, www.window-cleaning-supply.com

—★ Window Genie, ☎ (800) 700-0022, www.windowgenie.com

Snow and Ice Removal Service

Depending on your investment budget and on how much money you want to earn, there are a few methods for removing snow and ice during winter months. The most expensive of these is a snowplow and salt spreader mounted on a four-wheel-drive truck. This option will set you back about $2,000 to $3,000 for equipment, less the cost of the truck, but it gives you the potential to do the most work and earn the most income. The second option is a self-propelled snow blower as well as a manual salt spreader for de-icing. Both pieces of equipment are walk-behind models and require a truck or trailer to move from job to job. This is a good option for people wanting to earn extra money on nights and weekends. The third option is the good old Armstrong method. Armed with nothing more than a $20 shovel and bag of salt, you can remove snow and ice. Regardless of the method you choose, snow removal and surface de-icing is an easy service to start, operate, and sell. And even though this is a seasonal and weather-dependent opportunity, it is not uncommon for plow operators to earn $1,000 a day or more when the snow blows.

AT A GLANCE

 INVESTMENT: Under $1K–under $10K

 RATE: $15+

 SKILL LEVEL: 1

 RESOURCES

—★ Clintar Groundskeeping Services, ☎ (800) 361-3542, www.clintar.com

—Plows Unlimited, snowplow and snow removal equipment, ☎ (877) 214-7569, www.plowsunlimited.com

—The Boss Snowplow, snowplow and snow removal equipment, ☎ (800) 286-4155, www.bossplow.com

Yard Maintenance

Offer clients a host of yard and property cleanup and maintenance services by starting a general yard maintenance service. Cut grass, provide rubbish removal, trim trees and hedges, and offer lawn aeration and garden tilling. Concentrate your marketing efforts on securing customers who are prepared to sign up for regular service, and offer financial incentives to persuade them to do so. Most of the equipment needed to operate a yard maintenance service is relatively inexpensive; to keep start-up costs to a minimum, equipment such as mowers, tillers, leaf blowers, and weed eaters can be purchased secondhand or rented on a as-needed basis until you have earned enough to buy them. On average, you should have no problem charging in the range of $15 to $30 per hour. Providing you offer great service, and because yard maintenance can be hard work, there should be no shortage of homeowners prepared to part with a few dollars per month to have their yards professionally maintained and kept in tiptop condition. If you will be operating in northern climates, offer leaf raking in the fall and snow clearing and de-icing services in the winter for a year-round operation.

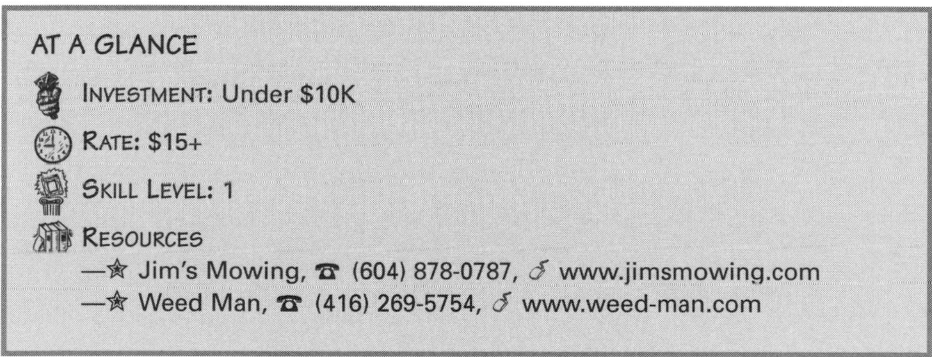

AT A GLANCE

INVESTMENT: Under $10K

RATE: $15+

SKILL LEVEL: 1

RESOURCES

—☆ Jim's Mowing, ☎ (604) 878-0787, www.jimsmowing.com

—☆ Weed Man, ☎ (416) 269-5754, www.weed-man.com

Small-Spaces Landscaping

Condominiums, townhouses, and lofts are being constructed in record-breaking numbers across the United States and Canada, and this building boom has spawned an entirely new and super red-hot industry which is called small-spaces landscaping. Where are these small spaces? They include sundecks, patios, decks, balconies, rooftops, and courtyards for both residential and commercial locations such as professional offices and restaurants. Home and property owners want to have beautiful outdoor spaces to enjoy, but when your outdoor space is limited to a ten-by-ten foot balcony, most don't know how to combine both function and flowers in such a small space. That's when they call in a professional small-spaces landscaper. Capitalizing on your knowledge of plants, flowers, and design, you can offer customers a specialized landscaping service that transforms their small outdoor space into a lush, yet still highly functional living space. Planters, gazebos, seats, water features, flowers, ivy, sunshades, heaters, and barbeques are just a few of the elements you will have to work with and plan for. Income is earned in three ways. One, planning and installing the small-space garden; two, purchasing products wholesale that will be used in the garden and selling them to clients at retail; and three, ongoing monthly fees to maintain and upgrade the garden area as required.

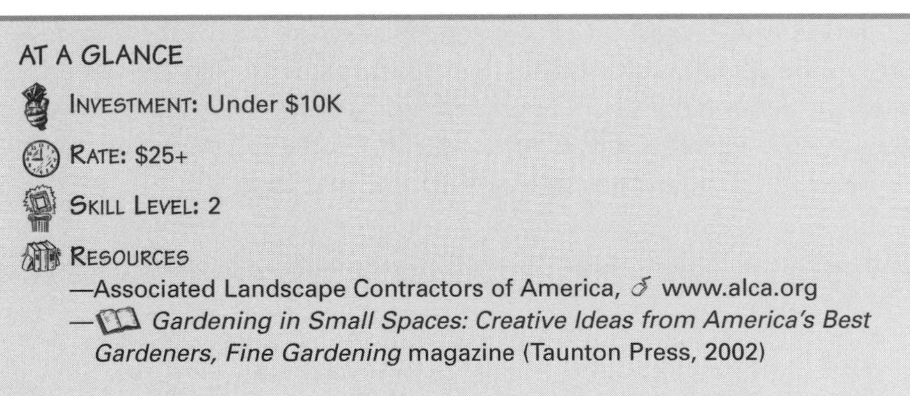

AT A GLANCE

INVESTMENT: Under $10K

RATE: $25+

SKILL LEVEL: 2

RESOURCES

—Associated Landscape Contractors of America, www.alca.org

—*Gardening in Small Spaces: Creative Ideas from America's Best Gardeners, Fine Gardening* magazine (Taunton Press, 2002)

Stump Removal

Cutting down a tree is the easy part—getting rid of the stump is the tough part of the job. And that is why homeowners, landscapers, and tree trimmers will be more than happy to pay you a handsome fee to perform stump-removal services. The fastest and most efficient way to get rid of a tree stump is to grind it out using a stump-grinding machine. Though care is needed to operate stump-grinding machines, they are easy to master nonetheless. These machines are relatively expensive and you will need suitable transportation such as a truck or trailer to move the machine to and from job sites. Stump-removal rates fall in the range of $75 to $300 each, depending on size, so return on investment is quick. Once again, market the service to landscape companies, general contractors, road and sidewalk contractors, tree-trimming services, and by running advertisements in the classifieds section of your community newspaper. This is a great part-time business that can easily generate an extra thousand dollars a month, and much more for ambitious entrepreneurs.

AT A GLANCE

 INVESTMENT: Under $10K

 RATE: $25+

 SKILL LEVEL: 2

 RESOURCES

—Alpine Magnum, stump-grinder manufacturer, ☎ (360) 357-5166, www.alpinemagnum.com

—Rayco, stump-grinder manufacturer, ☎ (800) 392-2386, www.raycomfg.com

---

Awning Cleaning

Many businesses are switching from traditional box signs to commercial awning signs to advertise their businesses and brand their operating locations. All these awnings have one thing in common: they need to be cleaned on a regular basis to project a good corporate image for the businesses they are promoting. This opens up a great opportunity for the enterprising entrepreneur to cash in and profit by starting an awning-cleaning service. The best way to get customers is simply to put on some comfortable walking shoes and start knocking on doors. Visit retailers and offices in your area that have awning signs and pitch your service. Remind them about the benefits of good first impressions. This may seem an old-fashioned and time-consuming way to promote the business. However, if you set a goal of talking with ten potential customers a day and can close two of these presentations, you will then have 40 new clients in a month's time, and be well on your way to establishing a solid and profitable business.

AT A GLANCE

 INVESTMENT: Under $10K

 RATE: $25+

 SKILL LEVEL: 1

 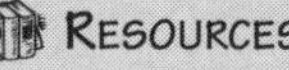 RESOURCES

—Awning Cleaning Source, products and training, www.awningcleaningsource.com

—National Register of Professional Awning Cleaners, www.awningpro.com

Line Painting

Help give your fellow humans the directions they need by starting a line-painting service. Line painting is needed in parking lots to delineate spaces, show handicap zones, directions, and reserved parking areas. Line painting is also needed for sports fields and running tracks, temporary marking for special events, and for interior uses such as marking zones and directions in warehouses and factories. Walk-behind paint-striping machines for both pavement- and turf-marking are available at a relatively modest cost, in the range of $1,500 to $5,000, along with reusable stencils for marking. You will also need a truck or trailer to move the equipment from job site to job site and a power washer or blower to clean surfaces before applying traffic paint. In all, an initial investment of less than $10,000 will get you started. Customers include commercial property owners, property managers, developers, and warehouse owners, as well as sports field and running track contractors, paving contractors, sports clubs, and schools. This is a great opportunity for anyone wanting to earn in excess of $25 per hour on a full- or part-time basis. Line painting is also an easy skill to learn and the service is always in demand.

AT A GLANCE

 INVESTMENT: Under $10K

 RATE: $25+

 SKILL LEVEL: 1–2

 RESOURCES

—Fast Line Manufacturing, paint-striper equipment and supplies, ☎ (800) 565-1564, www.fastline.net

—Seal Master, paint-striper equipment and supplies, www.sealmaster.net

—Trusco Manufacturing, paint-striper equipment and supplies, ☎ (800) 327-8859, www.truscomfg.com

Litter Pickup

If you are looking for an easy service to sell that requires no special skills or experience, yet still has excellent income potential and a start-up investment of only a few hundred dollars, then a litter pickup service might be just what you've been searching for. Armed with only a rake, shovel, garbage can, and a pair of gloves, you can be cleaning up litter for paying customers in your community. Ideally, these customers will be retailers, professionals, and other business owners who need to project a good business image. Having litter in and around their businesses in parking lots, lawns, flowerbeds, and sidewalks is obviously not the image they want to project. Create a detailed promotional flier outlining services and litter pickup fees and distribute it to retailers, service providers, and professionals with storefronts and parking lots. In exchange for a flat monthly fee, visit customers' business locations daily to pick up any litter lying in close proximity to their shops—sidewalks, entranceways, flowerbeds, lawns, and parking lots—and in no time you will be well on your way to building a profitable business.

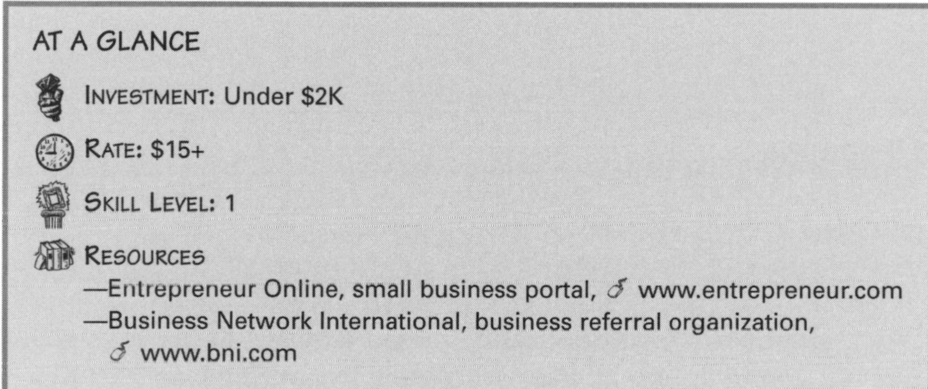
AT A GLANCE

INVESTMENT: Under $2K

RATE: $15+

SKILL LEVEL: 1

RESOURCES
—Entrepreneur Online, small business portal, www.entrepreneur.com
—Business Network International, business referral organization, www.bni.com

Pooper-Scooper Service

Believe it or not, you can make a very comfortable living by starting and operating a doggie pooper-scooper service in your community. In fact, this service has really taken off in the past few years and new pooper-scooper services are popping up daily across the country. This is an easy business to start requiring little investment, no special skills, and minimal equipment to operate. You will need reliable transportation, a cell phone, garbage buckets, shovels, gloves, a good pair of rubber boots, and that's about it. Basically, if you can handle a shovel and plastic bags, and can put up with less than aromatic smells, you're qualified to run a pooper-scooper service. If not, you can still cash in on this booming growth business by marketing and managing the service while hiring others to do the dirty work. Spread the word about your pooper-scooper service by advertising in local newspapers, pinning fliers to bulletin boards, and through dog-related businesses and clubs in the community. Most services charge a flat monthly rate of between $30 and $60 to stop by customers' homes or businesses weekly to clean up their yards, which takes no more than ten minutes per visit.

AT A GLANCE

INVESTMENT: Under $2K

RATE: $15+

SKILL LEVEL: 1

RESOURCES

—American Dog Owners Association, www.adoa.org

—Pooper Scooper, directory of dog waste removal services, www.pooper-scooper.com

—★ Wholly Crap, ☎ (330) 448-1700, www.whollycrap.com

Dog Grooming

Tap into the highly lucrative dog grooming industry by becoming a dog groomer, or as groomers prefer to be called, a *canine cosmetologist*. There are an estimated 30,000,000 pet dogs in North America, and most owners think nothing of spending a bundle on a regular basis to keep their pampered pooches well-groomed. Not all dog groomers are professionally trained and certified. I do recommend, however, that you invest in the training to become a professional dog groomer if this is a service you want to sell. Dog owners are a conscientious bunch and most do not like to leave their best friends in the care of the inexperienced. Both of the associations listed below offer dog grooming training workshops and exams across the United States and Canada to become a Certified Master Groomer. This is a service you can easily operate from a homebased grooming studio, or a commercial storefront. You might even want to consider a mobile operation so you can service clients who don't have transportation, or who have dogs with health problems that keep them from traveling. The profit potential is excellent, as many groomers report earnings in the range of $50,000 after expenses.

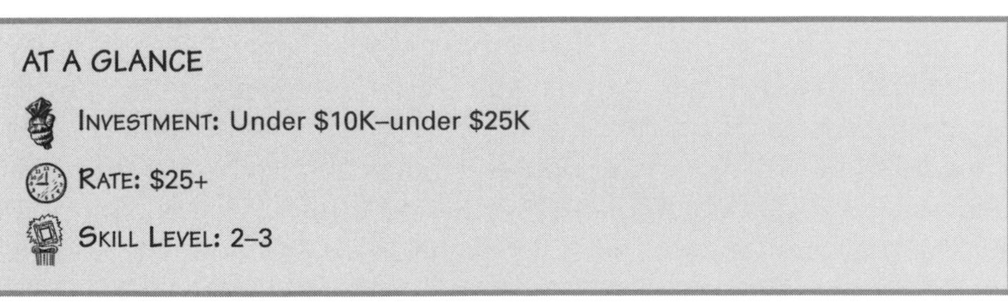

AT A GLANCE

INVESTMENT: Under $10K–under $25K

RATE: $25+

SKILL LEVEL: 2–3

RESOURCES

—*From Problems to Profits: The Madson Management System for Pet Grooming Businesses*, Madeline Bright Ogle (Madson Group, 1997)

—National Dog Groomers Association of America, ☎ (724) 962-2711, www.nationaldoggroomers.com

—★ Wag'n Tails, ☎ (631) 513-0304, www.wagntails.com

—Western Professional Dog Groomers Association, ☎ (604) 476-6637, www.wags.ca

---

Dog Walker

A dog-walking service is perfectly suited for people with time, patience, and a love for dogs. Best of all, with an investment of just a few hundred dollars you can be up and running your own full- or part-time dog-walking service in no time. There are various styles of multilead dog walking collars and leashes available that will allow three or more dogs to be walked at the same time without becoming tangled in the leash. Acquiring this equipment is important because it will reduce frustration and enable you to walk many dogs at the same time, which in turn will increase revenues and profits. Design a promotional flier detailing your dog-walking service and qualifications, and distribute the fliers to businesses that are frequented by dog owners, such as grooming locations, kennels, pet food stores, animal shelters, and community centers. Once word is out about your dog-walking service, it should not take long to establish a base of 20 or 30 regular clients. Dog-walking rates are in the range of $6 to $12 per hour, per dog. Again, walking multiple dogs at a time gives you your best income and profit potential.

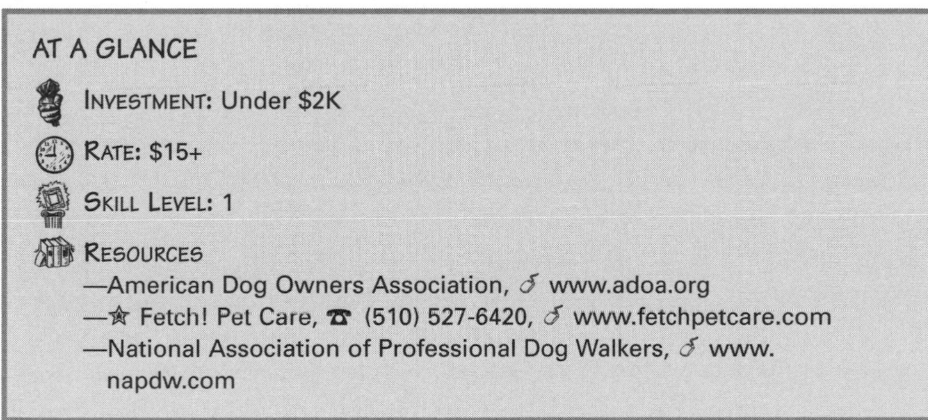

AT A GLANCE

INVESTMENT: Under $2K

RATE: $15+

SKILL LEVEL: 1

RESOURCES

—American Dog Owners Association, www.adoa.org

—★ Fetch! Pet Care, ☎ (510) 527-6420, www.fetchpetcare.com

—National Association of Professional Dog Walkers, www.napdw.com

Pet Sitting

Lots of people have pets that cannot be boarded or left with friends or family when the need arises—pets with chronic health conditions, exotic pets that are difficult to take care of, for example. Likewise, many people prefer to have their dogs, cats, and other pets in the safety and familiar surroundings of home as opposed to an unfamiliar boarding environment. When these pet owners want or need to be away from home there is only one solution available—hire a pet-sitting service to come to their homes and take care of their beloved pets while they are away. If you want to work on a small scale, you can be the pet sitter, but if your intention is to operate full-time with an eye to growth, you will need to hire or contract additional pet sitters. Good candidates for the job include pet-loving retirees and students. Market your pet-sitting services through pet-related businesses in your community such as veterinarians, pet food retailers, dog trainers, dog walkers, and pet-grooming services. Remember, many people also hire pet sitters for short periods of time—a weekend away, a night out, or time off for family events. Therefore, you will need to develop fee schedules for long- and short-term pet-sitting jobs.

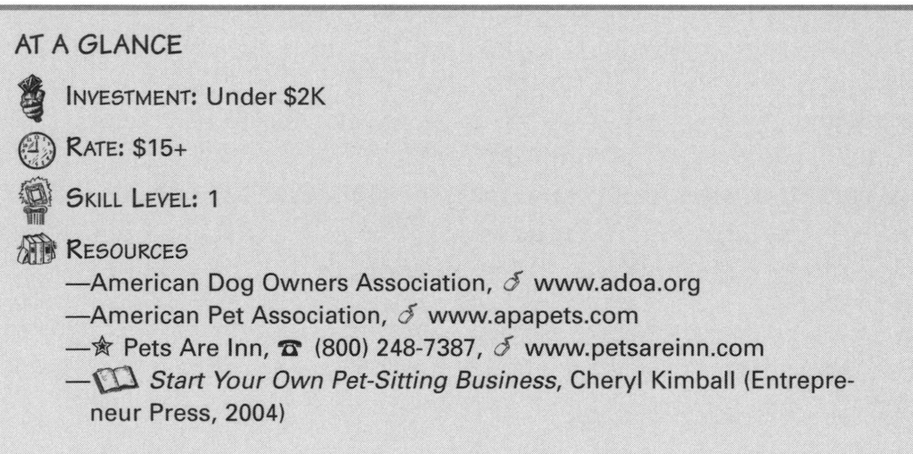

AT A GLANCE

INVESTMENT: Under $2K

RATE: $15+

SKILL LEVEL: 1

RESOURCES

—American Dog Owners Association, www.adoa.org

—American Pet Association, www.apapets.com

—Pets Are Inn, (800) 248-7387, www.petsareinn.com

—*Start Your Own Pet-Sitting Business*, Cheryl Kimball (Entrepreneur Press, 2004)

Doggie Day Care

Day-care facilities for dogs are becoming increasingly popular, especially as more and more caring dog owners are realizing the benefits of leaving their beloved dogs at day care with other dogs instead of at home alone while they are at work. Dogs, like people, are social creatures and need contact with people and other dogs to become well-behaved and confident. However, a doggie day care should not be confused with a kennel, which boards animals for short- and long-term time spans. A doggie day care is strictly a drop off in the morning and pick up in the evening, or anytime during the day, type of operation. If space allows and your neighbors don't mind the barking, you can open at home. A better alternative is to rent commercial warehouse space and convert it into a doggie day spa, complete with water features, fenced outdoor space, and indoor couches to ensure your clients have all the creature comforts they are used to at home. One innovative doggie day-care center in my community recently installed web cams throughout their facility so people at work could log on to the web site and see live footage of their dogs playing with other dogs. Current rates are in the range of $15 to $25 per day, with discounts for weekly service.

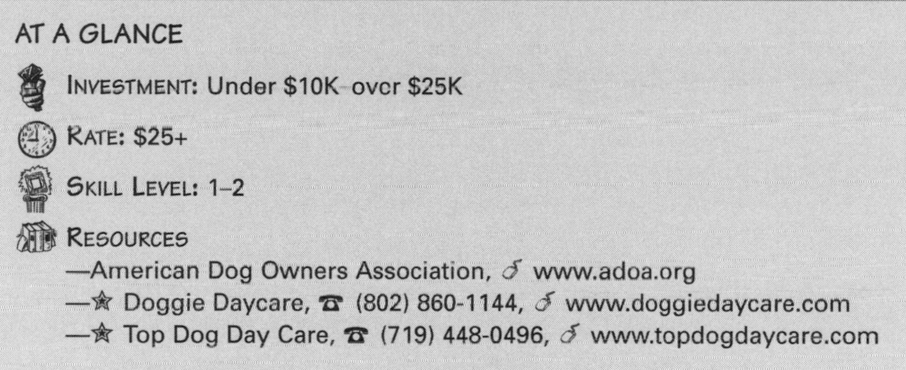

AT A GLANCE

INVESTMENT: Under $10K–over $25K

RATE: $25+

SKILL LEVEL: 1–2

RESOURCES

—American Dog Owners Association, www.adoa.org

—★ Doggie Daycare, (802) 860-1144, www.doggiedaycare.com

—★ Top Dog Day Care, (719) 448-0496, www.topdogdaycare.com

Dog Obedience Training

Dog obedience training is a multimillion-dollar industry, and continues to grow by double digits as more and more dog owners realize the benefits of professional obedience training. Training classes can be held at your home in a one-on-one or group format, or if your home is not suitable you can travel to your customers' homes and train one-on-one. Likewise, you can also strike deals with schools and community centers to hold dog obedience classes on weekends and nights. Many trainers are currently not certified by a recognized association, although that trend is changing. If you are serious about making dog obedience training your career, I strongly suggest that you receive professional training to become an instructor and obtain the required certifications. Not only can certification be used as a powerful marketing tool when persuading people that you are the right trainer for their dog, but having the proper credentials will also mean that you can charge a premium for your services. Current rates for in-home training are in the range of $30 to $50 per hour and many trainers create dog-training packages for their customers, which include a set amount of training classes and course materials in print and video formats.

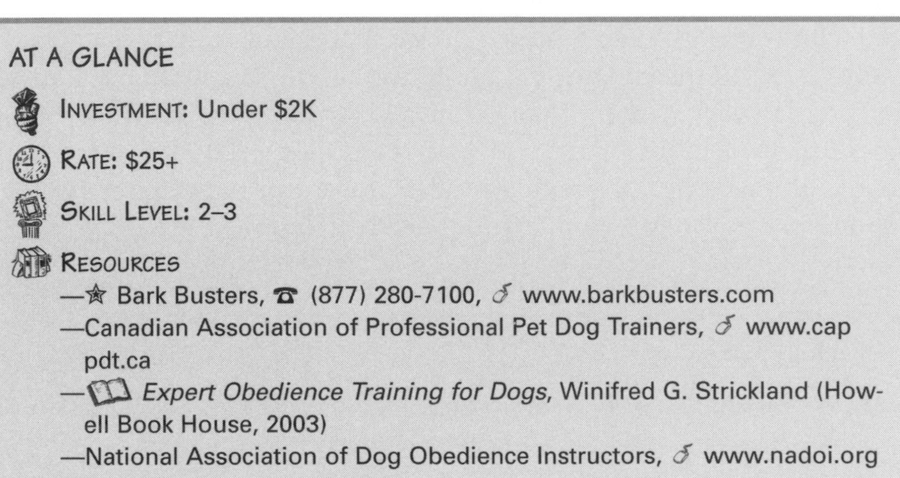

AT A GLANCE

INVESTMENT: Under $2K

RATE: $25+

SKILL LEVEL: 2–3

RESOURCES

—★ Bark Busters, ☎ (877) 280-7100, www.barkbusters.com
—Canadian Association of Professional Pet Dog Trainers, www.cappdt.ca
—*Expert Obedience Training for Dogs*, Winifred G. Strickland (Howell Book House, 2003)
—National Association of Dog Obedience Instructors, www.nadoi.org

Pet Photography

As an animal lover, I cannot imagine a business that would be more fun and rewarding than operating a pet photography service. Unfortunately, I am not a very good photographer, but if you are and you love pets, then what are you waiting for? Start a pet photography service! Owners of dogs, cats, reptiles, horses, champion livestock, birds, and even fish can all be potential customers. Full-time or part-time, operate the service on a mobile basis, from a homebased studio, or from pet shops, or combine all to cover all the bases. Making the experience fun for pets and their owners will also go a long way toward securing repeat business and a ton of referrals, so liven things up with pet costumes, themed backdrops, and by offering pet videotaping services, complete with music, titles, and special effects. Likewise, to boost profit potential also offer a wide assortment of products that customers can have their pets' photographic images transferred onto—key tags, greeting cards, calendars, mugs, hats, T-shirts, sports bags, and bumper stickers.

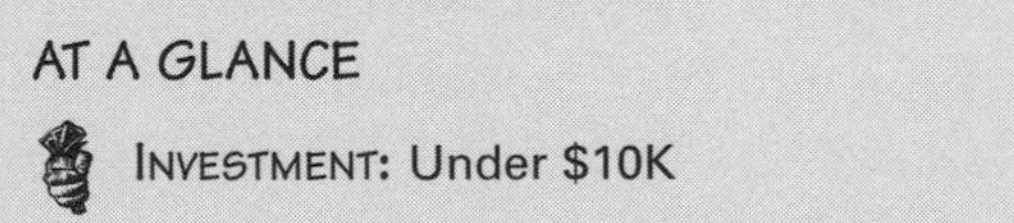

AT A GLANCE

INVESTMENT: Under $10K

 RATE: $25+

 SKILL LEVEL: 2–3

RESOURCES
—American Dog Owners Association, www.adoa.org
—American Pet Association, www.apapets.com
—★ The Visual Image, ☎ (800) 344-0323, www.thevisualimageinc.com

Portrait Photography

Calling all hobby photographers! Why not profit from your skills by starting a portrait photography service? As with pet photography, you can work at it full-time or part-time and operate the service on a mobile basis by going to your client's home, office, or business, or from a homebased studio requiring clients to come to you. Also, like pet photography, you can easily increase profits by simply offering to place images on a wide variety of products including greeting cards, calendars, mugs, and T-shirts. Photo greeting cards and calendars are especially popular. Promote the business by utilizing print media such as fliers, newspaper ads, and Yellow Pages advertisements, as well as by working with local retailers who will allow you to set up a weekend portrait studio in their location on a revenue-splitting basis. Also do not overlook potential clients at sports clubs, charity organizations, social clubs, and corporations, as most put together an annual yearbook featuring photographs of employees, members, and volunteers.

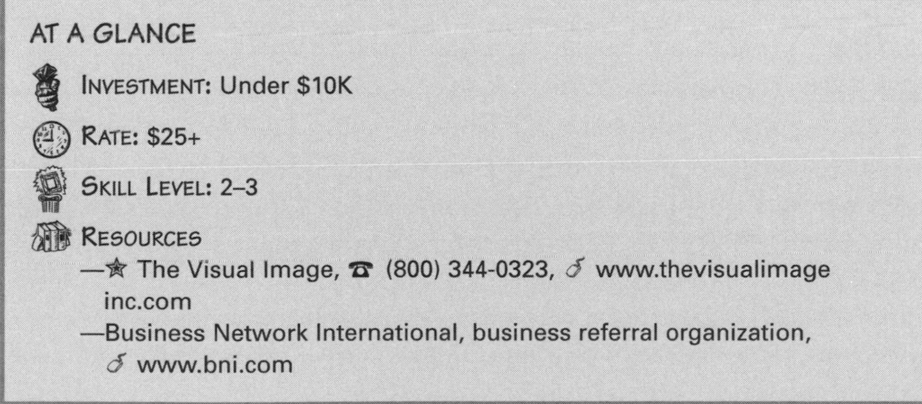
AT A GLANCE

INVESTMENT: Under $10K

RATE: $25+

SKILL LEVEL: 2–3

RESOURCES
—★ The Visual Image, ☎ (800) 344-0323, www.thevisualimageinc.com
—Business Network International, business referral organization, www.bni.com

Freelance Photography

There are two very good reasons why the internet has breathed new life into the freelance photography industry. First, using e-mail, it is now very easy to send pictures to publishers, editors, copywriters, marketers, and designers all around the globe in a matter of moments. Second, billions of photographic images are needed to fill the now more than four billion (and climbing) web pages. In addition to the internet, there are millions of print publications, media companies, retailers, marketers, organizations, government agencies, and others who need new photographs every day to add meaning to newspapers, newsletters, magazines, brochures, catalogs, and presentations. Needless to say, people with fantastic photographic skills have the opportunity to earn a great living taking and selling photographs. You can contract with publishers, or post your photos on any one of the many stock photography services online. People browse the selection and purchase photographic images that they need. You are paid a one-time fee, or a royalty each time the image is downloaded, depending on your agreement with the image broker.

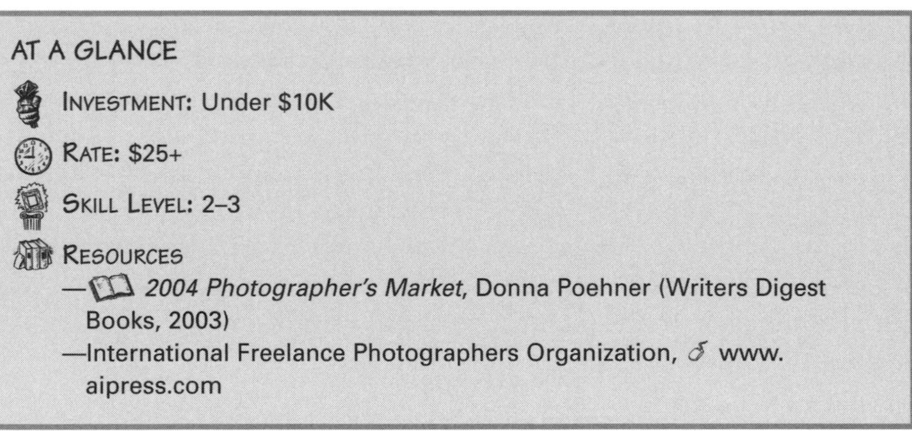

AT A GLANCE

INVESTMENT: Under $10K

RATE: $25+

SKILL LEVEL: 2–3

RESOURCES

—*2004 Photographer's Market*, Donna Poehner (Writers Digest Books, 2003)

—International Freelance Photographers Organization, www.aipress.com

Aerial Photography

Aerial photography equipment is available in various styles, including telescopic aluminum masts that can be outfitted with a camera and extended to heights reaching over 100 feet. There are also helium-filled blimps available ranging in size from 5 feet to 25 feet, that can be outfitted with cameras that reach heights of up to 1,000 feet. The blimps are safely operated from the ground by a tether line or remote control. Surprisingly, the blimp option is not very expensive. Good-quality blimps, complete with photographic gear and a transportation trailer, can be purchased new for less than $10,000, or up to as much as $25,000. Regardless of whether you choose to use a telescopic mast or a helium blimp, both can be outfitted with film or digital still or video cameras. Potential clients include government agencies, homeowners, property developers, corporations, marinas, campgrounds, amusement parks, golf courses, outdoor-event organizers, mining and forestry sites, and sporting-event organizers—basically, any person or business that wants or needs aerial photographs of his or her home, building, event, or property. It takes a bit of learning to operate the equipment, but the manufacturers listed below do provide basic training. Rates are excellent because this is a highly specialized niche service.

 INVESTMENT: Under $25K

 RATE: $50+

 SKILL LEVEL: 2–3

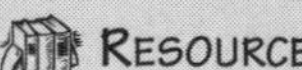

—Altafoto Manufacturing, aerial photography equipment manufacturer, www.altafoto.com

—Southern Balloon Works, aerial photography equipment manufacturer, (800) 348-4903, www.southernballoonworks.com

Vacation Property Rental Agent

If you live in a busy tourist area, there is probably a good chance that you can start and flourish by operating a vacation property rental agency. It is not uncommon for people to purchase vacation homes and condominiums in hopes that for part or all of the year they will be able to rent them to tourists to help offset the costs of financing, maintenance, taxes, insurance, and utilities. Unfortunately, rental income often fails to materialize, as the property owners do not understand how much time and work is involved in renting the properties—marketing, booking, cleaning, repairs, and lots more. Not to mention that most owners are sometimes hundreds—if not thousands—of miles away. As a result, many vacation properties sit vacant when not being used by the owners. This creates a terrific opportunity to rent these properties for the owners on a revenue-splitting basis. In addition to marketing and renting the properties, you will also be responsible for cleaning and light maintenance to ensure that they stay in tiptop condition and attract top dollar for rental. Start small, representing one or two vacation property owners, and run the service from home. As the business grows, so too can your time commitment until you are at the point of operating a profitable full-time going business concern. The same business concept can also be applied to recreational vehicles and boats, if they are your interests.

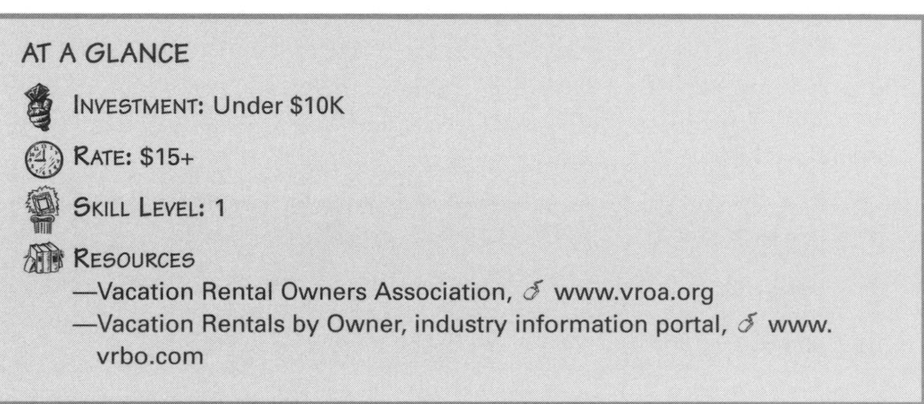
AT A GLANCE

INVESTMENT: Under $10K

RATE: $15+

SKILL LEVEL: 1

RESOURCES
—Vacation Rental Owners Association, www.vroa.org
—Vacation Rentals by Owner, industry information portal, www.vrbo.com

Apartment and House-Finder Service

Finding a new home or apartment to rent can be a very time-consuming and daunting task. That's why many people needing to rent a home enlist the services of a professional apartment and house-finder service. The service can be operated from home and on the web, or you can rent an office location for client visits, as well as build a web site to feature available properties for rent. This business is competitive. You might want to consider specializing in one or more of the following types of rentals: roommate listings, short-term furnished and unfurnished accommodations, long-term furnished and unfurnished accommodations, executive accommodations, rentals that allow pets, student housing, vacation properties, or niche properties such as penthouses only, parking stalls, floating accommodations, or artist lofts. You also have a couple of options in terms of fees. You can charge renters a fee to find the right place to suit their needs. Or you can charge the landlord or building owner a fee to list his or her properties with your service.

AT A GLANCE

INVESTMENT: Under $10K

RATE: $15+

 **SKILL LEVEL:** 1

 **RESOURCES**

—American Association of Small Property Owners, www.aaspo.org
—Building Owners and Managers Association of Canada, www.bomacanada.org
—National Apartment Association, www.naahq.org
—National Property Managers Association, www.npma.org

House Sitting

Who might need a house sitter? Surprisingly, quite a few people, including people going on vacations lasting longer than a week, traveling business owners and executives, people whose homes are being renovated and who don't want to be there but still want their home to be occupied for security reasons, just to name a few. House sitters not only provide peace of mind and security, but they also look after watering the plants and lawn, feeding the cat, collecting mail, light housecleaning duties, and taking care of any emergency situations that may arise while the homeowner is away, such as calling in a plumber if a pipe bursts. The next logical question is, Who would house sit? Once again, surprisingly there are quite a few people interested in house-sitting positions, including students, singles, retirees, or someone looking for a change of pace. You have a couple of options for how you establish a house-sitting service. First, you can operate as a referral service, bringing together people wanting house-sitting services and those who want to house sit. Second, you can employ house sitters on an on-call basis and assign them to jobs as they become available. Increasing revenues can be as easy as adding additional, but complementary, services like pet sitting, dog walking, baby sitting referrals, and a nanny service.

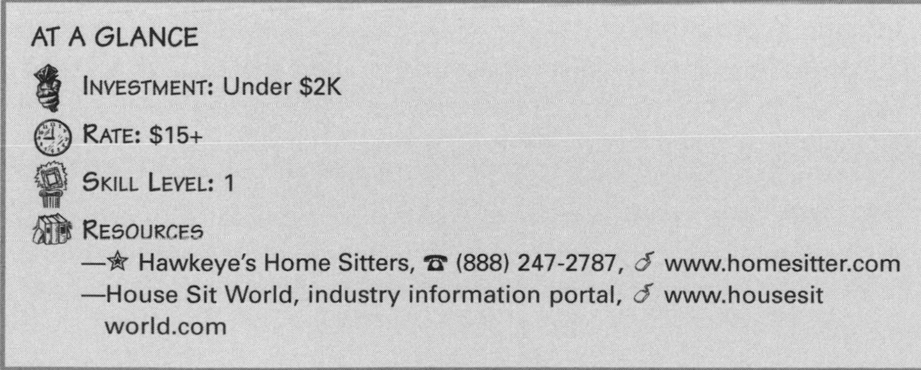

AT A GLANCE

INVESTMENT: Under $2K

RATE: $15+

SKILL LEVEL: 1

RESOURCES

—★ Hawkeye's Home Sitters, ☎ (888) 247-2787, www.homesitter.com
—House Sit World, industry information portal, www.housesitworld.com

Moving Service

Local residential or commercial moving rates are currently in the range of $60 to $90 per hour for two movers and a truck, making this service potentially very profitable, especially if you hire additional movers to handle more work and increase billable hours. Providing clients with additional services and products can also increase revenues and profits. These can include packing and unpacking services, and selling moving supplies such as cardboard boxes, garment boxes, tape, and bubble wrap. The downside to selling moving services is the investment; new trucks and equipment are very costly, and even secondhand trucks and equipment in good condition will set you back thousands. As a result, you need to carefully research the market and plan the business to minimize risk and maximize the potential for success. Additional concerns include liability insurance, workers' insurance, and a moving and storage license because some municipalities require all moving companies, regardless of size, to be licensed.

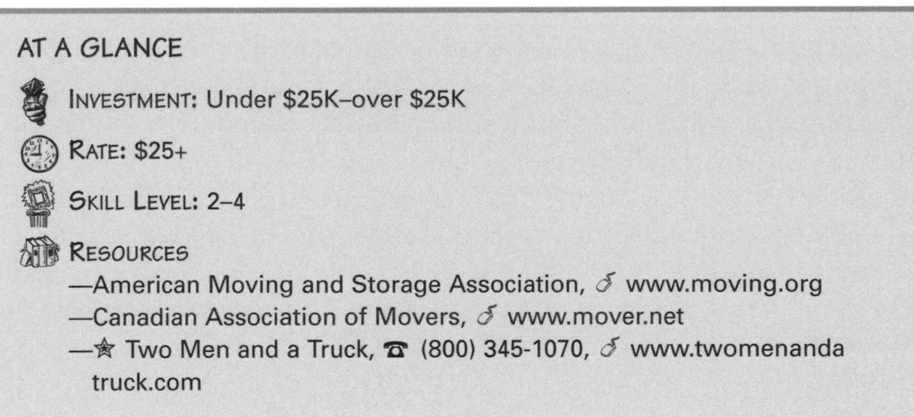
AT A GLANCE

INVESTMENT: Under $25K–over $25K

RATE: $25+

SKILL LEVEL: 2–4

RESOURCES
—American Moving and Storage Association, www.moving.org
—Canadian Association of Movers, www.mover.net
—★ Two Men and a Truck, ☎ (800) 345-1070, www.twomenanda truck.com

Real Estate Appraiser

Real estate appraisers are specialists in estimating the value of land and the structures on that land. Real estate appraisals are commonly required when people buy a home, sell a home, apply for or renew a mortgage, for insurance purposes, to settle estates, and to settle divorce cases. It is the job of the real estate appraiser to prepare a written description of the property, and draw a diagram of the property that shows structures. Appraisers must also verify legal descriptions of the property with county or city records, along with an estimated market value. Fair-market values are based on factors such as property condition, the values of homes in close proximity, and building replacement costs, using building valuation manuals and professional cost estimators. The keys to success in this industry are alliances. You need to build working relationships with other professionals who commonly need, or whose clients need, real estate appraisal services. These professionals include mortgage brokers, bankers, real estate brokers, real estate agents, and real estate lawyers.

AT A GLANCE

INVESTMENT: Under $25K

RATE: $50+

SKILL LEVEL: 4

RESOURCES

—Appraisal Institute of Canada, ☎ (613) 234-6533, www.aicanada.ca

—National Association of Real Estate Appraisers, ☎ (320) 763-7626, www.iami.org

—The American Society of Appraisers, ☎ (703) 478-2228, www.appraisers.org

Mortgage Broker

Help people fulfill their dreams of home ownership by becoming an independent mortgage broker. The primary function of the mortgage broker is to bring together people who want to borrow money to buy real estate with lending institutions that advance funds for the purpose of real estate purchases. It should be noted that the rules and policies for obtaining a mortgage broker's license differ among states and provinces, but you can contact the associations listed on the following page to find out about training and licensing requirements in your area. Once a mortgage broker has received an application from a client and checked credit and work references, the next step is to send the application to one or more lending institutions for acceptance or rejection. Mortgage brokers are typically paid a commission by the lending institution that advances the mortgage funds, ranging anywhere from a few hundred dollars to thousands of dollars, depending on the mortgage amount. Sometimes, however, in more difficult funding scenarios—second, third, or bridge financing, for instance—a mortgage broker will also charge the borrower a fee to cover the extra work involved in securing suitable financing. Most mortgage brokers handle finding residential mortgages for their clients, but you can also work with clients who want to renew their mortgages, increase their mortgage amounts, take out second or third mortgages, use equity for bridge financing, or purchase commercial properties, vacant land, income properties, or vacation properties. This is very much a business that thrives on referral and repeat business, so be sure to build working relationships with numerous real estate brokers and agents.

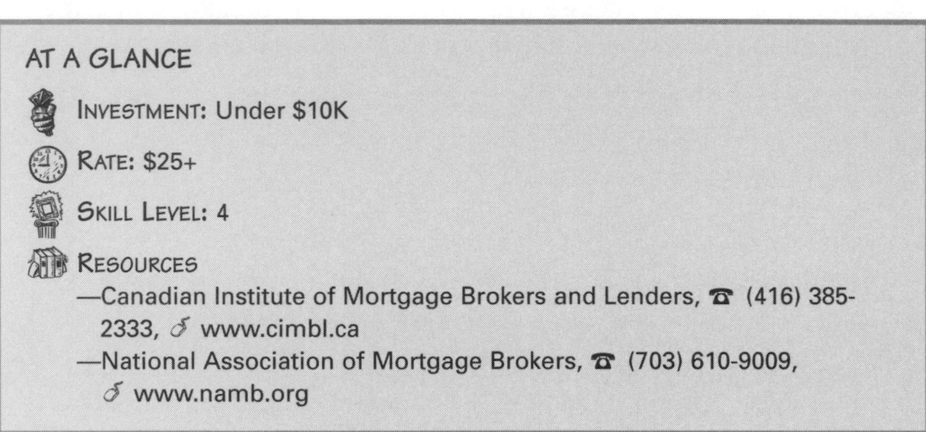
AT A GLANCE

INVESTMENT: Under $10K

RATE: $25+

SKILL LEVEL: 4

RESOURCES

—Canadian Institute of Mortgage Brokers and Lenders, ☎ (416) 385-2333, www.cimbl.ca

—National Association of Mortgage Brokers, ☎ (703) 610-9009, www.namb.org

---

Real Estate Listing Preparation Service

Real estate agents are quick to tell you that a home that has been professionally prepared to be listed will always sell faster, and for more money, than a home that has not been prepared to be listed. That is why real estate agents will become your number-one referral source if you choose to start a real estate listing-preparation service. Cracked windows, peeling paint, and rotten porch boards all leave a lasting impression with potential homebuyers—the wrong impression! When you see a rusty car you automatically think it must also run like junk. Homes are no different—peeling paint instantly conjures up the impression that the wood behind it must be rotten. Utilizing your handyperson skills you can conduct minor repairs, fix what needs to be fixed, and basically give your clients' homes a general spruce-up prior to the listing. It is not uncommon for the seller to be rewarded by getting multiple times their investment back when selling, because structural and cosmetic deficiencies always add up to a lower negotiated selling price.

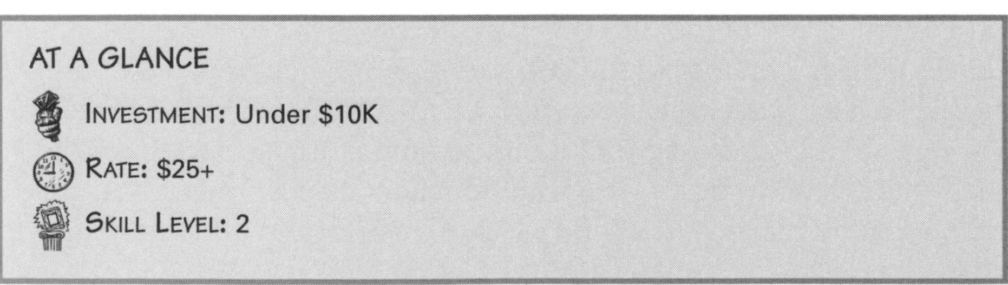
AT A GLANCE

INVESTMENT: Under $10K

RATE: $25+

SKILL LEVEL: 2

Resources
—📖 *2004 National Repair and Remodeling Estimator*, Albert S. Paxton (Craftsman Book Company, 2003)
—Canadian Real Estate Association, www.crea.ca
—National Association of Realtors, www.realtor.com

Apartment Preparation Service

By offering a full line of services that includes painting, carpet cleaning, minor repairs, and trash removal, you can help busy landlords and property managers, properly prepare an apartment for rental, making sure it's in great condition and able to demand top dollar. Advertise your apartment preparation services in traditional ways utilizing newspaper and fliers, as well as by joining landlord associations and contacting property management services. On average, you should be able to charge in the range of $25 to $35 per hour, plus materials and markup. The benefits to landlords are obvious: the better the condition of the apartment, the higher the rent will be, probably attracting a more conscientious renter. And of course, there will be much less work for the landlords. In short, landlords will easily recoup your fees and more through higher rents. You will need to invest in suitable transportation and equipment such as ladders, steam cleaners, and vacuums, but these are all relatively inexpensive and an investment of less than $10,000 will be more than sufficient.

AT A GLANCE

Investment: Under $10K

Rate: $25+

Skill Level: 2

Resources
—American Association of Small Property Owners, www.aaspo.org
—Building Owners and Managers Association of Canada, www.bomacanada.org
—National Apartment Association, www.naahq.org
—National Property Managers Association, www.npma.org

Relocation Consultant

What does a relocation consultant do? Actually, the list of duties is quite comprehensive. Relocation consultants assist people who are moving domestically or internationally with important issues, such as:

- Conducting a needs analysis to create an overall relocation plan to meet each client's specific needs
- Creating a profile of their client's new community, including identifying and detailing:
  - Schools and educational facilities
  - Hospitals and health-care facilities
  - Community maps
  - Recreational and entertainment facilities
  - Social service agencies, community associations, business clubs, sports associations, and social clubs
- Assisting in helping clients find short- or long-term accommodations if renting, and supply a realtor referral list if buying
- Help to hire qualified movers and arrange for transportation of pets and automobiles
- Provide clients relocating internationally with cultural awareness tip sheets, translation services, expatriate association information, customs clearances, import documents, and a referral list covering basic service and product providers

In short, relocation consultants ensure that clients experience a smooth transition to their new home and communities. Key to success in this business is your ability to build a wide network of business alliances that can refer people to your service, and these include realtors, immigration lawyers, and moving companies.

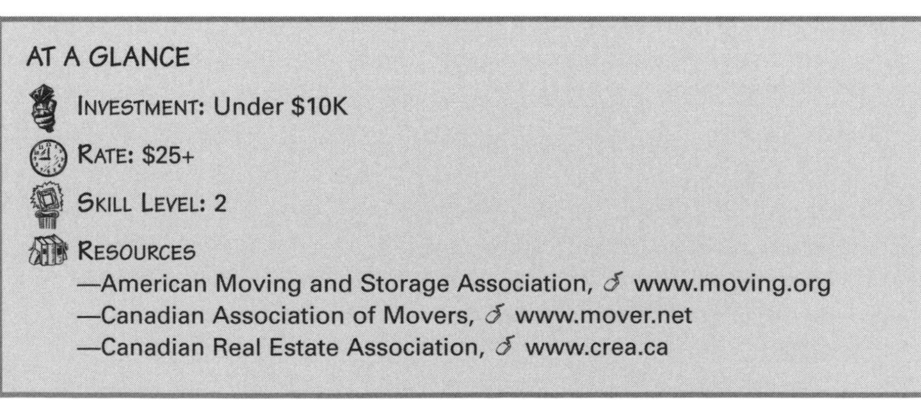

AT A GLANCE

INVESTMENT: Under $10K

RATE: $25+

SKILL LEVEL: 2

RESOURCES
—American Moving and Storage Association, www.moving.org
—Canadian Association of Movers, www.mover.net
—Canadian Real Estate Association, www.crea.ca

—Employee Relocation Council, www.erc.org
—National Association of Realtors, www.realtor.com

Packing Service

Anyone who has ever moved will be quick to agree that the worst part of the job is packing and unpacking items, mainly because it is slow, tedious, and back-breaking work. These same reasons are what make starting a packing service such a great idea, especially if you have a strong back and are not afraid of a little hard work. Moving companies specializing in both residential and office moving will be your main source of work because they can subcontract or refer your service to their clients. You can also run classified ads in your local newspaper under the "Moving" heading, and post fliers on bulletin boards throughout the community to get the telephone ringing. Billing rates should be in the range of $15 to $20 per hour, and you can earn additional money by selling packing supplies such as boxes, hangers, bubble wrap, and tape, and by hiring additional people to work as packers during busy periods.

 INVESTMENT: Under $2K

 RATE: $15+

 SKILL LEVEL: 1

 RESOURCES
—American Moving and Storage Association, www.moving.org
—Canadian Association of Movers, www.mover.net

Property Manager

Residential and commercial property managers are busy people because they have lots of work to do on behalf of their clients. These duties often include preparing annual management plans; preparing budgets and monthly financial statements; maintaining good tenant-owner relations; organizing tradespeople to conduct repairs; negotiating, preparing, and executing leases; and managing deposit accounts, just for starters! Running a property management service is ideal for people with a real estate background, project management experience, construction management experience, or a property administration background. However, anyone can start this venture on a small or part-time basis and gain valuable on-the-job experience, which can be leveraged to grow the business. Both of the associations listed below also offer property management training and certification programs, which is a wise investment especially for people who want to make a career of property management. Fees vary depending on the property being managed and the services provided, but you can expect to earn in the range of $25 to $40 per hour.

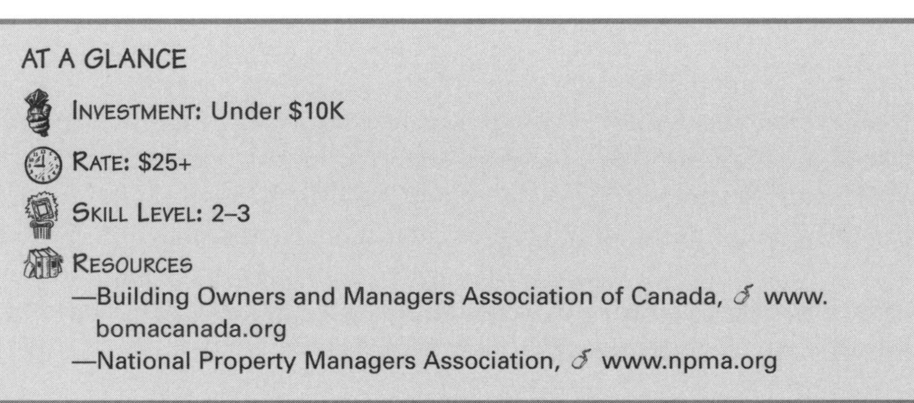

AT A GLANCE

INVESTMENT: Under $10K

RATE: $25+

SKILL LEVEL: 2–3

RESOURCES
—Building Owners and Managers Association of Canada, www.bomacanada.org
—National Property Managers Association, www.npma.org

Residential Security Consultant

In this era of heightened security, security consulting goes well beyond selling homeowners simple monitored alarm systems. Today's security consultants spend considerable time with each client, assessing and evaluating the entire family's security needs to develop an individualized security plan. The security plan takes into account home, personal, identity, and virtual security. Home security includes alarm systems, creating security zones within the home, security lighting, reinforcing doorjambs, upgrading window and door locks, as well as simple proactive security measures such as keeping bushes, trees, and shrubs clear of windows and entrance doors. Personal security includes self-defense training, handheld security devices, and training in how to spot suspicious behavior. Identity and virtual security includes taking measures to ensure that criminals cannot highjack a person's identity in the real world or online, as well as creating security firewalls to prevent critical information from being stolen from personal computers. Residential security consulting is ideally suited to entrepreneurs with a law enforcement, military, or security background. However, with the proper training and the ability to pass police clearance, any person with the desire can become a residential security consultant.

AT A GLANCE

 INVESTMENT: Under $10K

 RATE: $50+

 SKILL LEVEL: 2–3

 RESOURCES

—National Crime Prevention Council, www.ncpc.org
—The International Association of Professional Security Consultants, www.iapsc.org
—★ The McGruff® Safe Kids Total Identification System, (888) 209-4218, www.totalidsystem.mcgruff-safe-kids.com

Locksmith

Working as a locksmith on a mobile basis, from home, or from a retail storefront, you can offer customers a wide range of locksmithing services ranging from key cutting, installing new passage sets, emergency entries, sales of locks, safes, and related equipment, and installation. In the United States there are more than 30,000 locksmiths, of which 50 percent are self-employed and reporting earnings in excess of $50,000 per year after expenses. Needless to say the time and money invested in locksmith training is money well spent. In both the United States and Canada, locksmiths are required to be licensed and bonded, but all states and provinces have their own training and licensing requirements. You can contact the associations listed below to inquire about training and licensing requirements in your area, or visit the Locksmith Schools Directory, www.trade-schools.net/directory/locksmithing-schools.asp, which lists locksmith schools offering both classroom and correspondence locksmith training.

AT A GLANCE

 INVESTMENT: Under $25K

 RATE: $25+

 SKILL LEVEL: 3–4

 RESOURCES

—Associated Locksmiths of America, (214) 827-1701, www.aloa.org
—National Locksmith Association of Canada, (800) 589-4701
—★ Pop-a-Lock, (337) 233-6211, www.pop-a-lock.com

Self-Defense Training

Self-defense training is big business—kids, students, single mothers, housewives, executives traveling overseas, government employees, celebrities, sports figures, politicians, school teachers, security guards, and just about anyone who wants and needs to feel safe and secure are potential customers. This opportunity will really appeal to people with a martial arts, military, or law enforcement background—the more qualified and the better your credentials, the more your training services will be in demand. Training can be conducted in a group format or on a one-on-one basis at your school location or the clients locations, including their homes, businesses, or offices. Never before has self-defense training been as popular as it is right now. Literally hundreds of thousands of people sign up for new classes every month and are prepared to shell out big bucks to learn the skills they need to keep themselves and family members safe. Rates vary from a few dollars per hour, per student, when training a group, to as much as $200 per hour when training one-on-one.

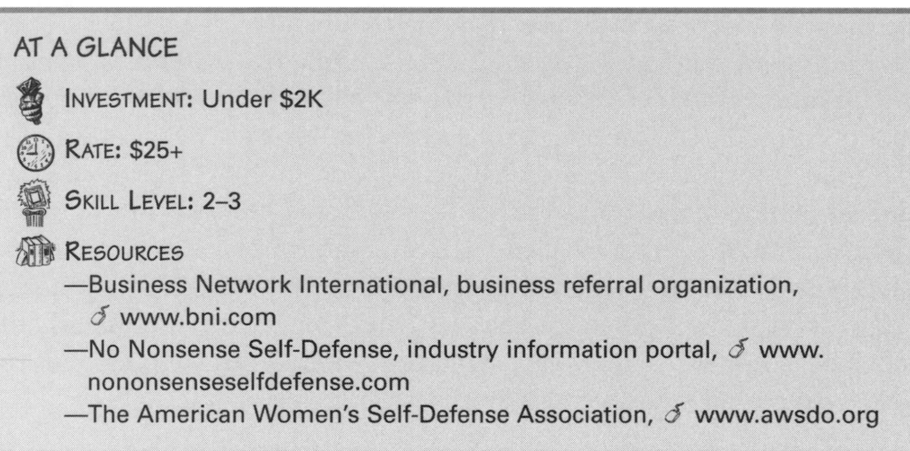

AT A GLANCE

INVESTMENT: Under $2K

RATE: $25+

SKILL LEVEL: 2–3

RESOURCES

—Business Network International, business referral organization, www.bni.com

—No Nonsense Self-Defense, industry information portal, www.nononsenseselfdefense.com

—The American Women's Self-Defense Association, www.awsdo.org

Product Assembly Service

I know I am not alone when I say that there are far too many products sold today that have to be assembled by the purchaser, and assembling these products is never as easy as advertised. We've all been in this annoying situation: We fight and struggle to get three or four boxes home, only to fight and struggle for another few hours to assemble a few bookcases. Herein lies the opportunity—start a product assembly service. It can be started for peanuts, less than $500, and marketed through retailers who do not currently offer product assembly services to their customers; additional revenues can be earned if you also provide delivery services at the same time. You will need to buy basic tools such as a cordless drill, hand tools, and a socket set, along with moving equipment like blankets, a dolly, and suitable transportation if you will also be offering delivery services. Retailers of products that must be assembled after purchase will be your big market, but at the same time do not overlook the possibility of building alliances with home and office movers because moving often requires furniture and equipment to be disassembled for the move and reassembled after the move.

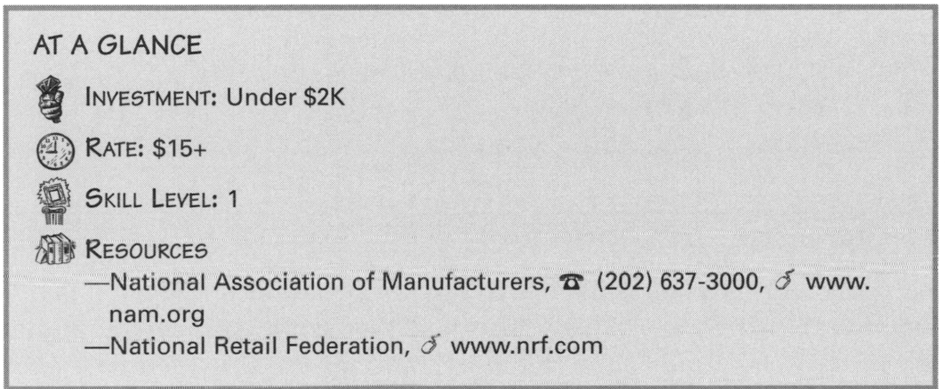

AT A GLANCE

INVESTMENT: Under $2K

RATE: $15+

SKILL LEVEL: 1

RESOURCES

—National Association of Manufacturers, ☎ (202) 637-3000, www.nam.org

—National Retail Federation, www.nrf.com

Private Investigator

Assignments handled by private investigators run the gamut from spousal surveillance to insurance fraud investigation, medical investigation, witness protection, abduction investigation, security surveillance, and lots more. Mainly, though, the majority of private investigators are kept busy with cases of a domestic nature—cheating spouses, tracking down natural parents, finding long-lost family members, and finding ex-spouses and deadbeat dads who are not keeping up with child support and alimony payments. Ideally, people entering this field will have a military, law enforcement, or security background, and of course, an interest in investigative work. Fees vary widely depending on the type of investigative work performed and related expenses, but it is not uncommon for highly specialized private investigators to earn well into the six-figure range. In the United States and Canada, all states and provinces require private investigators to be licensed and bonded, but each state and province has its own requirements for the licensing process. Contact the associations listed on the next page to inquire about training and licensing requirements in your area.

AT A GLANCE

 INVESTMENT: Under $10K

 RATE: $25+

 SKILL LEVEL: 3–4

 RESOURCES

—National Council of Investigation and Security Services, ☎ (800) 445-8408, www.nciss.org.

—Private Investigators Association of British Columbia, www.piabc.com

—*The Complete Idiot's Guide to Private Investigating,* Steven Kerry Brown (Alpha Books, 2002)

Party Tent Rentals

Renting party tents is a fantastic opportunity for people who are searching for an easy way to earn extra money. Just think of all the people, companies, and organizations that routinely rent large tents for outdoor events—wedding planners, catering companies, event and corporate planners, charity organizations, retailers hosting under-the-tent sales and clearance events, and sports teams and clubs, to name just a few. New party tents can be expensive, up to $5,000 or more for large ones, but with a little bit of research it is possible to buy secondhand party tents in good condition for about half the cost of new and even less if you are prepared to make a few repairs. As a rule of thumb, large party tents require about one hour for two people to set up and about the same time to disassemble, while one person can erect and disassemble smaller tents in half that time. Depending on tent size, rental rates are in the range of $200 to $400 per day, including delivery, setup, and disassembly. Extra income can also be earned by renting tables, chairs, lighting, and PA systems.

AT A GLANCE

 INVESTMENT: Under $10K

 RATE: $ varies

 SKILL LEVEL: 1

RESOURCES
—Celina Tent, party tent manufacturer, ☎ (866) 438-8368, www.gettent.com
—Starrett Brothers, party tent manufacturer, ☎ (800) 433-9116, www.tentmanufacture.com

Limousine Service

Limousines are no longer limited to stretched Cadillac and Lincoln automobiles. Today's limos include mile-long Hummers, vintage Rolls Royces, and theme vehicles with built-in hot tubs, grand pianos (complete with a pianist), and even disco themes, complete with the mirror ball and mini dance floor. In most areas of the United States and Canada, a special business and driver's license known as a chauffeur's license is required to operate a limousine service and drive the vehicle. Therefore, be sure to check into regulations in your area before making any investments. If you cannot acquire a limousine plate you may be able to purchase one if any are for sale, but expect to shell out big bucks, up to $100,000. Limousine plates and licenses are in high demand, mainly because it is not uncommon for operators to earn six-figure incomes. Advertising in newspapers, Yellow Pages directories, and school newspapers approaching graduation time is sure to get the telephone ringing. Likewise, contact hotels, nightclubs, wedding and event planners, celebrity handlers, and larger corporations to drop off business cards and fliers and to let them know about the limo services you provide so they can have their guests and clients whisked around town in style.

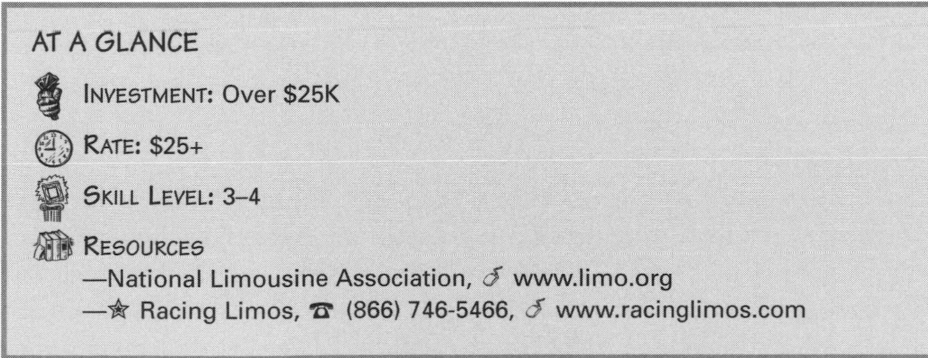

AT A GLANCE

INVESTMENT: Over $25K

RATE: $25+

SKILL LEVEL: 3–4

RESOURCES
—National Limousine Association, www.limo.org
—★ Racing Limos, ☎ (866) 746-5466, www.racinglimos.com

Wedding Planner

Long gone are the days when a great shindig of a wedding could be put on for a couple thousand dollars. Now the cost of a typical wedding can easily exceed $10,000, $20,000, and even $30,000. It's easy to see why many couples now realize that spending $1,000 to hire a professional wedding consultant is not only money wisely spent, but also a very cheap insurance policy on their substantial wedding investment. It is the duty of the wedding consultant to plan the wedding, hire caterers, screen musicians or disc jockey services, book a reception hall, find a florist and help to create table centers and bouquets, make a lot of suggestions, and fix a myriad of last-minute crises. In other words, the consultant does everything required to plan and carry out an unforgettable, perfect wedding. If you like to plan a party, are well organized, and thrive in a chaotic atmosphere, it's likely that providing wedding-planning services would be right up your alley. There are more than 8,000 professional wedding planners in the United States, and needless to say, the industry is competitive. At the same time, however, more than 2.5 million people get hitched each year, so the opportunity to succeed and profit is available to those willing to get out there and make things happen.

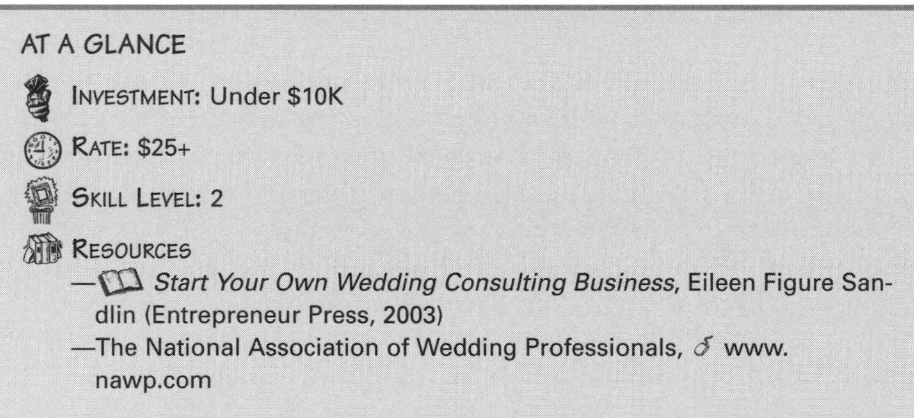

AT A GLANCE

INVESTMENT: Under $10K

RATE: $25+

SKILL LEVEL: 2

RESOURCES

—*Start Your Own Wedding Consulting Business*, Eileen Figure Sandlin (Entrepreneur Press, 2003)

—The National Association of Wedding Professionals, www.nawp.com

Makeup Artist

There are numerous occasions when professional makeup artistry is needed, such as for the bride on her wedding day, people working in film, in the fashion industry, going for important job or organizational interviews, public speaking engagements, and for special occasions such as parties, reunions, and dates. Or just for people who want a makeover to feel more confident. What makes makeup artistry such a great opportunity is the flexibility it offers. You can work on a mobile basis, full- or part-time, and travel to your client's location. You can establish an independent shop or join forces with an established hair salon, day spa, or nail studio. Or you can freelance for cosmetic companies and work from retail cosmetic counters. You will want to build working relationships with wedding planners, event planners, and people in the fashion industry. Additionally, cosmetology training is recommended. Contact the associations listed below to inquire about class availability in your area.

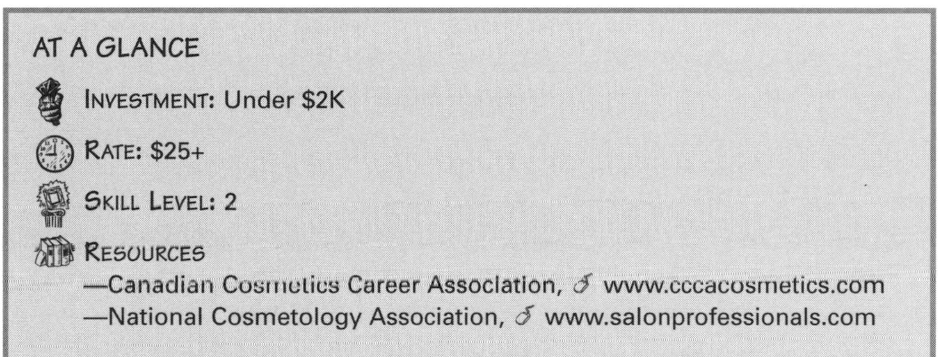

AT A GLANCE

INVESTMENT: Under $2K

RATE: $25+

SKILL LEVEL: 2

RESOURCES

—Canadian Cosmetics Career Association, www.cccacosmetics.com
—National Cosmetology Association, www.salonprofessionals.com

---

Honeymoon Consultant

A perfect wedding is not perfect without a perfect honeymoon. Without question, the honeymoon trip is the most important trip that people take. Consequently, lots of research and planning is required to make sure the most important trip of a lifetime turns out to be the best trip of a lifetime. Unfortunately, that's not always the case. Why? Simply because newlyweds spend so much time fussing over wedding plans, they sometimes don't have the time or energy left to plan for the perfect honeymoon. That's where you step in; operating as a honeymoon consultant, you can make sure your clients' honeymoon vacation is the experience of a lifetime. Help them select a destination that is suited to their personalities, make travel arrangements, book accommodations, and arrange activities and events, planning for even the smallest of details like a camera, film, currency conversions, travel and health insurance, and passports. In short, you attend to every detail that goes into planning and executing the trip of a lifetime. Remember, there is no cookie-cutter honeymoon stuff here. The honeymoon package you create for your clients must be unique, and developed strictly for each client based on their specific needs and wants.

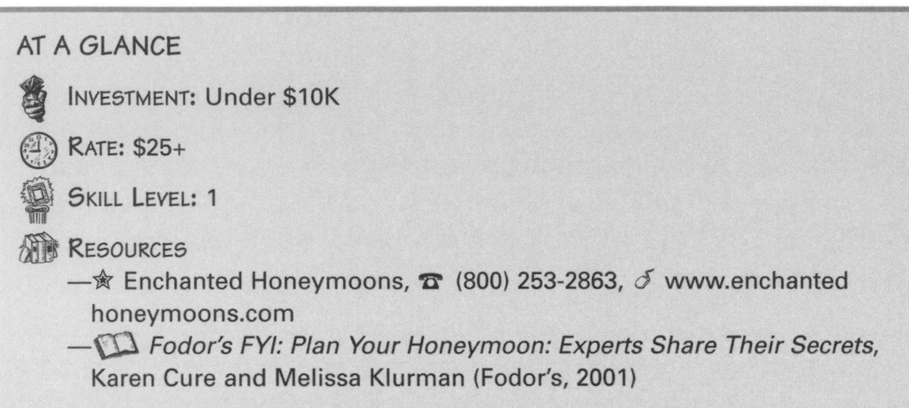

AT A GLANCE

INVESTMENT: Under $10K

RATE: $25+

SKILL LEVEL: 1

RESOURCES

—Enchanted Honeymoons, (800) 253-2863, www.enchantedhoneymoons.com

—*Fodor's FYI: Plan Your Honeymoon: Experts Share Their Secrets*, Karen Cure and Melissa Klurman (Fodor's, 2001)

Holiday and Event Decoration Service

One of the hottest new services to sell is holiday and event decoration services. Not only is there the potential to earn big bucks and have a lot of fun doing it, but the business also has minimal start-up investment and skill requirements. Holiday and event decorators offer clients a wide variety of services—everything from installing Christmas lights, to decorating banquet halls for wedding receptions, to "creeping-out" a house, business, or office for Halloween celebrations. Establishing working relationships with wedding planners, event planners, and retailers can go a long way toward gaining valuable referrals. In addition to Christmas and special occasions, you can also help decorate customers' homes, stores, and offices for anniversaries, Halloween, Easter, New Year's Day, and Fourth of July celebrations. To provide clients with holiday and special event decorating services, you will need basic tools like ladders, a cordless drill, and hand tools, along with a creative flair and suitable transportation. Decorations may be purchased wholesale and marked up for retail, providing an additional revenue source. Ultimately, your work will be your greatest advertisement, so be sure to use site signs promoting your service, hand out lots of business cards, and send press releases to the media when you have done a bang-up job on a house or office, or business.

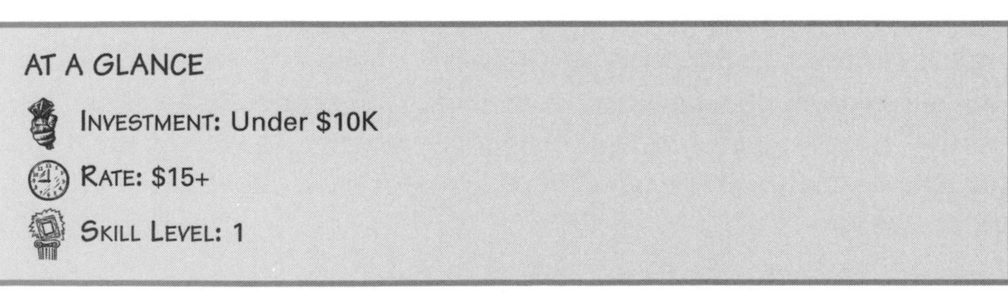

AT A GLANCE

INVESTMENT: Under $10K

RATE: $15+

SKILL LEVEL: 1

 RESOURCES

—★ Christmas Décor, ☎ (800) 687-9551, www.christmasdecor.net

—Four Seasons General Merchandise, ☎ (323) 582-4444, www.4sgm.com

Errand Service

Let's face it; today's busy lifestyles mean that most working people just don't have time for even the simplest of errands, such as taking the family pet to the veterinarian for a routine checkup, buying Aunt Sue a birthday present, or picking up the kids after school. Which is great news if you're a multitasker looking to start your own simple, inexpensive, yet potentially very profitable business. An errand service can be operated with nothing more than a cell phone and reliable transportation. Land clients by networking, and by creating a simple marketing brochure explaining the services you provide along with your contact information. The brochures can be pinned to community bulletin boards, hand-delivered to homes and businesses, and distributed with the local newspaper. A few promotional items such as pens and memo pads emblazoned with your company logo, name, and telephone number given out to potential customers will go a long way as a gentle reminder of your fast, reliable, and affordable errand services. This is the kind of business where growth is fuelled by referrals, so customer service and satisfaction are the most important goals.

AT A GLANCE

 INVESTMENT: Under $10K

RATE: $15+

 SKILL LEVEL: 1

 RESOURCES

—International Concierge and Errand Association, www.iceaweb.org

— *Start Your Own Personal Concierge Service*, Lisa Addison (Entrepreneur Press, 2002)

Rental Business

Working from home or a rented commercial space, you can earn big profits renting just about every and any type of product or equipment imaginable. Top rentals include tools, small watercraft, portable hot tubs, construction equipment, recreational vehicles, movie props, musical instruments, office furniture and equipment, canoes and kayaks, and camping equipment. Rental businesses have long been a popular moneymaker, mainly because although not everyone can afford to purchase a $50,000 recreational vehicle, most people can afford to shell out a few hundred to rent one for a week. Start-up costs can be high depending on the types of products and equipment that you purchase to rent. However, you can minimize costs by purchasing these items in good condition secondhand. Or you may even elect to find owners of the products you want to rent and start a rental pool, keeping a percentage of the fees for providing management services. As a general guideline, small items typically rent for 3 to 5 percent of their value per day, 10 percent per week, and 20 percent on a monthly rental.

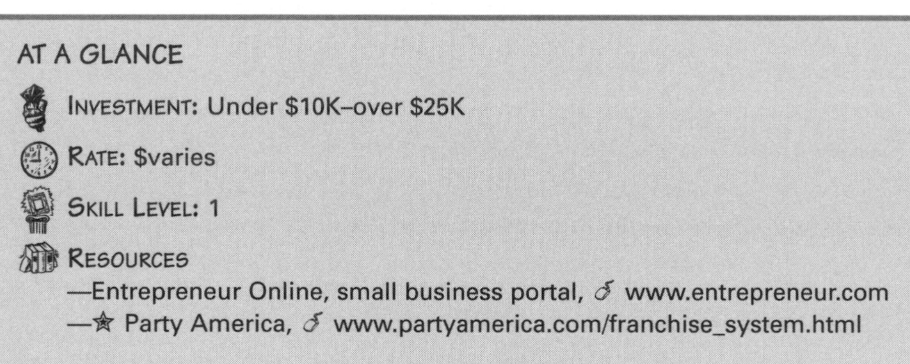

AT A GLANCE

INVESTMENT: Under $10K–over $25K

RATE: $varies

SKILL LEVEL: 1

RESOURCES

—Entrepreneur Online, small business portal, www.entrepreneur.com

—★ Party America, www.partyamerica.com/franchise_system.html

Sharpening Service

Who needs sharpening services? Lots of people and businesses do, such as restaurateurs, caterers, and butchers needing kitchen-knife-sharpening; saw-blade sharpening for contractors, carpentry shops, and mills; scissors sharpening for hair stylists, barbers, tailors, and seamstresses; and surgical-equipment sharpening for doctors, dentists, and hospitals. Depending on the type of equipment you purchase, you can offer customers free pickup of their items to be sharpened, take these items to your workshop to sharpen them, and return them to the customer the same day or the following day. The second option is to operate the business on a mobile basis, from a fully equipped van or trailer, and sharpen items right at your client's location. The easiest way to market sharpening services is to put on a comfortable pair of shoes and get out in the community and talk to businesspeople in need of sharpening services. This may seem old-fashioned, but when you stop to consider that all these items need to be sharpened on a regular basis, you are not just landing one sale, but potentially a customer for life.

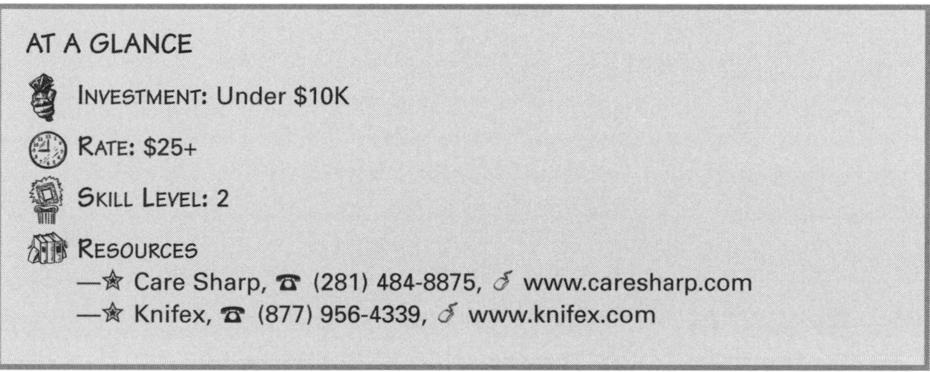

AT A GLANCE

INVESTMENT: Under $10K

RATE: $25+

SKILL LEVEL: 2

RESOURCES

—☆ Care Sharp, ☎ (281) 484-8875, www.caresharp.com
—☆ Knifex, ☎ (877) 956-4339, www.knifex.com

Disaster Planning and Preparation Service

Earthquakes, floods, hurricanes, tornadoes, blizzards, and wildfires wreak havoc and destruction of enormous magnitude and increasing intensity, thanks to a changing global climate. We cannot control these forces of nature, but with careful planning we can be prepared when disaster strikes. Being prepared for a natural disaster can literally mean the difference between life and death. There are two ways to generate revenues from this business. The first is to provide disaster-planning services, and the second is to sell disaster-related products. Both can also be combined to maximize profit potential. Services can include one-on-one consulting with clients to identify potential threats in disaster situations and teach how to react in these situations, and drafting emergency action plans to respond to a wide variety of natural-disaster situations. Products can include the sale of first-aid kits, backup generators, emergency lighting, and nonperishable food products and water. Services and products can be marketed to residential homeowners and renters, businesses, corporations, and organizations. The requirements for starting this specialized consulting service include first-aid training, disaster-response training, and knowledge of natural disaster situations and how to create proactive responses and action plans. Basically, people with an emergency services background will flourish in this unique venture. Given the frequency and widely publicized severity of many natural disasters, successfully marketing this type of business should not prove difficult.

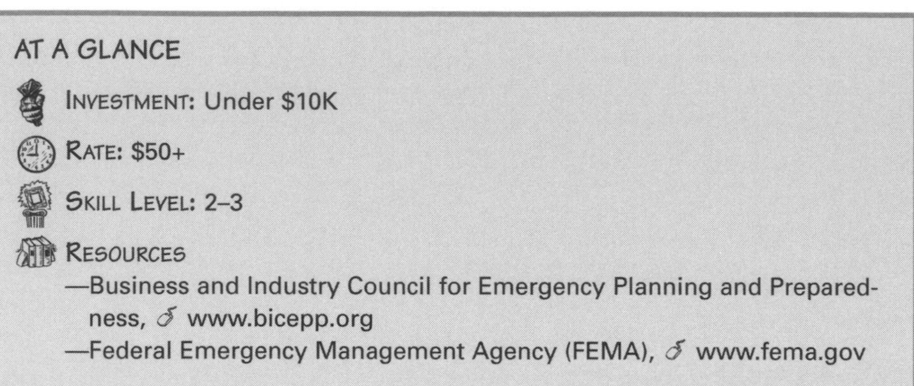

AT A GLANCE

INVESTMENT: Under $10K

RATE: $50+

SKILL LEVEL: 2–3

RESOURCES

—Business and Industry Council for Emergency Planning and Preparedness, www.bicepp.org

—Federal Emergency Management Agency (FEMA), www.fema.gov

Closet Organizing

Closet organizing took the home renovation industry by storm back in the '80s, and although it faded from popularity for a few years, it has returned with a vengeance, once again becoming one of the most popular interior renovations that homeowners are undertaking. Don't be too concerned if you lack the carpentry skills to transform unorganized closets into neatly organized mini clothing warehouses, complete with built-in shelves, drawers, ironing boards, and garment racks. You can concentrate on designing, marketing, and managing the business while hiring carpenters and handymen to perform the installations. You will, however, need a workshop outfitted with carpentry equipment and tools, as well as suitable transportation. Promote your services through advertising in newspapers, coupon and flier deliveries, subcontracting for homebuilders, interior designers, and renovation companies, and by exhibiting at home-and-design consumer shows, which can often generate a few hundred excellent leads from a single event.

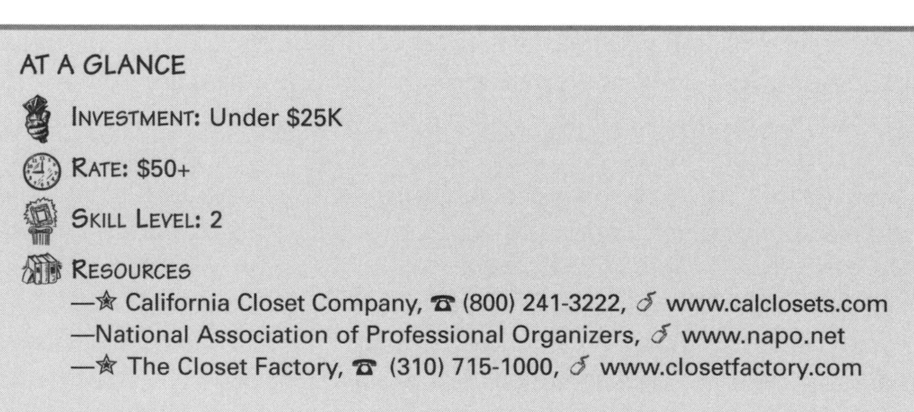

AT A GLANCE

INVESTMENT: Under $25K

RATE: $50+

SKILL LEVEL: 2

RESOURCES

—★ California Closet Company, ☎ (800) 241-3222, www.calclosets.com

—National Association of Professional Organizers, www.napo.net

—★ The Closet Factory, ☎ (310) 715-1000, www.closetfactory.com

Event and Party Planner

If you love to plan and host parties and special events, then starting an event and party planning service will be right up your alley. Event and party planners share common personality traits; they are detail-oriented, well-organized, good communicators, and very creative. In a nutshell, event and party planners are responsible for organizing and hosting special events such as wedding anniversaries, birthdays, graduations, and award ceremonies for their clients. Duties can include creating and sending out invitations, selecting event locations, decorations, arranging for entertainers and speakers, selecting caterers and menus, and just about everything else that is required to pull a special event together and put it on without a hitch, including arranging to get everything cleaned up after all the guests have left. Networking, networking, and more networking will be your main marketing tool for attracting and keeping new business, peppered liberally with advertising in newspapers, the Yellow Pages, and direct-mail fliers. You will also need to build a reliable team of contractors; businesses and individuals who you can call on and rely on to supply products and services required for hosting events on time and on budget. The more reliable your team is, the more successful and profitable your event and party planning service will be.

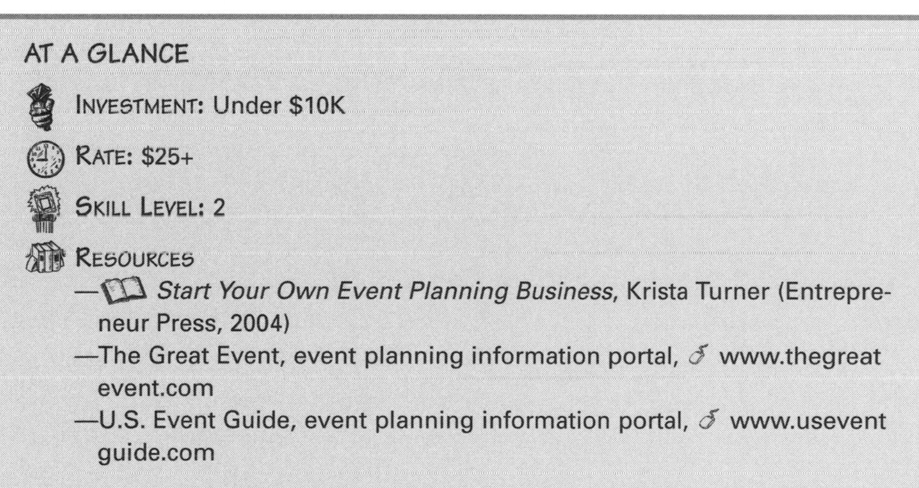

AT A GLANCE

INVESTMENT: Under $10K

RATE: $25+

SKILL LEVEL: 2

RESOURCES

—*Start Your Own Event Planning Business*, Krista Turner (Entrepreneur Press, 2004)

—The Great Event, event planning information portal, www.thegreatevent.com

—U.S. Event Guide, event planning information portal, www.useventguide.com

Party Entertainment Service

There is big money to be earned operating a party entertainment service and providing live entertainment for parties and special occasions—clowns, soloists, musical bands, magicians, singing telegrams, public speakers, spokespeople, acrobats, jugglers, comedians, adult-themed entertainers, and lots more. Kids parties, corporate events, social events, graduations, birthdays, anniversaries, weddings, trade shows, conventions, and Christmas parties are a lot more fun when there is live entertainment to keep guests entertained and in high spirits. Entertainers can be employed as contractors working on an on-call basis, and can be paid by way of revenue-sharing; the range of 60/40 in the entertainer's favor is the industry standard. Promote the service by running advertisements in your local newspaper and in the Yellow Pages, as well as by contacting wedding planners and event planners in your community and explaining the various types of entertainers your service provides, as well as rates. This service can easily be managed from home, and start-up costs are modest, with the bulk of the budget being spent on business setup and marketing to get the telephone ringing with eager customers wanting to book acts for their special occasions and events.

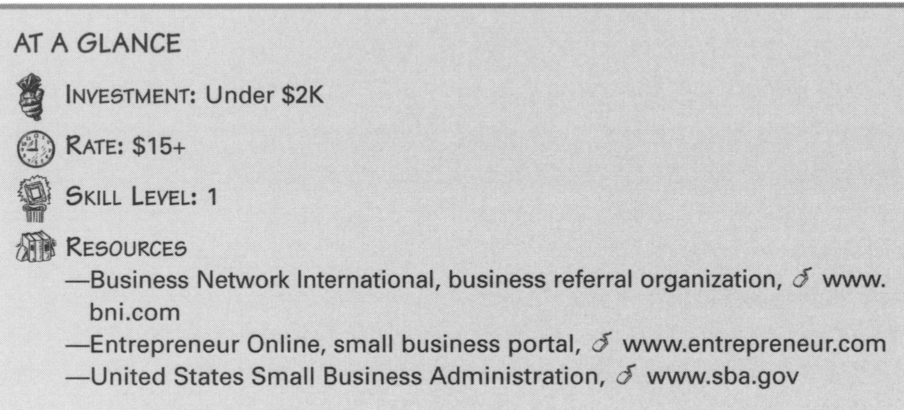

AT A GLANCE

INVESTMENT: Under $2K

RATE: $15+

SKILL LEVEL: 1

RESOURCES

—Business Network International, business referral organization, www.bni.com
—Entrepreneur Online, small business portal, www.entrepreneur.com
—United States Small Business Administration, www.sba.gov

Mystery Shopper

Go undercover and mystery-shop at clients' retail businesses, eat at clients' restaurants, and have clients' employees provide you with services, all in an effort to assess quality of employees and management, operational procedures, and customer-service policies. Many companies, organizations, and retailers have introduced mystery-shopper programs to their businesses, and for good reason. Mystery-shopper programs work extremely well at uncovering customer service, employee, or product and service problems. Mystery shoppers prepare a document detailing their findings, relaying their experiences, and making recommendations to clients upon completion of their visit(s). Recently, some have even begun to use small and concealed digital cameras to document their work and present their clients with an audiovisual record of their findings. Expanding the business is as easy as hiring additional mystery shoppers to work on a subcontract-as-needed basis. The industry is competitive, so the more relevant experience and training you can bring to the table, the better. These experiences would include managerial training, prior customer-service postings, retail selling, human-resources work, and time spent as an operations specialist. There are even mystery-shopper training courses available that can put you on the path to starting and operating your own mystery-shopper service.

AT A GLANCE

INVESTMENT: Under $2K

RATE: $15+

SKILL LEVEL: 2–3

RESOURCES

—*Mystery Shopper's Manual*, Cathy Stucker (Special Interests Publications, 2004)

—Mystery Shopping Providers Association, www.mysteryshop.org

—National Retail Federation, www.nrf.com

Garage and Estate Sale Promoter

Weekend profits await entrepreneurs with good marketing and organizational skills who become garage and estate sale promoters. Garage, lawn, and estate sales are hugely popular events in every community across North America. In fact, it is estimated that more than 60 million people go garage-sale-shopping annually, generating billions in sales. As a promoter, you can provide clients who do not have the time or gumption to hold their own sale with the service of organizing and conducting the sale for them. Duties include promoting, organizing, selling items, and cleaning up after everyone has gone home. In exchange for providing this valuable service you retain a percentage of the total revenues generated—25 percent for larger sales and up to 50 percent for smaller ones. Once you have found a client, be sure to canvas the immediate neighborhood and solicit for additional items. Why hold a small sale if you can increase revenues and profits by enlisting neighbors to provide items, too? Promote the sales with professional site signage and in community newspapers that do not charge for small classified ads or for garage sale postings.

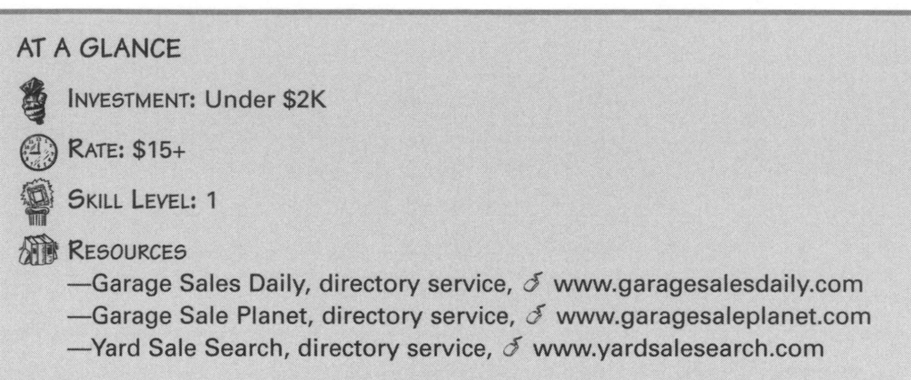

AT A GLANCE

INVESTMENT: Under $2K

RATE: $15+

SKILL LEVEL: 1

RESOURCES

—Garage Sales Daily, directory service, www.garagesalesdaily.com
—Garage Sale Planet, directory service, www.garagesaleplanet.com
—Yard Sale Search, directory service, www.yardsalesearch.com

Bed and Breakfast Operator

Substantial profits can be earned by converting your home into a bed and breakfast, catering to pleasure and business travelers. Just think, the money you earn renting rooms out by the day, week, or month, can be used to pay down your mortgage faster, send the kids to college, or to supplement your retirement income. B&B rates are in the range of $40 to $100 per night per person and include a light (or sometimes full and hearty) breakfast, hence the name. Promote your bed and breakfast through local tourist associations, via online directories, and by establishing alliances with independent travel agents and brokers. The biggest obstacle you might need to overcome in turning your home into a B&B will be zoning regulations. Some municipalities encourage B&Bs, while others prefer to keep guest accommodations within the confines of an established hotel/motel zone and out of residential neighborhoods. A trip to the city hall planning and zoning department will be your first stop to find out about local bylaws. Also consider creating a central theme, or individual theme rooms such as a Western room, rock-'n-roll room, and others, as themed B&Bs have recently become very popular and capture lots of valuable publicity in travel and leisure magazine articles.

AT A GLANCE

INVESTMENT: Over $25K

RATE: $ varies

SKILL LEVEL: 1

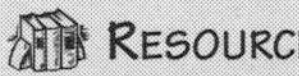
RESOURCES

—American Bed and Breakfast Association, www.abba.com

—*Start Your Own Bed & Breakfast*, Rob Adams (Entrepreneur Press, 2004)

Murder Mystery Parties

Whodunit murder mystery parties are hugely popular and the basis for a fun and exciting part-time business opportunity that can be kicked off for peanuts, yet has the potential to earn excellent profits. Clients can include individuals wanting to host an interesting dinner party for family and friends, corporations seeking fun social functions for employees or customers, and event planners searching for an extraordinary and unique experience for their clients. If you have writing aspirations and a creative flair, you can write the story and murder mystery party scripts; if you do, be sure to try to include your clients in the script—their likenesses, personalities, and names. If you are not a wordsmith, you can use a popular mystery theme or story as the basis of the mystery, or you can even purchase murder mystery scripts online. Rates for mystery dinner party services start at $25 per person plus the cost of a catered dinner, specialty props, and location rentals if the party is not held at the client's location.

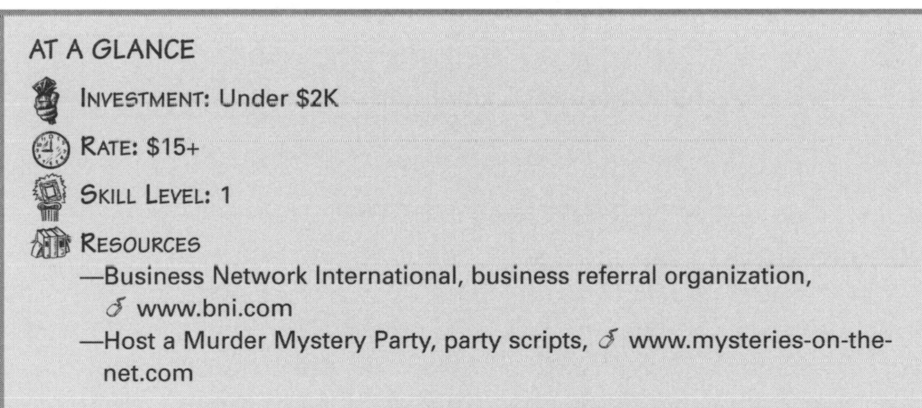
AT A GLANCE

INVESTMENT: Under $2K

RATE: $15+

SKILL LEVEL: 1

RESOURCES

—Business Network International, business referral organization, www.bni.com

—Host a Murder Mystery Party, party scripts, www.mysteries-on-the-net.com

Mobile Disc Jockey

Four things make starting and operating a mobile disc jockey service a wise decision for people looking to get into a fun and potentially profitable business, and these include:

- Disc jockey services are in high demand in a growth industry.
- The business can be started on a minimal investment, often less than $5,000.
- Operating overhead is almost nonexistent, especially once the business is established and enjoying repeat and referral business.
- The profit potential is excellent as rates are currently in the range of $250 to $500 per event, plus gratuities. Expanding the business is as easy as purchasing additional systems and hiring people to deejay.

You will need an excellent and varied music selection, deejay equipment, and reliable transportation, as well as an outgoing personality and talent for public speaking. Clients can include event and wedding planners, tour operators, restaurant and nightclub owners, corporations, and individual consumers seeking to secure disc jockey services for a celebration or special event.

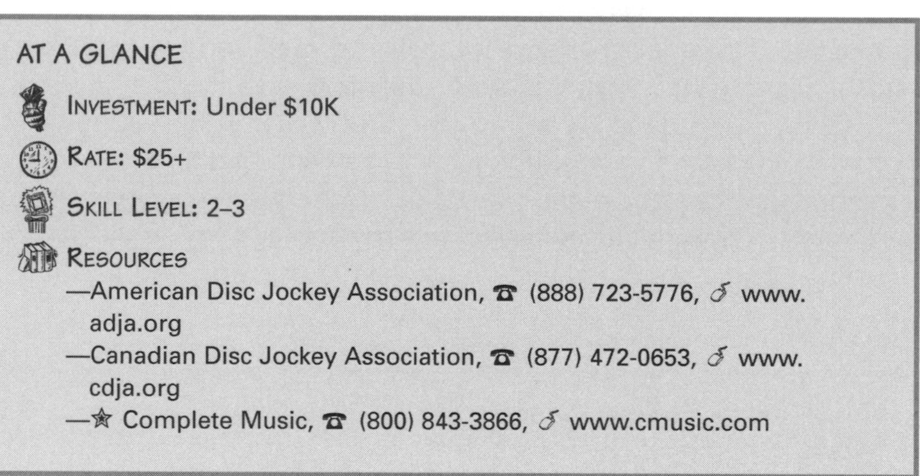
AT A GLANCE

INVESTMENT: Under $10K

RATE: $25+

SKILL LEVEL: 2–3

RESOURCES
—American Disc Jockey Association, ☎ (888) 723-5776, www.adja.org
—Canadian Disc Jockey Association, ☎ (877) 472-0653, www.cdja.org
—★ Complete Music, ☎ (800) 843-3866, www.cmusic.com

Balloon Service

With an investment of less than $1,000 you can start a part-time party balloon service and earn big profits on weekends and during holidays. Depending on your goals and ambition, you could even turn the business into a full-time lucrative going concern. Corporate events, grand openings, children's birthday parties, special occasions, graduations, retailer sales, weddings, and community events—the demand for party balloons is gigantic and continually growing. Marketing a party balloon service is best achieved by creating a basic yet detailed brochure describing your service and rates. Distribute it to party and event planners, wedding planners, children's stores, restaurants, banquet facilities, day-care centers, and catering companies. There are also many balloon manufacturers and printers who offer custom balloon printing services so you can also sell direct to businesses that want to advertise sales and special events with their names and logos featured on the balloons. Great add-on services to increase revenues include a party cleanup service, streamer and decoration supplies, and event-planning services, especially for children's birthday parties. You will need reliable transportation and basic equipment such as helium tanks for gas-filled balloons, and air compressors for blowing up cold-air balloons. But don't worry—this type of equipment is cheap to buy or rent and readily available in every community.

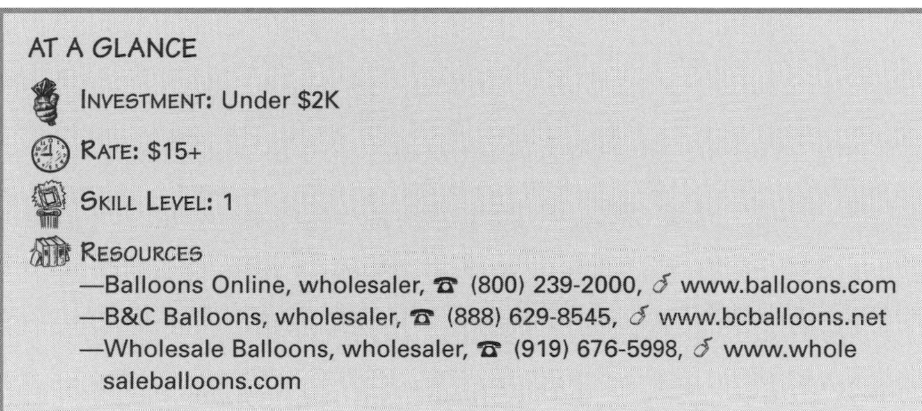

AT A GLANCE

INVESTMENT: Under $2K

RATE: $15+

SKILL LEVEL: 1

RESOURCES

—Balloons Online, wholesaler, ☎ (800) 239-2000, www.balloons.com

—B&C Balloons, wholesaler, ☎ (888) 629-8545, www.bcballoons.net

—Wholesale Balloons, wholesaler, ☎ (919) 676-5998, www.wholesaleballoons.com

Personal Trainer

Calling all fitness gurus! The time has never been better than right now to start your own personal fitness-trainer business teaching others how to live a more healthy life through the implementation and maintenance of exercise and nutritional programs. While there are currently no across-the-board certification requirements to become a personal trainer, anyone serious about operating this service for long-term success would be urged to take professional training to become certified. You can contact the associations listed on the next page for more information about certification programs offered in your area. Your target audience will include any person who wants professional guidance to become more fit. You can specialize and work one-on-one with busy executives, kids, or seniors at their offices or homes. Or, open your own fitness studio and offer one-on-one and group training programs to everyone. In addition to developing exercise programs to match each student's individual needs, personal trainers also provide fitness assessments and nutritional coaching.

AT A GLANCE

 INVESTMENT: Under $10K

 RATE: $25+

 SKILL LEVEL: 2–3

 RESOURCES

—★ Fitness Together, ☎ (303) 663-0880, www.fitnesstogetherfranchise.com

—International Fitness Professionals Association, (800) 785-1924, www.ifpa-fitness.com

—National Federation of Professional Trainers, (800) 729-6378, www.nfpt.com

---

Sports Coaching

Amateur sports coaching is a growing industry in all areas of North America. If you have sports coaching or playing experience in ice hockey, football, baseball, basketball, boxing, golf, tennis, soccer, or competitive diving, you can turn these experiences and skills into a profitable commodity by offering one-on-one sports coaching. Amateur athletes of all ages are turning to individual coaching to give them a competitive advantage on the field or course in the ring or pool. Parents are parting with up to $75 per hour to make sure their kids receive the professional sports coaching they need so they are not left behind. Adult athletes are also enlisting the services of freelance sports coaches to help them improve their game, get more enjoyment from their sport, and decrease the risks of injury. Market your sports coaching services by joining sports associations and networking with parents and adult athletes. Also develop a workshop or seminar platform on topics involving the benefits of your service and the sport you coach, which can be offered for free to all who want to attend, with the aim of recruiting students during and after the seminar.

 INVESTMENT: Under $2K–over $25K

 RATE: $50+

 SKILL LEVEL: 2

 RESOURCES

—Sports Workout, sports coaching training products and services, www.sportsworkout.com

—Velocity Sports Performance, (678) 990-2555, www.velocitysp.com

Bicycle Repair Service

Mechanically inclined entrepreneurs with an interest in cycling can earn a great income repairing bicycles right from the comfort of a homebased workshop. In addition to big profit potential, there are many other advantages to operating a bicycle repair service, including low overhead, huge demand for the service in an ever-growing sport, and you can work flexible full- or part-time hours. Even if you are not experienced in bicycle repairs, there are a number of schools offering bicycle mechanic courses that take only a few weeks to complete, such as those offered by United Bicycle Institute in Oregon. Key to marketing your services is to join bicycling clubs and organizations in your community, largely because members can become customers and refer other bicycling enthusiasts to your business. You can also work on a contract basis for bicycle retailers to handle their overflow work during the busy season. Likewise, advertising in your community newspaper and distributing fliers detailing the services you provide is sure to attract new business.

AT A GLANCE

 INVESTMENT: Under $10K

 RATE: $25+

 SKILL LEVEL: 2–3

 RESOURCES

—*Barnett's Manual: Analysis and Procedures for Bicycle Mechanics*, John Barnett (Velo Press, 2003)

—United Bicycle Institute, Oregon-based training school offering students certification courses in bicycle mechanics, www.bikeschool.com

Appliance Repair Service

Appliance repair is a great moneymaking opportunity for mechanically inclined entrepreneurs. Stoves, fridges, dishwashers, washers, dryers, central vacuum systems, and freezers are just a few of the home appliances that you will be able to repair at rates as high as $75 per hour. You will need home-appliance repair training, but certification courses can be completed in less than a year, and you can contact the associations listed below to find classes available in your area. Further training in commercial kitchen equipment will enable you to also repair restaurant and food services equipment such as grills, fryers, and commercial coolers. Advertise in the Yellow Pages and in your community classifieds. Offering customers a 24-hour emergency repair service, as well as an ironclad warranty on all work, is sure to get the telephone ringing. Also market your appliance repair services to apartment landlords and property managers. This venture is perfectly suited to be operated from a homebased workshop to handle major repairs, while minor repairs can be completed right at your customers' homes.

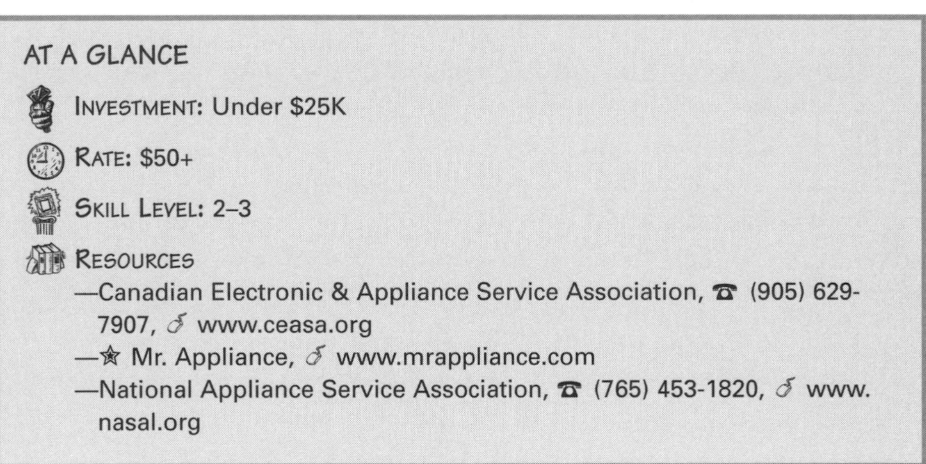

AT A GLANCE

INVESTMENT: Under $25K

RATE: $50+

SKILL LEVEL: 2–3

RESOURCES

—Canadian Electronic & Appliance Service Association, ☎ (905) 629-7907, www.ceasa.org

—★ Mr. Appliance, www.mrappliance.com

—National Appliance Service Association, ☎ (765) 453-1820, www.nasal.org

Framing Service

What must you have and know in order to sell framing and matting services? Framing and matting experience is helpful, but with a little bit of practice and trial and error, framing and matting can be mastered by just about everyone. Tools and equipment are also necessities. If you are purchasing standard-size frames from wholesalers, only basic tools will be needed. If you plan on building custom frames, you will need a power miter saw, glass cutters, clamps, and other hand tools, along with suitable workshop and storage space. You can set up your workshop at home, or rent appropriate space. Set up at home and work part-time to keep overhead low until the business is self-supporting; then you can move to a larger space if required. In addition to customers looking to have only one or two photographs or paintings framed, you can also market your services to higher-volume customers, including photographers, artists, retailers of prints and posters, schools (for framing diplomas and awards), and interior designers.

 **Investment:** Under $10K–over $25K

 **Rate:** $25+

 **Skill Level:** 2–3

 **Resources**

- —★ Big Picture Framing, ☎ (800) 315-0024, www.bigpictureframing.com
- —📖 *Home Book of Picture Framing: Professional Secrets of Mounting, Matting, Framing and Displaying Artworks, Photographs, Posters, Fabrics, Collectibles, Carvings and More,* Kenn Oberrecht (Stackpole Books, 1998).
- —★ The Great Frame Up, www.thegreatframeup.com

Flea Market Organizer

Flea markets are a multibillion-dollar business in the United States, and here is your opportunity to cash in on the boom by becoming a weekend flea market organizer and manager. Get started by renting commercial space in a highly visible area with lots of passing traffic, one that is large enough to be subdivided into smaller vendor booths—10-by-10, 10-by-20, and 20-by-20. If climate permits or during summer months, and if space allows, extra revenues can be earned by renting outside vendor stalls as well. Rents vary depending on factors such as booth size, location, equipment (tables included, etc.), and hours of operation, but generally are in the range of $3 to $10 per square foot per day. When booking vendors, try for a wide variety of products that will be offered for sale—antiques, electronics, kitchenware, food items, clothing, tools, toys, art, and sporting goods. Doing so will ensure broad appeal to a large target audience of flea market shoppers. Additional revenues can be earned by charging a gate fee, parking fees, having an onsite ATM, renting equipment, and providing shoppers with delivery services for the large items they buy. But be careful not to get too caught up in extra fees, because the bread and butter of the operation is booth rent. Vendor occupancy is much more important than charging a dollar to park. The investment to get this business up and running is larger than most featured in this book, once costs such as rent, deposits, renovations, equipment, signage, and marketing have been taken into account. But with that said, the profit potential is excellent, as are the long-term growth opportunities.

AT A GLANCE

 INVESTMENT: Under $25K

 RATE: $25+

 SKILL LEVEL: 1

 RESOURCES
- —Flea Market Guide, flea market directory service, www.fleamarketguide.com
- —Flea USA, flea market directory service, www.fleamarkets.com
- —The National Flea Market Association, (602) 995-3532, www.fleamarket.org

Day-Care Center

The escalating cost of living has made child day care a booming industry simply because many families require two full-time incomes to make ends meet. Day-care facilities can be homebased, operated from a storefront or office location, or in conjunction with an established business or office complex. Investment budget, business objectives, and demand will likely dictate what is the best operating location for you. In the United States and Canada, day-care facilities as well as child-care staff must obtain proper licensing and certification to meet minimum operating requirements. Because every state and province has its own individual licensing requirements, you will need to contact your regional municipal offices to make inquires, or contact the associations listed on the next page to inquire about certification and licensing requirements in your area. Once your center is open, you will find that the problem is not finding kids to fill your facility, but having to turn down parents daily because you are at your limit. Word-of-mouth advertising is generally all that is required for marketing in this industry.

AT A GLANCE

 INVESTMENT: Under $10K–over $25K

 RATE: $25+

 SKILL LEVEL: 4

 RESOURCES

—Canadian Child Care Federation, ☎ (800) 858-1412, www.cccf-fcsge.ca

—*Family Child-Care Contracts and Polices: How to Be Businesslike in a Caring Profession*, Tom Copeland (Redleaf Press, 1997)

—National Association of Child Care Professionals, ☎ (800) 537-1118, www.naccp.org

—★ Wee Watch Private Home Day Care, ☎ (800) 663-6072, www.weewatch.com

Nanny Match Service

The focus of this exciting opportunity is to match nannies and parents searching for a nanny. Hiring a nanny to help look after the kids and do light household chores has exploded in popularity over the past decade. This is mainly because today's hectic lifestyles keep all family members hopping from dawn to dusk, combined with the fact that many families need two breadwinners in the household to keep up with the cost of living. The solution for many parents is to hire a nanny to help care for the children and help out around the house. But for parents new to hiring a nanny, there are as many questions as the nanny solution answers. Where do you find a qualified nanny? How do you conduct a background check? How much do nannies get paid? If you choose to start a nanny match service, you must be able to provide parents answers to all these questions and many more. Revenues are earned by charging parents a fee to find a qualified nanny to meet their specific needs, to conduct a background and reference check, and to follow up periodically with parents to be sure that the arrangement is working.

AT A GLANCE

 INVESTMENT: Under $10K

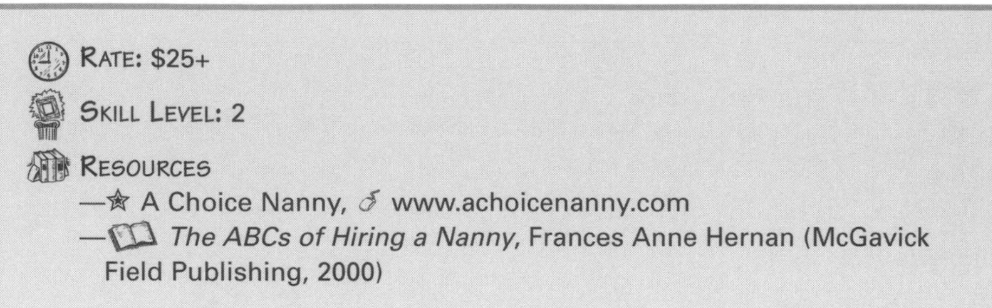

RATE: $25+

SKILL LEVEL: 2

RESOURCES

—A Choice Nanny, www.achoicenanny.com

—*The ABCs of Hiring a Nanny*, Frances Anne Hernan (McGavick Field Publishing, 2000)

Baby-Sitting Referral Service

There are three ways to earn money running a baby-sitting referral service. The first is to charge baby sitters a fee to join the service, be listed in the directory, and have access to parents seeking baby-sitting services. The second is to charge parents a fee to join the service so they have access to a suitable and qualified baby sitter(s) in their area. And the third way to earn money is to sell advertising space on your web site and in your monthly "Baby-Sitting Newsletter" to community businesses that want access to your customer base to advertise their products and services, especially child- and baby-related businesses. Combined, these three revenue streams have the potential to generate huge profits for the innovative entrepreneur with strong marketing and management skills. You can run the business from home or a commercial office space, depending on space requirements and whether you plan on having parents and sitters sign up in person or online. It will be important to develop a screening system for both potential baby sitters and parents looking for baby sitters, to offer peace of mind in terms of qualifications, suitability, and security.

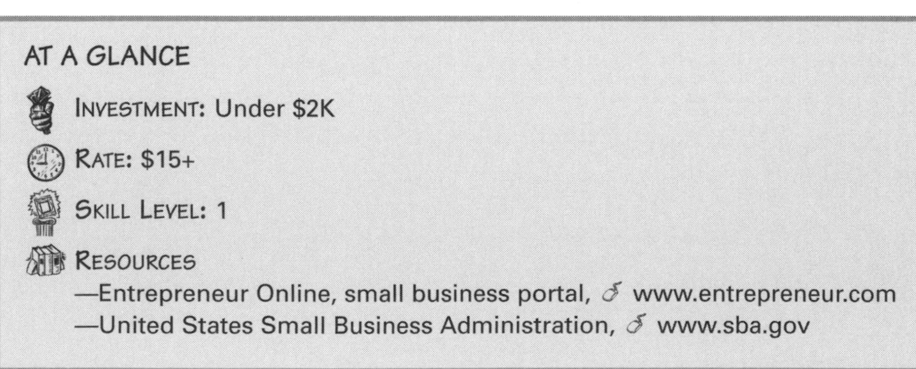

AT A GLANCE

INVESTMENT: Under $2K

RATE: $15+

SKILL LEVEL: 1

RESOURCES

—Entrepreneur Online, small business portal, www.entrepreneur.com

—United States Small Business Administration, www.sba.gov

Coin Laundry

Coin washers and dryers may only take spare change to clean clothes, but at the end of the year all that spare change can add up to thousands of dollars in profit. Coin laundries have been around for decades, and in spite of the fact that washer-dryer sets can often be purchased for less than $1,000, coin laundries continue to thrive and earn big bucks for their owners. Why? Simply because not everyone has the space, the septic capacity, or the need for their own laundry equipment, including students, business and pleasure travelers, and people living in small accommodations. The key to success in the coin laundry business is location. You must set up your laundry in an area comprised mostly of your target audience. Therefore, think college and university districts, areas close to campgrounds and RV parks, and areas with many apartment buildings. Offering additional services such as a laundry drop-off wash-and-fold service, ironing, alteration service, and a dry-cleaning depot can greatly increase revenues and profits. Likewise, selling products such as soaps and snacks from vending machines will also add a few hundred dollars a month to the pot.

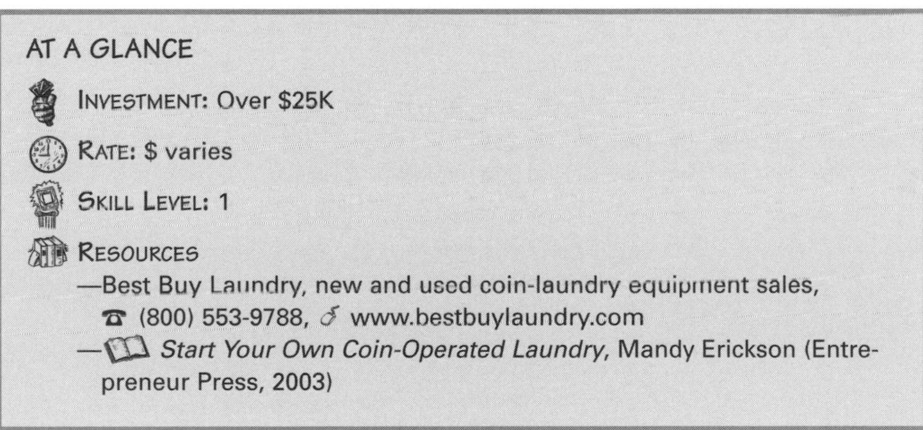

AT A GLANCE

INVESTMENT: Over $25K

RATE: $ varies

SKILL LEVEL: 1

RESOURCES

—Best Buy Laundry, new and used coin-laundry equipment sales, ☎ (800) 553-9788, www.bestbuylaundry.com

— *Start Your Own Coin-Operated Laundry*, Mandy Erickson (Entrepreneur Press, 2003)

Cloth Diaper Service

Let's face it: disposable diapers are not the best for a couple of reasons. First, they can often irritate a baby's skin. Second, they are not environmentally friendly. The solution is, of course, environmentally friendly cloth diapers made of natural fibers, which are soft to a baby's skin and can be washed and reused many times. When you stop to consider that a baby can go through as many as 4,000 diapers before being fully toilet-trained, you quickly realize the outstanding business opportunity that awaits entrepreneurs who start a cloth diaper delivery service. Depending on how much money you have to invest, there are a couple of options for starting a cloth diaper service. If money is plentiful, you can offer a complete service, including diaper supply, delivery, pickup, and cleaning. Or if funds are tight, you can simply supply delivery and pickup services and have an established commercial laundry wash the diapers at a reduced or bulk rate. Over the long term, option one will probably put more profits in your pockets than option two, as well as enable you to have more control over your business. Word-of-mouth marketing will be your main promotional tool, so be sure to get out and start the promotion train rolling by talking with as many new parents as you can.

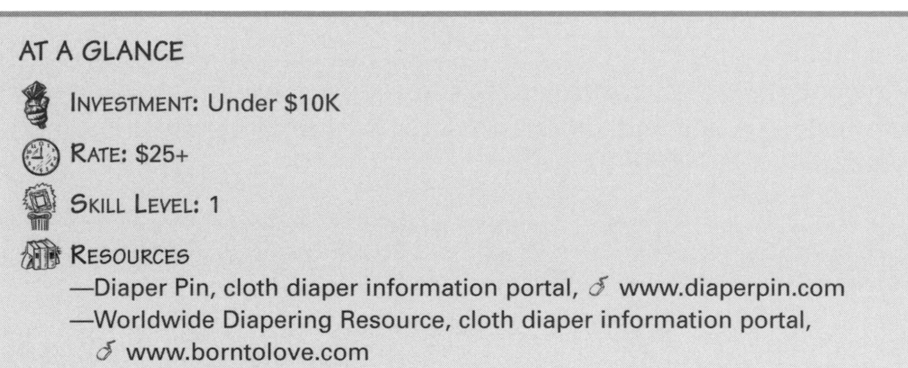

AT A GLANCE

INVESTMENT: Under $10K

RATE: $25+

SKILL LEVEL: 1

RESOURCES

—Diaper Pin, cloth diaper information portal, www.diaperpin.com

—Worldwide Diapering Resource, cloth diaper information portal, www.borntolove.com

Children's Party Service

A love of children and party planning are the two most important prerequisites for starting and operating a children's party service. This is a hot business opportunity! Just think of all the reasons a party is thrown for kids—birthdays, milestones, school-is-out, back-to-school, holidays, Halloween, special achievements, and recovery from illness, just to name a few. There are two ways to run this service. First, you can operate on a mobile basis and throw the party at your clients' locations. Second, you can host the parties from a fixed location requiring partygoers to come to you—your home, a rented space, or a restaurant or children's retailer with whom you have an arrangement. Regardless of whether you operate mobile or from a fixed location, duties remain the same—plan the party, decorate, provide entertainment, food, and beverages, stage games and contests, and make the event one heck of a lot of fun for kids and their parents. Rates will vary depending on the menu, entertainment, games, and frills, but start at about $20 per guest and go as high as $100 per guest for highly specialized and themed parties.

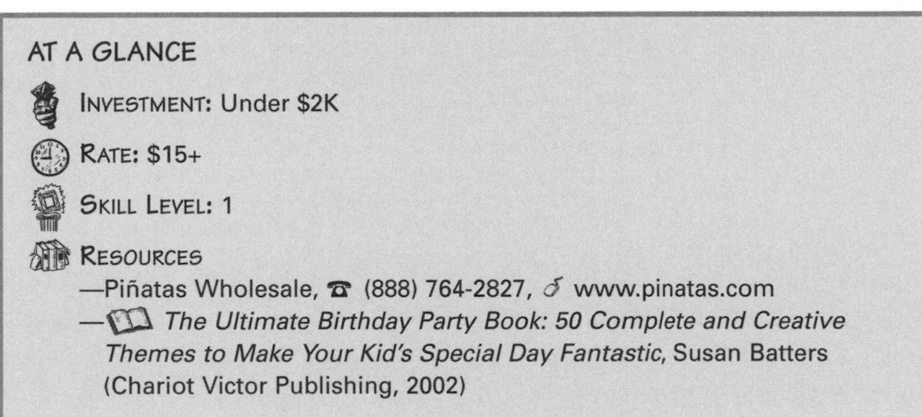
AT A GLANCE

INVESTMENT: Under $2K

RATE: $15+

SKILL LEVEL: 1

RESOURCES

—Piñatas Wholesale, ☎ (888) 764-2827, www.pinatas.com

—*The Ultimate Birthday Party Book: 50 Complete and Creative Themes to Make Your Kid's Special Day Fantastic*, Susan Batters (Chariot Victor Publishing, 2002)

Bouncy House Rentals

Bouncy houses are inflatable amusement games that children and adults absolutely love to bounce around in (and on) and they are available in a wide range of shapes, sizes, and themes such as castles and blimps. Renting bouncy houses is easy, and you can make incredible profits, up to $250 per day, just for delivering, setting up, and returning at the end of the day for pick up. This is perhaps one of the best part-time business opportunities available. New inflatable amusement games cost in the range of $2,000 for small basic models, and up to $15,000 for large, fully featured models. Used ones are available for about half the cost of new. In addition to renting these inflatables for children's birthday parties, they can also be rented to charities, sports and social clubs, and for corporate and community events. Setup is fast, taking one person approximately 30 minutes and about the same amount of time for dismantling and removal.

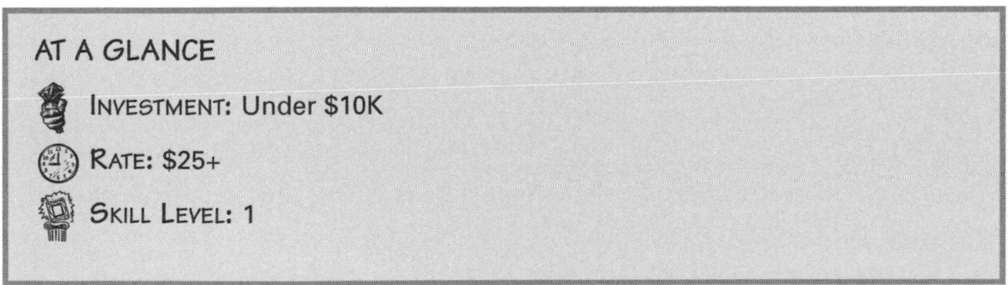
AT A GLANCE

INVESTMENT: Under $10K

RATE: $25+

SKILL LEVEL: 1

 RESOURCES

—China Inflatable, www.china-inflatable.com
—Discount Inflatable, (317) 657-5555, www.discountinflatable.com
—Moon Walker, (888) 840-5867, www.moon-walker.com

Dry-Cleaning Delivery

Dry-cleaning delivery services have recently exploded in popularity. In addition to starting your own dry-cleaning delivery service from scratch, there are also a number of franchise opportunities available all across the country for those who prefer a strength-in-numbers approach to business. Armed with little more than a cell phone to handle customer calls and reliable transportation, you can earn substantial profits picking up and delivering dry-cleaned garments. Revenues are earned by charging customers a small fee for picking up and delivering, as well as by charging dry cleaners a fee for supplying business, generally 10 to 15 percent of the dry-cleaning bill. The benefit to customers is that they don't have to worry about dropping off or picking up their dry cleaning, which can be delivered right to their homes, businesses, or offices. The benefit to dry cleaners is that they don't have to spend money on advertising to find new customers, because that's your job. In addition to advertising the service in the newspaper, through flier and coupon drops, and in your local Yellow Pages directory, also be sure to call on large-volume clients such as police departments, fire stations, hospitals, restaurants, corporations, and basically any other business or organization that requires employees to wear uniforms that must be regularly dry-cleaned.

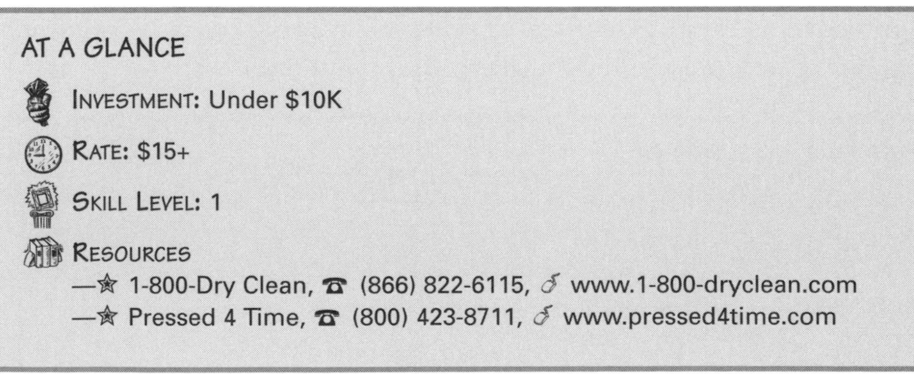

AT A GLANCE

INVESTMENT: Under $10K

RATE: $15+

SKILL LEVEL: 1

RESOURCES

—★ 1-800-Dry Clean, (866) 822-6115, www.1-800-dryclean.com
—★ Pressed 4 Time, (800) 423-8711, www.pressed4time.com

Silkscreening

Late-model silkscreen printing equipment is relatively small and portable, which means it can be set up in your garage, basement, or any spare room and used for printing logos and images on a wide variety of products for big profits. These products include T-shirts, mouse pads, bumper stickers, hats, sweatshirts, heat transfers, shower curtains, presentation covers, furniture, umbrellas, boomerangs, Frisbees, a wide range of advertising specialties, and sports and corporate uniforms. New and used screen-printing equipment is available for sale in most areas and through online dealers. Basic models are inexpensive, but more important, they can help you to realize huge profits. For example, the cost to purchase and screen-print a T-shirt is less than $5 each, including all materials; often less than that is needed if the shirts are purchased in large quantities. In turn, they can be sold retail for as much as $25 each and in the range of $7 to $12 each wholesale. Sell just 50 screen-printed T-shirts a week retail and you could earn as much as $50,000 a year in profits. Potential customers include small businesses, corporations, organizations, sports clubs and teams, and retailers for wholesale or consignment sales.

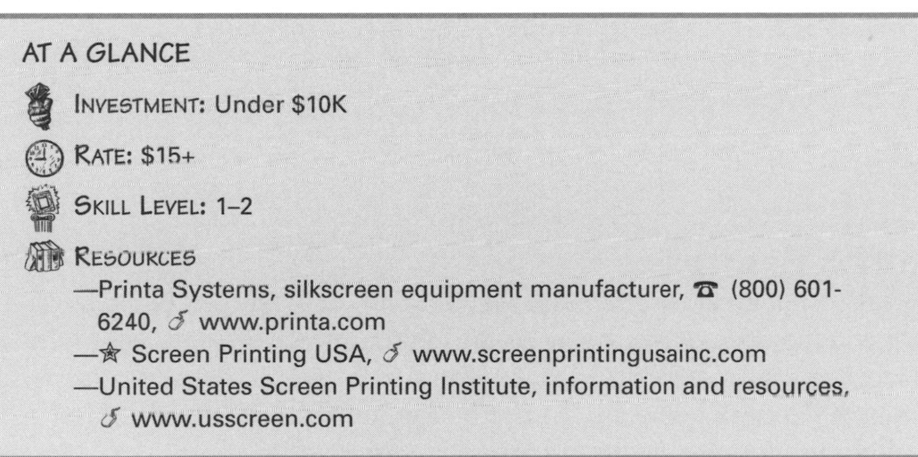

AT A GLANCE

INVESTMENT: Under $10K

RATE: $15+

SKILL LEVEL: 1–2

RESOURCES

—Printa Systems, silkscreen equipment manufacturer, ☎ (800) 601-6240, www.printa.com

—★ Screen Printing USA, www.screenprintingusainc.com

—United States Screen Printing Institute, information and resources, www.usscreen.com

Embroidery

Embroidery machines are available in multihead models enabling the operator to embroider six or more items at a time, which greatly increases productivity and profitability. Modern embroidery equipment is also computer-assisted. Designs can be created using a computer and specialty software and then automatically transferred to the embroidery machine to complete the stitching of the design onto the chosen garment. An embroidery service can easily be operated from home, but a small showroom should be established to display items that can be embroidered, as well as samples of embroidery options and designs for clients to choose from. Popular products include hats, T-shirts, sweaters, fleece garments, leather jackets, sports bags, and towels and linens. Marketing is as easy as creating a product catalog and marketing brochures and distributing the promotional package to potential customers such as sports associations, schools, corporations, government agencies, organizations, and charities. You might also want to consider hiring a commissioned salesperson to solicit for new business, preferably one with existing contacts that can be capitalized upon for immediate sales.

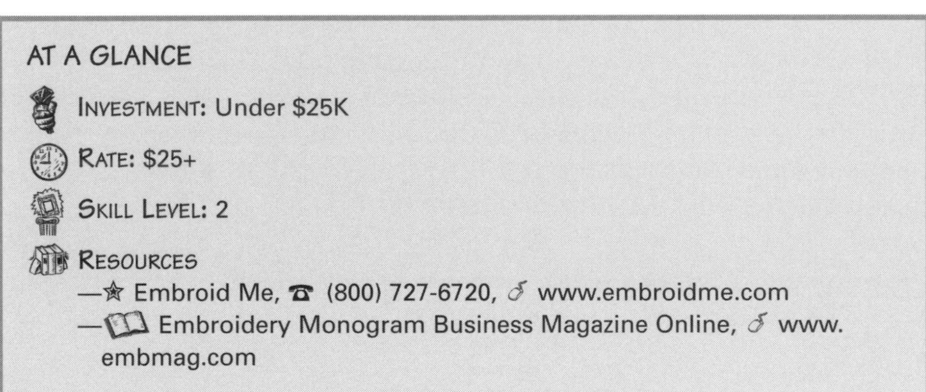

AT A GLANCE

INVESTMENT: Under $25K

RATE: $25+

SKILL LEVEL: 2

RESOURCES

—★ Embroid Me, ☎ (800) 727-6720, www.embroidme.com

— Embroidery Monogram Business Magazine Online, www.embmag.com

---

Alteration Service

Calling all homemakers, students, and retirees! It's time to capitalize on your sewing skills by providing garment and fabric alteration services right from a home work space, and earn a bundle of money in the process. Dry cleaners, fashion retailers, uniform retailers, bridal boutiques, drapery studios, and consignment clothing shops—all are potential customers for your service. In fact, all businesses that retail or rent clothing of any sort are potential customers. Put on a comfortable pair of shoes and start calling on these businesses in person, offering your alteration services. Offer free pickup and delivery, fast turnaround times, great service, and quality workmanship, all at fair prices. Your business clients benefit because they can offer alteration services to customers for free, ensuring repeat business. Or they can make it a profit center by marking up what you charge. Along with your sewing skills, you will need the tools of the sewing trade, and reliable transportation.

AT A GLANCE

INVESTMENT: Under $2K

RATE: $15+

SKILL LEVEL: 2

RESOURCES

—Bright Notions, sewing equipment and supplies, www.brightnotions.com
—Sew True, sewing equipment and supplies, www.sewtrue.com
—Wholesale Sewing Supplies, www.wholesalesewingsupplies.com

Tutor

For parents wanting the peace of mind of knowing that their children are receiving the best education possible, in-home one-on-one tutoring is usually the preferred teaching method. Utilizing your academic experience and knowledge of math, English, science, or history, you can start your own tutoring service and have an opportunity to earn between $25 and $40 per hour, depending on your qualifications and the material you teach. Tutoring classes can be held at your home, requiring students to come to you, or at your students' homes, requiring you to go to your students. Some low-income families can take advantage of tutoring programs for their kids associated with the *No Child Left Behind Act*, which provides tutoring for children who have learning disabilities. However, to qualify as a teacher in these programs, you need a teaching certificate. In addition to traditional tutoring, ESL (English as a Second Language) tutoring has exploded in popularity in the past decade, both for new immigrants and foreign students who need to master English for job and academic reasons.

AT A GLANCE

INVESTMENT: Under $2K

RATE: $25+

SKILL LEVEL: 2–4

RESOURCES

—National Tutoring Association, www.ntatutor.com

—★ Tutoring Club, ☎ (888) 674-6425, www.tutoringclub.com
—Tutor Nation, online portal bringing together tutors and students, www.tutornation.com

Dance Instructor

Providing you know how to dance, regardless of the style—tap, highland, ballroom, ballet, swing, break, modern, disco, flamenco, or line dancing—there is big money to be earned by teaching people how to dance. If space is available, open a dance studio right in your own home. If not, operate your dance classes in conjunction with a suitable partner or partners who do have the space—fitness center, community center, music shop, or a community college. Of course, you can also rent studio space, or even teach students right at their own homes. Expanding your business is as easy as hiring other dance instructors in the same or new styles to teach students and to work on a revenue-splitting basis. One-on-one instruction rates start at about $30 per hour, while group rates are less per student, but you can earn more by teaching numerous people to dance at the same time.

AT A GLANCE

INVESTMENT: Under $2K

RATE: $25+

SKILL LEVEL: 2

RESOURCES

—Dance Net, dance instructors' directory, www.dance.net
—★ Kinderdance International, ☎ (800) 554-2334, www.kinderdance.net
—Voice of Dance, dance instructors' directory, www.voiceofdance.com

Music Lessons

If you know how to sing, play guitar, piano, drums, a wind or string instrument well enough to teach others, then what are you waiting for? Capitalize on your talents and earn a great full- or part-time income by teaching customers how to play your instrument of choice. Classes can be conducted one-on-one or in a group format, from your home, at the student's location, from rented commercial space, or in conjunction with community programs, continuing education, or even at an established music store. Expanding the business requires nothing more than hiring other experienced musicians to teach students. Fees are split—basically, you find the students, your instructors teach the classes, and everyone profits. Lesson rates will vary depending on class size, skill level, and instrument, but on average, group lessons cost students $10 to $20 per hour, and one-on-one lessons in the range of $40 per hour plus the costs of instrument rentals or purchases, course materials, and sheet music.

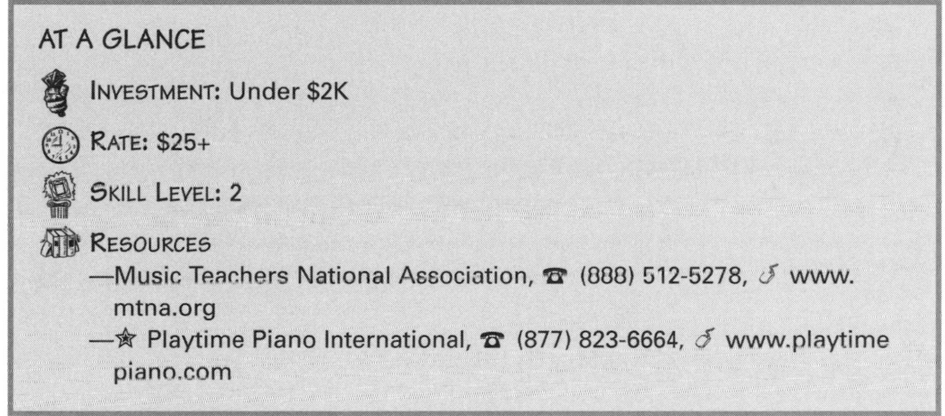
AT A GLANCE

INVESTMENT: Under $2K

RATE: $25+

SKILL LEVEL: 2

RESOURCES
—Music Teachers National Association, ☎ (888) 512-5278, www.mtna.org
—★ Playtime Piano International, ☎ (877) 823-6664, www.playtimepiano.com

---

Cooking Classes

Does everybody rave about the meals you prepare? If so, why not put your extraordinary cooking skills to work by teaching others how to be great cooks? Operating right from home on a small scale, you can teach students how to prepare fantastic meals. If you choose to operate on a larger scale, you will need to rent appropriate commercial space or partner with a restaurant or banquet facility and offer classes during nonbusiness hours. Either way, fantastic profits can be earned by teaching others how to make unforgettably tasty meals, desserts, and appetizers. You can earn additional profits by selling cookware and kitchen utensils to students, and even create and sell recipe books locally. One-on-one, students pay $20 to $30 per hour to learn how to prepare gourmet meals, and about half that amount when three to five are taught at the same time—less per student, but more income through volume. Needless to say, it does not take many students to earn an extra $1,000 per month working just a few nights and weekends.

Start-up costs are also minimal because chances are you will already have everything you need in terms of cookware and other tools of the cooking trade. Post fliers in grocery stores, retail shops, and at your local butcher shop advertising your classes. This is the kind of specialized service that people tend to talk about, so don't be surprised if you are quickly inundated with more students than you can handle.

AT A GLANCE

 INVESTMENT: Under $10K

 RATE: $25+

 SKILL LEVEL: 2

 RESOURCES

—*The Gourmet Cookbook: 1000 Recipes*, Ruth Reichl (Houghton Mifflin Co., 2004)

—Viva The Chef, www.vivathechef.com/franchise

Arts and Crafts Instruction

Knitting, painting, print-making, sculpture, stained glass, pottery, glass-blowing, and woodworking are just a few examples of arts and crafts that people are willing to shell out their hard-earned money to learn. If you have mastered any of these or other arts and crafts, why not be the person to train them and earn substantial profits for your efforts? Days, evenings, or weekends, arts and crafts can be taught from a homebased studio, rented commercial space, in partnership with a crafts retailer whose space you use, in conjunction with a community center or school, or even at a park if weather permits. Promote your classes through arts and crafts retailers, by running advertisements in the newspaper, networking at business and social functions, posting notices on community bulletin boards, and by exhibiting at arts and crafts shows. Creative entrepreneurs may even choose to film and broadcast their training classes via the internet to a worldwide student base. The options are nearly limitless when you have a skill that other people are willing to pay to learn. Rates will vary depending on how many people are in each class, material and equipment requirements, and the art or craft being taught. On average, independent arts and crafts instructors earn in the range of $25 to $50 per hour.

AT A GLANCE

 INVESTMENT: Under $2K

 RATE: $25+

 SKILL LEVEL: 2

 RESOURCES

—Arts and Crafts Association of America, ☎ (616) 874-1721, www.artsandcraftsassoc.com

—Canadian Crafts & Hobby Association, ☎ (403) 291-0559, www.cdncraft.org

---

Kayak Tours

Turn your passion for kayaking into a profitable full- or part-time enterprise by starting a kayak tour business. Offer outdoor enthusiasts various tour packages—a half-day beginners' course, a full day of paddling including basic training and lunch, and weeklong paddling excursions including overnight campouts on islands and beaches. Ideal locations for this type of venture are coastal areas of the United States and Canada, as well as states and provinces surrounding the Great Lakes. You will need to invest in five or six fiberglass or plastic touring kayaks and related equipment including life jackets, dry bags, spray skirts, and paddles, as well as suitable transportation for six, and a trailer to carry the kayaks and gear. Current rates are in the range of $65 per person for half-day tours, $120 for full day, and $1,200 for weeklong tours inclusive of transportation, overnight gear, and meals. Multiply these numbers by six and you have the potential to earn $3,000 per week and more having fun, enjoying your sport, and living it up in the great outdoors.

AT A GLANCE

 INVESTMENT: Under $25K

 RATE: $50+

 SKILL LEVEL: 2

 **RESOURCES**

—Ocean Kayak, sea kayak manufacturer, ☎ (360) 366-4003, www.oceankayak.com

—SEE Kayak, industry information portal, www.seekayak.com

—Trade Association of Paddlesports, ☎ (800) 755-5228, www.gopaddle.org

---

Survival and Outdoor Training

What would you do if you were trapped on a mountainside, in subzero weather, with a blizzard approaching? This may not seem like a very likely scenario for many of us, but if you are one of the many millions of outdoor enthusiasts across the country engaged in any number of outdoor adventure activities like skiing, snowmobiling, paragliding, hiking, ice-climbing, or whitewater kayaking, this scenario, or one with similar dire consequences, could happen. Operating a survival and outdoor training service is perfectly suited to people with a taste for adventure, but with a steadfast safety-first attitude. People with search-and-rescue, military, or fire training are good candidates for the job, but so are people who are willing to get the training needed so they can train others to play safe while enjoying their adventurous pursuits. You can contact the resources below to learn about becoming a certified instructor. You might also consider specializing in one or more types of survival training, such as avalanche rescue, mountain rescue, swift-water rescue, cold-weather or desert survival, wilderness first aid, or map, compass, and GPS training.

AT A GLANCE

 **INVESTMENT:** Under $25K

 **RATE:** $50+

 **SKILL LEVEL:** 3–4

 **RESOURCES**

—Equipped to Survive, survival training school directory, www.equipped.com/srvchol.htm

—National Association for Search and Rescue, www.nasar.org

—Survivalist, survival training school directory, www.survivalistbooks.com/survschools.htm

Automobile Detailing

There are two ways of cashing in on the booming automobile detailing industry. The first is to work on a mobile basis using a van or enclosed trailer as your base of operations and travel to your customers' locations—homes, businesses, or offices. The second option is to work from a fixed location like your home garage or a rental location and have customers come to you. Fixed-location or mobile, automobile detailing is a hot growth business with excellent upside income potential. Offer customers detailing and cleaning services such as washing, waxing, pin-striping, window-tinting, interior and engine shampooing, upholstery steam-cleaning, and chrome-polishing. If you choose to operate from a fixed location make sure to offer free pickup and delivery of clients' automobiles from their homes or offices. Market your services to new and used car dealers, fleet operators, in combination with valet parking services so customers can have their cars detailed while at lunch or other events, and through traditional advertising methods that include coupons, newspaper ads, and fliers.

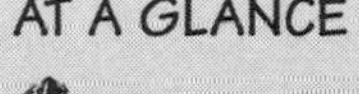

 INVESTMENT: Under $10K

 RATE: $25+

 SKILL LEVEL: 1–2

 RESOURCES

—★ Colors on Parade, ☎ (800) 726-5677, www.colorsfranchise.com

—Lane's Professional Car Care Products, ☎ (866) 798-9011, www.car-waxes.com

Courier Service

Start a courier service specializing in envelopes, small packages, or large shipments, or combine all package types and sizes to maximize profit potential. The least expensive way to get started in the courier industry is to subcontract your services to an established courier company, meaning that you supply the transportation and yourself to pickup and deliver parcels. But this option also leaves you with the lowest profit potential and ability to grow the business. A better option is to start your own courier service outright, and hire other owner/operators on a revenue-sharing basis to make deliveries, while you concentrate on marketing, managing, and building the business. In addition to suitable transportation, depending on the types of parcels you will be delivering, you will also need to invest in a courier's license, a two-way radio system, and moving dollies. Every municipality has its own regulations for issuing courier's licenses to both drivers and courier companies, so you'll need to take a trip to city hall or a transportation office to make inquiries about obtaining a license. Courier rates vary by size, weight, and parcel destination. Competition in the courier industry is stiff, but providing great customer service and reliability will go a long way toward ensuring long-term success.

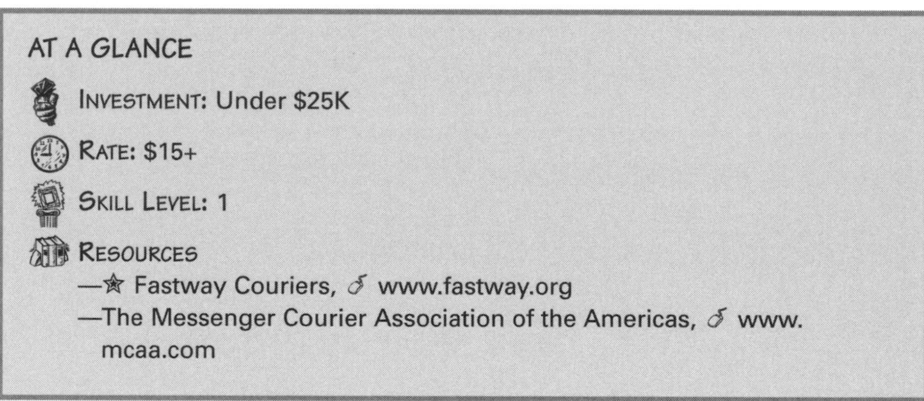

AT A GLANCE

INVESTMENT: Under $25K

RATE: $15+

SKILL LEVEL: 1

RESOURCES
—★ Fastway Couriers, www.fastway.org
—The Messenger Courier Association of the Americas, www.mcaa.com

Valet Parking Service

A driver's license, the ability to obtain third-party liability insurance, and an outgoing friendly personality are the three essentials for starting a special-events valet parking service. The business can be started with minimal cash and the profit potential is excellent, as rates for valet parking services are in the range of $50 to $70 per hour for a two-to-three person crew. And it goes almost without saying that tips can really add up! Market your valet parking services directly to consumers hosting parties and events, corporations hosting conventions and other event and wedding planners, trade show organizers, and charity groups and organizations. Uniforms worn by all staff and emblazoned with your business name and slogan, along with incredible customer service and a smile, will make a great impression on customers that is sure to secure lots of repeat business and word-of-mouth referrals.

202

AT A GLANCE

 **INVESTMENT:** Under $2K

 **RATE:** $15+

 **SKILL LEVEL:** 1

 **RESOURCES**

—United States Small Business Administration, www.sba.gov

—Valet Park, industry information and resources, www.valetpark.net

---

Mobile Oil Change

The oil change industry generates a whopping $15 billion in annual sales! Getting your piece of this very lucrative pie may be easier than you think, especially when you consider that specialized equipment is available, which enables the operator to quickly, and without mess, change oil at just about any location—home, office, business, or on the job site. Best of all, this equipment can be purchased for as little as $10,000 for the basic model. Many manufacturers of mobile oil-change equipment and products also provide training courses. That way, you can start to operate this service regardless of previous inexperience. Potential customers include private automobile owners, fleet owners, heavy equipment and construction equipment operators, and farmers. In addition to oil changes, you can also provide customers with hydraulic fluid changes, transmission fluid changes, and general lube services.

AT A GLANCE

 **INVESTMENT:** Under $25K–over $25K

 **RATE:** $25+

 **SKILL LEVEL:** 2–3

 **RESOURCES**

—Lube n' Go, distributor of mobile oil change equipment, products, and training, (888) 451-3981, www.lubengo.com

—★ Oil Butler International, (908) 687-3283, www.oilbutlerinternational.com

—Sage Oil Vac, distributor of mobile oil-change equipment, products, and training, (877) 645-8227, www.sageoilvac.com

Boat Cleaning

If you want to get into the highly lucrative and booming cleaning industry, but do not want to compete with the multitude of residential and commercial cleaning services, consider a boat-cleaning service. There is less competition, arguably more profit potential and, like residential and commercial cleaning, the number of potential customers is nearly unlimited. Boat cleaning is a very easy service to start because there are no special skills or equipment required to operate and market the business. Fliers describing the services you provide and a little bit of legwork to distribute the fliers at marinas and boating clubs are all that's required to get things rolling. Considering that you can get started on an initial investment of less than $1,000, the income potential at $20 to $30 per hour is excellent. If you have the equipment and necessary skills, also offer clients additional services such as in-the-water bottom-cleaning, sailboat rigging, haul-out bottom-painting, and woodwork or brightwork refinishing, as these services can command as much as $60 per hour. And if you *really* want to offer a unique service, purchase a small work boat equipped with steam-cleaning equipment, water tanks, and vacuums so you can go to any marina and offer same-day mobile service, working right from your work boat.

AT A GLANCE

 INVESTMENT: Under $10K

 RATE: $25+

 SKILL LEVEL: 1–2

 RESOURCES

—📖 *Boat Maintenance: The Essential Guide to Cleaning, Painting, and Cosmetics*, William Burr (International Marine, 2000)

—★ Super Clean Yacht Service, ☎ (949) 646-2990, www.supercleanyachtservice.com

Small Engine Repair

Mechanically inclined entrepreneurs have the opportunity to make fantastic full- or part-time cash repairing outdoor power equipment and small engines, right from a fully equipped homebased workshop, or from a small commercial storefront. Even if you do not have previous small-engine repair experience, there are numerous schools offering in-class and correspondence small-engine repair training, such as the one listed below. The list of equipment you can repair is almost unlimited: lawn mowers, outboard motors, gas trimmers, lawn tractors, snowmobiles, snow blowers, leaf blowers, and chainsaws are only the tip of the iceberg. There are additional revenue sources as well. The first is to establish a certified-warranty repair depot for outdoor power-equipment manufacturers. The second is to buy secondhand outdoor power equipment in need of repairs at dirt-cheap prices, fix it, and sell it for a profit right from your shop. And the third additional revenue source is to rent outdoor power equipment and tools to local homeowners and contractors. Combine the three with the repair side of the business and you could easily generate in excess of $100,000 per year in sales.

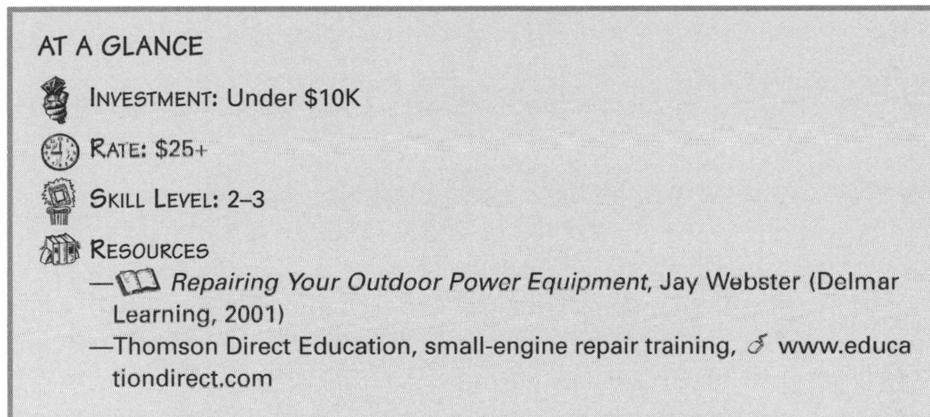

AT A GLANCE

INVESTMENT: Under $10K

RATE: $25+

SKILL LEVEL: 2–3

RESOURCES

—*Repairing Your Outdoor Power Equipment*, Jay Webster (Delmar Learning, 2001)

—Thomson Direct Education, small-engine repair training, www.educationdirect.com

---

Dent Removal

Using specialized equipment, you can remove small dings and dents in vehicles caused by hail, minor collisions, and door bumps, all without the need for new paint, and on a mobile basis right at your customer's location—home, office, or business. Potential clients include private automobile owners, automobile fleet owners, new and used car dealers, and insurance companies. Operating on a mobile basis enables you to get started with limited funds, keep your overhead low, and more importantly it gives you the ability to go to where the business is available, with no geographical limitations. Many distributors and manufacturers of dent removal tools and equipment also provide training, which is reasonably priced and requires only a few weeks to complete. Hence, even if you have no previous auto body repair experience, you can still start and operate this business.

Extra money may be earned by offering clients paint touchup services, automobile detailing services, and window tinting.

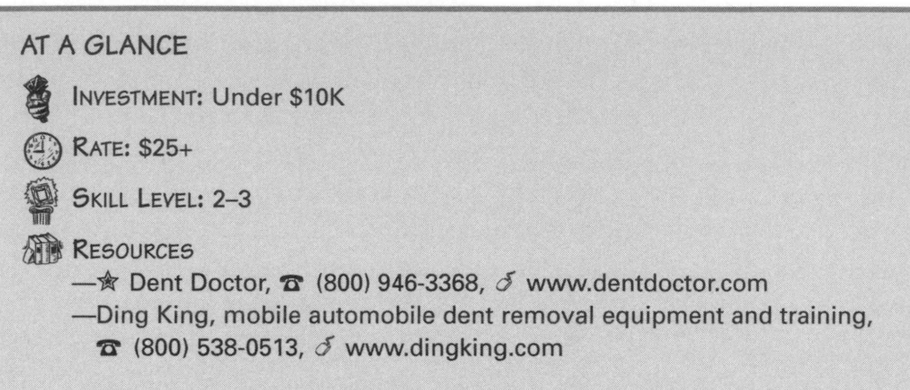

AT A GLANCE

INVESTMENT: Under $10K

RATE: $25+

SKILL LEVEL: 2–3

RESOURCES

—★ Dent Doctor, ☎ (800) 946-3368, www.dentdoctor.com

—Ding King, mobile automobile dent removal equipment and training, ☎ (800) 538-0513, www.dingking.com

---

Community Delivery Service

Equipped with nothing more than a cell phone to handle incoming and outgoing customer calls, coupled with reliable transportation, you can offer clients in your community fast and convenient delivery and/or pickup services for dry cleaning, spirits, fast foods, medications, event tickets, groceries, pet foods, flowers, or just about anything else imaginable. The business is also easily expanded simply by putting your marketing and management skills to work. Concentrate on promoting your services and securing new customers, while hiring subcontracted drivers with their own automobiles to handle the pickups and deliveries on a revenue-split basis. Maximize the efficiency of the operation by installing two-way radios in each vehicle linked to a central dispatcher, thereby limiting downtime and nonproductive travel time. In addition to advertising with promotional fliers, in the newspapers, and via direct-mail coupons, also be sure to strike deals with restaurants, grocery stores, pharmacies, liquor stores, and other retailers to handle their delivery services.

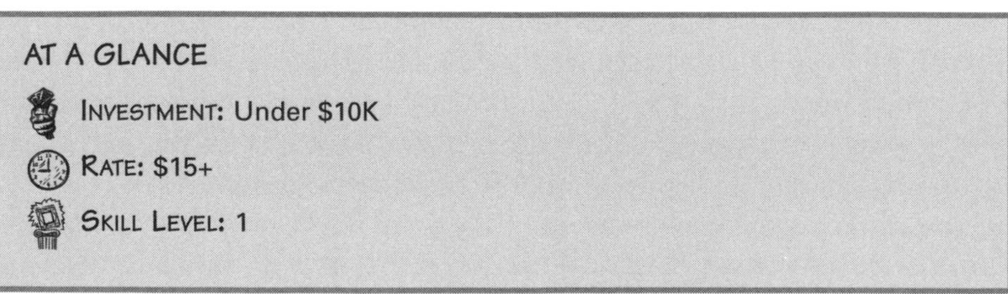

AT A GLANCE

INVESTMENT: Under $10K

RATE: $15+

SKILL LEVEL: 1

RESOURCES
—★ Dine-In Delivery, ☎ (303) 604-6840, www.dine-indelivery.com
—Entrepreneur Online, small business portal, www.entrepreneur.com

---

Automobile Paint Touch-Up

The future is bright for a mobile automotive paint touch-up service, especially when you consider that there are more than 130 million vehicles registered in the United States. Bumper scuffs, key scratches, stone chips, and just about every other type of minor automobile paint damage can be quickly and easily fixed at the customer's site using special equipment and color-matching paint. In addition to car, truck, van, and motorcycle owners, other potential customers include new and used car dealers, fleet owners, and insurance companies. Don't fret if you do not have paint touch-up experience, because many distributors of mobile automobile painting equipment and products also offer low-cost training workshops that can be completed in less than a few weeks. The investment to get started in your own mobile automobile paint touch-up service is reasonable—under $10,000, including equipment, business setup, supplies, and a modest marketing budget. Extra income may be earned by also providing small dent and ding removal services and automobile detailing services.

AT A GLANCE

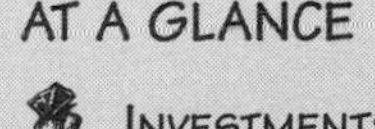

INVESTMENT: Under $10K

RATE: $25+

SKILL LEVEL: 2–3

RESOURCES
—★ Chips Away, ☎ (800) 837-2447, www.touchup.biz
—Paint Bull, automotive paint touch-up products, equipment, and training, ☎ (989) 793-2200, www.paintbull.com

---

Mobile Car Wash

Here is a simple business that is perfectly suited to entrepreneurs seeking to sell an in-demand service with the added benefits of flexible working hours, low overhead, minimal start-up costs, zero prior experience requirements, and excellent profit potential. Operating a mobile car wash means that you go to your client's location—home, business, or office. You need only basic equipment such as a portable pressure washer mounted on a truck or trailer, scrub brushers, shop vacuum, rags, and buckets to offer on-site car-washing services. The market potential is enormous, especially when you consider that there are more than 130 million vehicles registered in the United States. Promote with fliers, discount coupons, advertisements in your local newspaper, and through personal contact (knocking on doors). Talk with car dealers, construction companies, courier services, and other businesses that have equipment and fleet vehicles that need to be cleaned on a regular basis, and pitch the benefits of your service—mobile, high quality, fast, convenient, and great value. Securing customers who can become repeat customers is the best way to fly because it is much easier and more profitable to find a repeat customer than it is to continually find new ones.

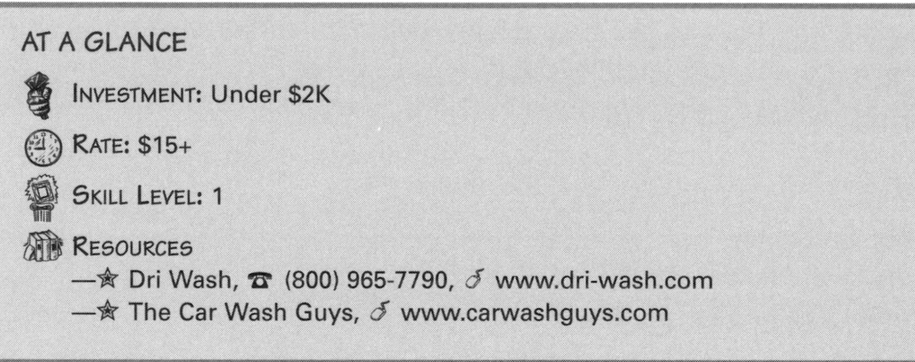

AT A GLANCE

INVESTMENT: Under $2K

RATE: $15+

SKILL LEVEL: 1

RESOURCES

—★ Dri Wash, ☎ (800) 965-7790, www.dri-wash.com
—★ The Car Wash Guys, www.carwashguys.com

Boat Broker

Highly ambitious entrepreneurs with boating experience have the potential to cash in big on the boating boom by starting a boat brokerage service. However, before you get too excited at the prospect of selling boats, you should know that some states require boat brokers to be licensed. At present, though, there are no across-the-board regulations, and each state has its own regulations. You can contact either of the boat broker associations listedon the next page to find out licensing regulations in your state. Or you can enroll in the National Yacht Brokers Certification Program, ☎ (410) 263-1014, www.cpyb.net, but only people with prior boat sales experience are eligible for the program. The cost and time to obtain a license (if required in your state) may still be a wise investment because thousands of pre-owned motorboats, sailboats, and personal watercraft are bought and sold annually, generating billions in sales. Securing just a tiny portion of this very lucrative market may be easier than you think, especially when you consider that you can operate from home and travel to marinas to list, show, and sell, enabling you to keep start-up costs to a minimum. Or if investment funds are plentiful, you can lease space at a marina that has no boat brokerage and offer full brokerage services on site. Generally, boat brokers or boat sales consultants charge a 10 percent commission upon the successful sale and transfer of the boat to the new owner. The commission rate can be as high as 25 percent for boats with a value of less than $5,000, and as low as 3 percent when selling boats in the million-dollar price range.

AT A GLANCE

INVESTMENT: Over $25K

RATE: $50+

SKILL LEVEL: 3–4

RESOURCES
—United States Boat Brokers Association, www.usboatbrokers.com
—Yacht Brokers Association of America, www.ybaa.com

Pedicab Service

Peddle your way to big profits by starting a pedicab taxi/tour service. A ride through the park, a sightseeing tour around town, or a relaxing ride to and from a restaurant—tourists and locals alike love to take in a region's sights and sounds from a ride in a pedicab. Pedicabs are available in a wide range of styles, purposes, and price points. There are basic two-occupant models all the way up to models that will accommodate six people, and even others that are equipped with storage space (but no seating) for urban parcel delivery instead of people. New pedicabs start at about $3,500, and half that amount if used. Ride rates are currently about $1 per minute, with a minimum charge of $5. The business can easily be expanded from a one-person operation by purchasing multiple pedicabs and hiring drivers to operate them on a revenue-split basis. Also, don't forget to sell the highly visible and valuable space on the back of the pedicab to local business advertisers. This space can easily generate an additional $500 per month and more in large urban centers. Be sure to build alliances with hotels, tourist associations, event planners, restaurants, and travel agencies so they can refer your pedicab service to their customers. Additional profits may also be earned by selling photograph mementos, T-shirts, hats, and postcards.

AT A GLANCE

 INVESTMENT: Under $10K

 RATE: $15+

 SKILL LEVEL: 1

 RESOURCES

- —Main Street Pedicab Manufacturing, ☎ (303) 295-3822, www.mainstreetpedicabs.com
- —McKay Insurance Agency, pedicab commercial general liability insurance, ☎ (641) 842-2135, www.mckayinsagency.com
- —Premier Pedicab Manufacturing, ☎ (509) 467-4954, www.tipke.com

---

Community Tour Guide

If you live in an area frequented by tourists and are a real people-person, why not consider starting a personal tour guide service? It can be started for virtually peanuts, and has the potential to generate an income that can easily top $50,000 per year if you work at it full-time. Promote your tours aggressively by building contacts with businesses and individuals who can refer your personally guided tours to their clients. These people and businesses include coach and taxi drivers, event planners, hotels, restaurants, and travel agents. In addition to the usual fare of stopping at the oldest building, the best beach, and area museums, also show some of the more unusual sights in your community—crime scenes, television or movie set locations, past or present celebrity houses, and human enclaves like ethnically exotic neighborhoods. Personal tour guides are charging $150 to $200 for half-day tours, and up to $350 for full-day tours plus the cost of transportation and tickets to events and attractions. Provide clients with an unforgettably fun experience combined with incredible service and you will have the two main ingredients to secure lots of referral and repeat business. Also market your services to corporations that want to treat their visiting out-of-town customers, employees, and executives to a special event.

AT A GLANCE

INVESTMENT: Under $10K

RATE: $15+

SKILL LEVEL: 1–2

RESOURCES

—Rezcity.com, (201) 567-8500, www.rezcity.com

—*Start and Run a Profitable Tour Guide Business*, Barbara Braidwood, Susan Boyce, and Richard Cropp (Self-Counsel Press, 2000)

Adventure Travel Agent

How about ice-climbing in Finland, deep-sea fishing off Australia, base-jumping in Africa, or a Mayan ruins tour in a hot-air balloon? Have fun and earn incredible profits arranging the adventure of a lifetime for clients by starting a specialty adventure travel agency. Forget about run-of-the-mill tours of Paris and those mundane amenity-packed hotels in the Caribbean, and concentrate instead on your client's need for adventure by offering the most unique vacation adventures available. To get started, market the adventure vacation packages in company newsletters, and online chat rooms, advertise in specialty sports and recreation publications, exhibit at sports and recreation shows, and use e-mail broadcasting. Once established, repeat business and referral business should go a long way toward attracting a steady flow of profits. Speaking of which, income is earned either by charging clients a fee for organizing the adventure trip, or by charging host companies and accommodation providers a fee for marketing their accommodations and activities to your clients. You can charge for both, but you will need to establish a standard pricing formula. With a little imagination, motivated entrepreneurs can earn a substantial living arranging adventure vacations for people who are seeking something out of the ordinary. This can be especially fulfilling if you also share the same enthusiasm for adventure travel and recreation.

AT A GLANCE

INVESTMENT: Under $10K

RATE: $25+

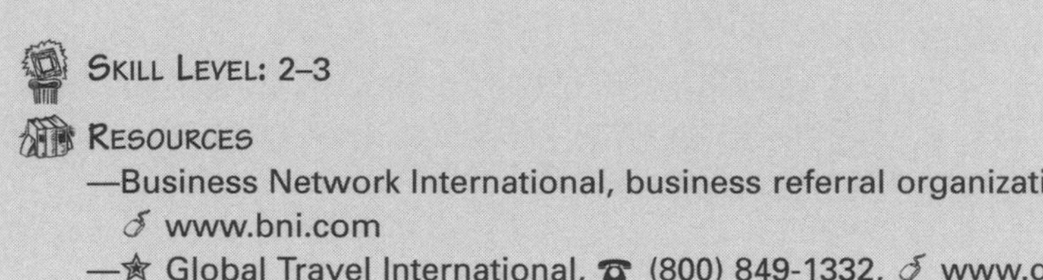
SKILL LEVEL: 2–3

RESOURCES

—Business Network International, business referral organization, www.bni.com

—★ Global Travel International, ☎ (800) 849-1332, www.globaltravel.com

Cruise Ship Travel Agent

Working from the comforts of a homebased office, you can plan and book cruise vacations-of-a-lifetime for your clients. Travel consulting experience is recommended for this opportunity; if you do not have experience, I would advise you to contact the National Association of Commissioned Travel Agents to inquire about training courses in your area. You could also choose a franchise cruise agent business, which provides all franchisees with intensive training in the areas of marketing, administration, and reservation booking. The cruise travel agent industry is competitive, but at the same time it is also the fastest-growing segment of the travel industry. Key to success in this business is marketing. You have to tap in to the demographic groups that are most likely to take a cruise—which include the 50-plus crowd and newlyweds—and target your marketing efforts to these groups. You might also want to consider specializing in a niche area of the cruise holiday industry, such as singles-only and alternative lifestyle cruises.

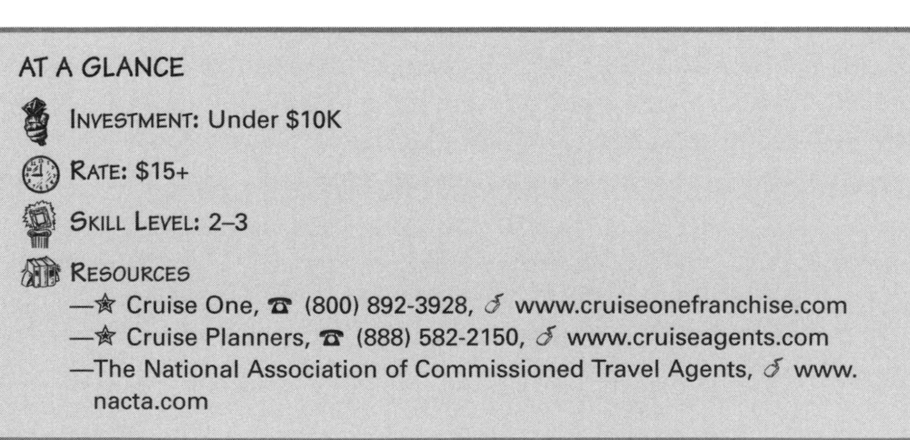
AT A GLANCE

INVESTMENT: Under $10K

RATE: $15+

SKILL LEVEL: 2–3

RESOURCES

—★ Cruise One, ☎ (800) 892-3928, www.cruiseonefranchise.com

—★ Cruise Planners, ☎ (888) 582-2150, www.cruiseagents.com

—The National Association of Commissioned Travel Agents, www.nacta.com

Singles-Only Event Promoter

Two things make starting a singles-only event promotion business a safe bet in terms of the potential for success and profitability—a 50 percent divorce rate, and people choosing to stay single much longer than in decades past. Lots of 25-, 30-, 35-, and even 40-year-olds are still looking for Mr. or Mrs. Right. The result is a whole bunch of single people looking to meet other singles for fun, friendship, and maybe even love. Plan and host singles events such as pub nights, group outings to concerts and sporting events, local and international travel destinations, bingo nights, Saturday morning wilderness hikes, and Thursday night potluck dinners. Providing the events are unique, fun, and exciting, word will spread fast, precluding any need of costly advertising and promotion once the business is established.

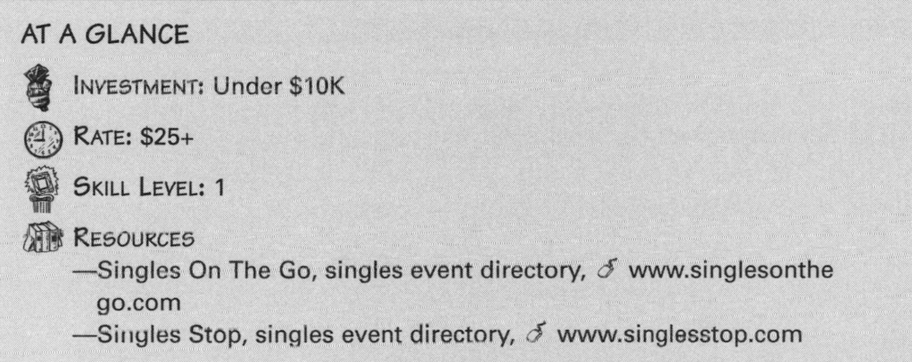

AT A GLANCE

INVESTMENT: Under $10K

RATE: $25+

SKILL LEVEL: 1

RESOURCES

—Singles On The Go, singles event directory, www.singlesonthego.com

—Singles Stop, singles event directory, www.singlesstop.com

Site Sign Installations

If you are searching for a simple, part-time, and low-cost service to sell that requires no previous experience or special skills, a site sign installation service just might fit the bill perfectly. Site signs are the small temporary signs typically used by realtors to advertise a home for sale; politicians use them to promote their runs for office; and construction firms that employ painters, roofers, and landscapers use them to promote the products and services they sell. These signs are stuck into the ground in front of homes so that passing motorists and pedestrians will take notice of what is being advertised or promoted. Installing site signs is very easy and only requires basic tools such as a sledgehammer and shovel. Current rates are in the vicinity of $20 to $30 for each sign delivered, installed, and removed at a later date. The easiest way to get started is to call on realtors and businesses in your area that typically use site signs, and pitch the benefits of your service—fast, convenient, reliable, and fairly priced.

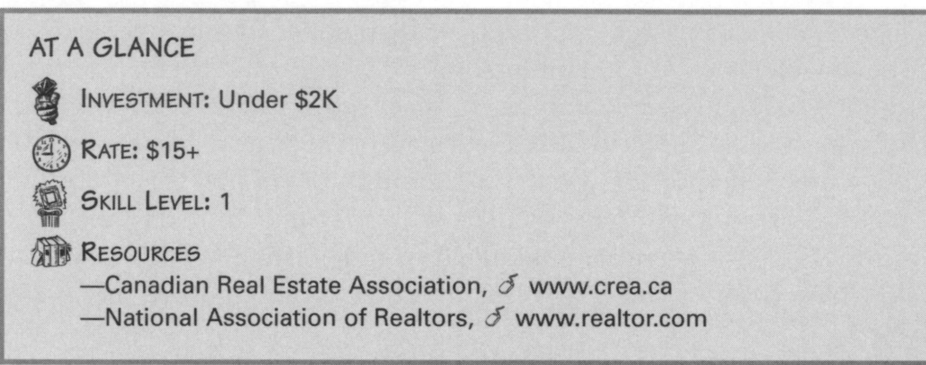

AT A GLANCE

INVESTMENT: Under $2K

RATE: $15+

SKILL LEVEL: 1

RESOURCES
—Canadian Real Estate Association, www.crea.ca
—National Association of Realtors, www.realtor.com

Board-Up Service

We have all been witness to the changing global climate over the past few decades, which has noticeably increased the ferocity and frequency of hurricanes, tornadoes, tropical storms, blizzards, and gales, resulting in millions of dollars' worth of property damage every time one of these weather disasters happens. While you might not be able to anticipate these weather patterns, you can, however, help home and business owners be more prepared when the weather does turn foul by starting a board-up service. Board-up work is actually quite simple; you go to your client's home or business and measure all windows, cut plywood panels to fit, label each panel for the corresponding window, install quick-assembly hardware on the exterior window trim, and presto! The next time the weather turns ugly, your customers can have their windows professionally boarded-up in a matter of moments. The boards can be stored when not needed, and when the need does arise, each is already sized and ready to install. This means no long waits at the lumberyard with hundreds, if not thousands, of other anxious people trying to buy plywood and fasteners to board up their windows before the storm hits.

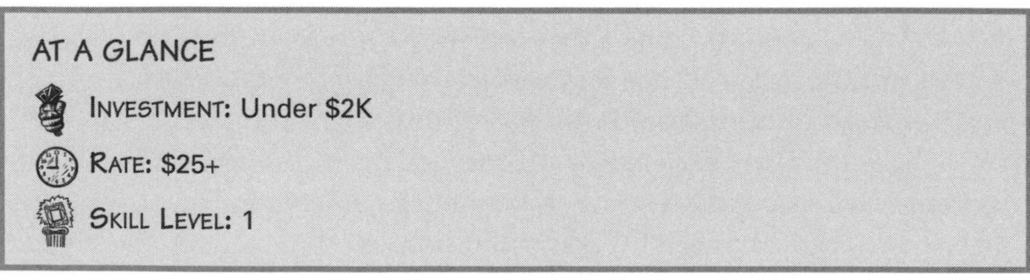

AT A GLANCE

INVESTMENT: Under $2K

RATE: $25+

SKILL LEVEL: 1

 RESOURCES

—Entrepreneur Online, small business information portal, www.entrepreneur.com

—United States Small Business Administration, www.sba.gov

Personal Shopper

If you love to shop, this is the opportunity for you. Earn great money and have fun by starting a personal shopping service assisting people who are too busy to shop, who don't like to shop, or who can't get out to do their own shopping. Lots of busy and well-heeled people hire personal shoppers to select gifts for any number of special occasions, including birthdays, births, weddings, Christmas, and anniversaries. And it's not just new products they're after: personal shoppers are also hired by interior designers and collectors to rummage through flea markets, consignment shops, antique dealers, and garage sales for collectibles, art, books, antiques, and funky home and office decor. Corporations hire personal shoppers to purchase the perfect gifts for customers, prospects, business partners, investors, employees, and executives, as well as to purchase products for gift bag giveaways at special events, ceremonies, and seminars. Seniors and other people who may find it difficult to get around, or who can't get out of their homes, hire personal shoppers to purchase groceries, clothing, and other home and personal products. Best of all, no experience is required to get started. If you love to shop, are creative, and don't mind networking with business owners, corporate executives, and people from all walks of life, you're qualified to become a personal shopper.

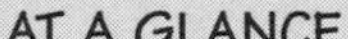

AT A GLANCE

 INVESTMENT: Under $2K

 RATE: $25+

 SKILL LEVEL: 1

 RESOURCES

—Elance Online, outsourcing and services marketplace, www.elanceonline.com

— *Get Paid to Shop: Be a Personal Shopper for Corporate America*, Emily Lumpkin (Forte Publishing, 1999)

INDEX